NANKING
1937

NANKING 1937

MEMORY
AND
HEALING

Foreword by Perry Link

Fei Fei Li, Robert Sabella and David Liu
editors

AN EAST GATE BOOK

M.E. Sharpe

Armonk, New York
London, England

An East Gate Book

Library of Congress Cataloging-in-Publication Data

Nanking 1937 : memory and healing / edited by Feifei Li, Robert Sabella, and David Liu.
   p. cm. —
"East gate book"
Includes bibliographical references and index.
ISBN 0-7656-0816-2 (alk. paper) — ISBN 0-7656-0817-0 (pbk.: alk. paper)
  1. Nanking Massacre, Nanjing, Jiangsu Sheng, China, 1937. 2. Nanjing (Jiangsu
Sheng, China)—History—20th century. 3. Nanking Massacre, Nanjing, Jiangsu Sheng,
China, 1937—Historiography. 4. Nanjing (Jiangsu Sheng, China)—History—20th
century—Historiography. I. Li, Feifei, 1976– II. Sabella, Robert, 1948– III. Liu, David,
1977–

DS797.56.N365 N36 2001
951.04′2—dc21
                                                 2001034216

This book is dedicated to all the victims and survivors
of the Nanking Massacre

Contents

Foreword

Perry Link

The end of the twentieth century brought to the world a certain mood of looking back and taking stock. In part, *fin-de-siecle* thinking is only arbitrary: It arises because year numbers are round, and this "roundness" comes, ultimately, only from the accident that human beings evolved with ten fingers. But there are more substantive reasons for looking back. The twentieth century far exceeds any other for the number of human deaths caused by other humans. I do not mean ordinary murders, whose history is immemorial and probably incalculable. I mean wars, genocides, and human-caused famines, in each of which areas the twentieth century has set records by wide margins. Another reason for retrospection stems from the end of the Cold War. The collapse of the bipolar standoff that had dominated the world for nearly half a century has led to a shift in attention toward smaller-scale problems—in Somalia, Iran, Yugoslavia, Rwanda, East Timor, and elsewhere—as well as to settling old scores: Can Augusto Pinochet be held accountable for torture and terror in Chile? Will Ta Mok, Khieu Samphan, and Nuon Chea be brought to justice for genocide in Cambodia? Will Swiss banks return money taken from Holocaust victims? Can "truth in reconciliation" work in South Africa? Some have tried to look at twentieth-century disasters more broadly, asking how we might try to measure or compare the essentially incalculable ravages of Hitler, Stalin, and Mao. Others wonder how long the human species will be able to survive its twentieth-century invention of nuclear weapons.

Retrospection has raised the problem of memory, which has recently become a hot topic in the academic world. Memory is of course an important resource in the project of looking back, but human recollection is also notoriously faulty, especially when severe pain and suffering are involved. Memory retains certain details while deleting others, and in the conversion of raw impressions into a coherent story, the remembering mind can even supply details that were not originally there. This happens especially when the rememberer needs self-protection or seeks to suit the perceived expectations of an audience. Hence it happens that perpetrators, victims, and bystanders to an atrocity can each recall it differently, even when no party intends to be lying.

In spite of these problems, a broad consensus persists that memory is valuable. Not only is it essential in our efforts to picture the past; another widespread article of faith is that memory of man-made disaster can help us to avoid its recurrence. In a 1993 book called *Against Forgetting*, Carolyn Forché collects poems written during or about twentieth-century trauma: the Armenian Genocide, World War I and World War II, Stalin's and Mao's repressions, the Spanish Civil War, the Indo-Pakistani and Middle-Eastern wars, the Korean and Vietnam wars, various cases of repression in Latin America and Africa, apartheid in South Africa, and the struggle for civil rights in the United States.[1] Forché's book not only assumes that humankind is better off remembering its suffering; it further assumes—and in considerable measure shows—that human responses to disaster are in essential ways similar: pain, memories of pain, and poems that express pain are easily understandable from one culture and historical situation to the next. The work of groups like Amnesty International and Human Rights Watch is based in similar convictions (1) that human suffering and fundamental human rights do not vary with time, place, or culture, and (2) that drawing attention to suffering and to rights abuse is ameliorative.

Broadly speaking, I share these assumptions, but find the second less simple than it first appears. To turn a spotlight on suffering can, first of all, violate the dignity of the victim. When the Japanese writer Ōe Kenzaburō (who was, incidentally, an early supporter of the conference on which the present volume is based) visited Hiroshima twenty years after the dropping of the atomic bomb on that city, he found some of the victims resentful of his probes. One wrote to him that "people in Hiroshima prefer to remain silent. . . . They do not like to display their misery for use as 'data' in the movement against atomic bombs or in other political struggles."[2] Similarly, Primo Levi found that the earliest wishes of many Holocaust victims after 1945 were not to draw public attention to what had happened but to struggle to return to normal patterns of life.[3] Yet, in other cases, victims have actively called for public scrutiny. Ding Zilin, whose son was killed in the Beijing Massacre of 1989, has campaigned tirelessly for an official accounting of exactly what happened on June 4, 1989, and who was responsible; and many

Holocaust victims, after recovery from initial shock, have sought commemoration, asked reparations and supported "Holocaust studies." Ōe
Kenzaburō, after visiting Hiroshima, concludes that victims must have
"first right" in the matter of whether or not to examine the past.[4]

A related risk in looking back at atrocities and seeking to "come to
terms" hides inside the assumption that things can in fact be made right
again. The German term *wiedergutmachung*, as Vera Schwarcz points
out in her chapter of this book, seems to suggest that restoration is possible. The word "reparations," often used by victims as well as by perpetrators, seems to hold out the same promise. Yet the poet Dan Pagis
(whom Schwarcz quotes in her essay) mocks this promise with powerful irony: "The scream back into the throat. . . . The smoke back to the
chimneys. . . . Nothing is too late." Moreover the idea of reparation
raises the difficult question—in one sense an absurd question—of how
to convert an irremediable loss into a monetary figure. No one can put
smoke back into a chimney, or someone's dead grandmother back into
her rocking chair; how can we dare to assign dollar amounts to such
things? The impossibility of an answer can seem an argument in principle against all reparation, but the conclusion does not follow. Even if
we cannot restore a *status quo ante*—which alone would be full "reparation"—there remains a significant choice between doing a partial reparation, however fractional, and doing nothing.

The question of whether "doing something" should include punishment of perpetrators can also be more complex than it first appears. Few
would argue that leaders responsible for systematic murder and torture—
Ta Mok, Pinochet, and others—should be "brought to justice." Victims
and their families receive spiritual comfort when this is done; more
broadly, humanity as a whole seems to gain, both in the present and
possibly for the future, by promotion of the principle that certain behavior is unacceptable no matter where committed or by whom. "Is not the
destruction of humans in Prague," wrote Vaclav Havel in 1984, "a destruction of all humans?"[5] But what kinds of punishments are appropriate? Let us sidestep for the moment the controversial question of whether
capital punishment is ever justified. In the cases of wars, genocides, and
other large atrocities, we need to consider the related question of how
large a group shares responsibility.

Chinese people have often felt, and with good reason, that the 1945
war crimes trials in Tokyo did not address the atrocities of World War II
as squarely as did the parallel trials in Nuremburg. Although certain

Japanese generals were tried and executed, should not the Japanese emperor also have been held responsible—either as an active participant in warmaking or as a symbol of the Japanese nation? Why shouldn't Japan pay reparations to China, as Germany has to Israel? At an emotional level, many Chinese even half a century later tend to hold all Japanese to some extent responsible for wartime atrocities. To what extent is this justified? Honda Katsuichi is a Japanese journalist who has done much to expose the Japanese army's flagrant excesses during the war; in this sense he is a friend of China. But he declines personal responsibility. Born in 1933, he points out that he was, at the time, a mere four-year-old who knew nothing of what happened.[6] Is this all right? Is a second generation free from responsibility for the acts of its forebears? In matters such as the return of stolen property, it is fairly clear that a second generation inherits a responsibility to set things right. But what about moral responsibility? When the descendants of victims present the descendants of perpetrators with grievances, there arises a danger of institutionalizing antagonism and nursing animosity among people who might otherwise begin to grow beyond these angers. On the other hand, who can look at the granddaughter of a victim and tell her to set aside the question of who murdered her grandmother? The dilemma about how a second generation can seek justice can be solved in part by government action. A state can issue apologies or reparations to another state—even after many years have passed—without implying that individual descendants are personally responsible for the atrocities committed by their ancestors.

If such a role were all that governments thought about, they might play it fairly easily; but in the real world, politics pushes moral questions around. For decades the government of postwar Japan avoided the issue of Japan's war guilt, and for many years, as well, no Western government and neither of the Chinese governments (Communist or Nationalist) saw fit to press the issue. Each side had "good" political reasons for its inaction, as the chapters by Ian Buruma and Takashi Yoshida in this volume indicate. Locked in a long-term political rivalry after 1945, the two Chinese governments sought diplomatic and trade (including investment) relations with Japan, and hence were not inclined to confront the Japanese government with an unpleasant issue. To raise specifically the Nanking Massacre was awkward for the Nationalists because the debacle seemed to symbolize their defeat—a defeat that in 1949 took on the greater humiliation of banishment to Taiwan. For the

Communists, too, Nanking presented a special awkwardness because it was, at the time it was attacked, the Nationalists' capital; to champion its case would lend glory to a rival. Later, when popular resentment of the Communist government swelled after the Great Leap Forward and the Cultural Revolution, that government faced the additional problem that stimulation of popular anti-Japanese feeling might get out of hand and turn against the Communists' own rule.[7] For its part the United States government, as victor in the Pacific war, was positioned to press the war guilt issue, but also had political reasons not to do so. Douglas MacArthur, who led the postwar U.S. Occupation of Japan, took steps to shield the Japanese emperor from war responsibility in order to stabilize the Occupation. In addition, the U.S. government and other Western governments sought to secure Japan as an ally in the emerging Cold War with the Soviet Union and felt that this effort could be undermined by pressing the war issue too hard. Hence we can understand (remembering that "understand" does not have to mean "approve of") a number of reasons why governments of several kinds have chosen to remain silent about the Nanking massacre.

It is more difficult to understand the long silence of the Chinese people themselves. Surveys show that fifty years after the end of the war, popular Chinese resentment of the Japanese invasion remained strong.[8] It is easy to confirm such survey results by inquiring about the war among virtually any Chinese people old enough to remember it. The resentment is strong; why has it gone unexpressed for so long?

One obvious contributing factor is government repression. When it is state policy in China not to raise an issue, discussion of that issue is limited to unofficial oral networks and to expressions in public that are, at most, veiled and occasional. Another factor is the almost continual turmoil that plagued China from the war through the end of the Mao years—a civil war, a series of tumultuous social campaigns, a tremendous famine, "class struggle," and much more. Dramatic events so dominated daily life that to turn attention to the disasters of a bygone day would seem a luxury. A third factor is that—as noted above—victims sometimes need some distance in time before they revisit painful events through memory. It can be too hard to look squarely at horrible facts right after they have occurred, and survivors—unfairly but truly—can feel guilt or shame.[9] Holocaust studies did not grow rapidly until three or four decades after the Holocaust; a similar time lag appears in Japanese literary accounts of the dropping of atomic bombs on Hiroshima and Nagasaki; in China the excesses of late Maoism found quick but superficial expression in the "scar" literature of 1979–1980, but society's deeper wounds remain largely unaddressed even now.

To me, though, all these factors together do not fully explain the long silence of the Chinese people over Nanking. I feel there is another cause, although I admit that it is hard to pinpoint. I believe that a deep sense of Chinese cultural pride has played a role. This is a justifiable pride, a pride seated in the notion that a few centuries earlier (in Tang times, for example) China was the largest, strongest, wealthiest, most highly cultured, and most cosmopolitan place on earth. When "barbarian" invasions occurred, the power of Chinese culture had converted the barbarians to Chinese ways. In 1937 something so grossly ugly and humiliating as the Nanking Massacre seemed to Chinese sensibility so profoundly wrong—especially when suffered at the hands of "lesser" Japan—that, I believe, in a sense it deserved only to be ignored. (There is a tendency in Chinese culture—observable in several contexts—to blur the line between "what is" and "what ought to be" by obliterating things that ought not to have happened.[10]) From the late 1930s through the early 1960s China produced many works of fiction and film about the war with Japan, but none showed the Chinese losing, let alone suffering outright massacre. There were, to be sure, famous stories about foreign insults to China—such as the sign at a Shanghai park that, at least in legend, read "No Dogs or Chinese Allowed."[11] But such stories focused on the warped mentality of those who delivered the insults; they did not portray a devastated China.

In 1997 Iris Chang's best-seller *The Rape of Nanking: The Forgotten Holocaust of World War II* shattered Chinese quiescence over Nanking.[12] The book is eloquent and powerful, but it is worth noting that the author, although connected to Nanking by stories passed through her parents from her grandparents' generation, is an American separated from the massacre by space, time, and culture. Chang writes and lectures in English, and many of the people in her enthusiastic audiences are overseas Chinese who are similarly removed from firsthand experience of the massacre. Hence we see here again that people who stand a certain distance from disaster seem to find crying out somewhat easier.

For Chang and her audience some of the obvious barriers to expression—government repression, need for recovery time, and so on— are largely absent. Another important difference in their case is the difference between firsthand and secondhand experience of pain. In daily life we take this distinction so much for granted that we easily overlook it. Consider a simple toothache. Phenomenologically speaking, what we mean by "toothache" is two very different things. If we look at someone who has a bad toothache, we see certain images: a contorted face, a hand gripping the jaw, perhaps the whole person jumping up and down. We also may hear sounds: "Ow!" "Oooooh-h-h!" "Dammit!" or maybe just "I have a toothache." All or any of this can be what we mean to report when we say "X has a toothache." But this is for a third-person X. When X is oneself, notice how the same statement reports a very different kind of thing: There are no visual images, no sounds, and no language—just that sharp and highly unpleasant sensation inside the mouth. We should reflect on how it is that two such very different kinds of impression can both be accurately reported as "toothache."[13]

If such is true for toothaches, can it not be true for massacres? When Iris Chang feels pain, it is a pain several layers removed from the original sensations of the massacre victims. Her grandmother's pain is closer; it comes from memories of the terrible scenes themselves. But her grandmother's pain itself must have been layered by the time she spoke with Iris's generation; she must have repeated the stories several times, and the pain she felt with later tellings probably was less than during earlier, fresher tellings; and the pain associated with any of her storytelling must have been much less than the shock and pain experienced in witnessing original events. None of this, of course, brings us to the widest gap of all—that between the pain of witnessing the murders and, for the victims, of suffering them.

To point out that the pain in Iris Chang's memory is several layers removed from the original pain of victims is not to denigrate the value of her writing. Indeed, it is admirable that she can take indirect impressions so deeply to heart and can feel a responsibility to speak for an older generation that for its own reasons has remained silent. But questions can arise when embrace of the problem comes to involve other feelings and attitudes. Second-generation Chinese-Americans, for example, commonly face the problem of whether and how to preserve some elements of "Chineseness" in their cultural identities. Ian Buruma has expressed doubt that identifying with a massacre is the best of choices:

> It is, it appears, not enough for Chinese-Americans to be seen as the heirs of a great civilization; they want to be recognized as heirs of their very own Holocaust. In an interview about her celebrity, Chang related how a

woman came up to her in tears after a public reading and said that Chang's account of the massacre had made her proud to be Chinese-American. It seems a very peculiar source of pride.[14]

Buruma is not saying that Nanking should be forgotten; indeed, he has written extensively on how Japan's war in Asia has been and should be remembered.[15] He is questioning one of the secondary uses to which memory of Nanking can be put.

Over the years the variety of these secondary uses has been considerable. Fei Fei Li points out in the introduction to this book how a "multiplicity of perspectives" has grown from the Nanking massacre. Victims, perpetrators, and third parties have had differing viewpoints; so, in some ways, have earlier and later generations; and the policies of governments have diverged not only from one another but sometimes, especially in the case of China, from the popular feelings of the governed peoples.

Before the 1980s China's Communist government did not permit any unofficial expression of anti-Japanese feeling in public; as Japan's investments in China grew during the Deng Xiaoping years, popular Chinese resentment of "economic imperialism" seems to have obliged Deng to permit at least some popular sentiment about Japan to surface, although Beijing University students were stopped when they protested in the streets. By 1998, when the Communist Party leadership was consciously stoking Chinese nationalism in order to strengthen its own hand, Deng's successor, Jiang Zemin, demanded on a trip to Japan that the Japanese government apologize in writing for its invasion of China in the 1930s. Ignoring the bloody history of his own regime, Jiang claimed that his generation had a duty to pass history on to the next generation.

The difficulties of "passing history" to later generations are more famous in the case of Japan, where postwar textbooks have downplayed or ignored Japan's invasions of its neighbors and where many in the younger generation now seem never to have heard of the Nanking Massacre. Yet memory in Japan is not as weak as outsiders sometimes fear. Some Japanese scholars, and a few courageous politicians, have urged that Japan face its past squarely. (See the chapters by Kasahara Tokushi, Onuma Yasuaki, and Takashi Yoshida.) Their opponents at the other end of the spectrum of Japanese opinion have been called "revisionists" because of their radical claim that events such as the Nanking Massacre simply did not happen—or at least did not happen in remotely the way

that the Chinese side claims. But by their very eagerness to deny atrocities, the revisionists not only take memory seriously but implicitly un-
derscore the tenet that atrocity in war is wrong. This is not the same as
obliterating history or claiming that it has no moral significance.

Some of the debates that the Japanese revisionists have stimulated
have shed more heat than light. Passions are sometimes expressed, for
example, in arguments over numbers: Did 300,000 people die, or only
10,000? Numbers can seem to be metaphors for the size of the wrong-
ness involved, but in the end they cannot measure some of the important
and probably unmeasurable questions about how painful the Massacre
was to its victims, how deep the insult to China's dignity, how much and
what kind of an apology is due, and so on. Of course the number of
victims is important, and should be established as accurately as possible; but by themselves numbers cannot represent the moral significance of a massacre.

Some of the partisans in recent debates have also fallen into self-
undermining exaggeration. In her paper for the Princeton conference,
for example, Iris Chang wrote that "the Yangtze River ran red with blood
for days" after the Nanking Massacre.[16] Here she was passing along,
uncritically, a popular Chinese hyperbolic phrase that could not possibly have been literally true. She held as well that the story of the Massacre survived "because the Japanese campaign for total obliteration of
the city fell a few souls short."[17] In fact, many more than a few witnessed and survived the events. On the other hand, Higashinakano Shudo,
in a cool, precise style quite different from Chang's, produces positions
that strain credulity just as much. Although he does not say so bluntly,
the argument in his chapter of this volume amounts to the following: At
the time of the Nanking events, international law prohibited the killing
of prisoners of war (POWs). In order to qualify as a POW, one had to be
a "belligerent," meaning a person who had engaged in battle. The people
killed at Nanking had not been belligerents (had not "laid down arms,"
since they had never taken them up). Therefore they were not POWs.
Therefore killing them did not violate international law.

The student-organized conference at Princeton represented a wide
variety of viewpoints. It set the difficult but admirable goal of seeking,
as much as possible, a unified picture of what happened and an understanding of how various later interpretations have come about. At its
best the conference resembled a sort of courtroom in which every person present was like a juror weighing different testimonies. Was, for

example, the rape of Nanking a military policy ordered from Tokyo or a case of soldiers running amok? Some addressed this question by observing that Nanking was China's capital at the time and that it makes sense that an invading army would have had orders to hit it hard in order to break the back of Chinese national resistance. There was also some evidence adduced that imperial orders to sack Nanking were probably issued, as well as evidence that such orders, and especially their connection to Japan's Emperor Hirohito, were covered up. On the other hand, as Haruko Taya Cook's paper in this volume shows, there is evidence that Japanese soldiers were under regulations and could be punished for violations. That the possibility of such punishment had at least some credibility is indirectly confirmed by accounts from the Chinese side that women were killed immediately after they were raped. This was done, according to the accounts, partly in order to prevent report of the rapes. But Japanese soldiers would not have feared reports to a Chinese authority; if they killed in order to hide evidence of rape, it must have been to hide it from Japanese authorities.

To "reason" in this way about hideous facts can seem insensitive or even a bit disgusting. Who are we, sitting in comfortable rooms at Princeton University or elsewhere, to coolly extract "implications" from the story of a woman who was raped and then bayoneted? Aware of this problem, the student organizers of the Princeton conference took pains to allow the expression of understandable outrage, even while seeking to keep reason as the governing principle of the meetings. The sense that moral questions (and not just "national interests") have a place in international relations pervaded the conference. Most participants agreed that to pass moral judgment on the Japanese who were responsible for the Nanking Massacre is appropriate. In its finest moments, however, discussion transcended the question of nations and rose to a human plane, recognizing that neither savagery nor victimhood belongs particularly to any one people. In a conference summary, Norman Itzkowitz, a Princeton professor of Near Eastern studies, observed that to demonize an adversary, to take satisfaction in destroying him or her, to teach hate from one generation to the next, and so on, compose a dangerous pattern of human behavior that affects human beings at many levels. To claim that such tendencies are a permanent mark of only one or another portion of humanity does not solve the problem, but only illustrates it. To me, the most heartening aspect of the Princeton conference came in observing how a group of young undergraduates, representing a new generation of Chinese, could address the complex and contentious topic of Nanking with an intellectual clarity and a moral probity that their elders, including people of several nationalities, have seldom matched.

Notes

1. Carolyn Forché, ed., *Against Forgetting: Twentieth-Century Poetry of Witness* (New York: W.W. Norton, 1993).

2. Ōe Kenzaburō, *Hiroshima Notes* (New York: Grove Press, 1996), pp. 19–20.

3. Primo Levi, *The Drowned and the Saved* (New York: Vintage Books, 1989), chapter 3.

4. Ōe, *Hiroshima Notes*, p. 109.

5. Vaclav Havel, "Politics and Conscience," in *Living in Truth* (London: Faber and Faber, 1984), p. 149.

6. Honda Katsuichi, *The Nanjing Massacre: A Japanese Journalist Confronts Japan's National Shame*, transl. Karen Sandness (Armonk, NY: M.E. Sharpe, 1999), p. xxv.

7. In 1982, as Ian Buruma points out in chapter 1, the Chinese government finally addressed the "textbook issue" partly as a salve to rising popular Chinese concern about the economic role of Japan in post-Mao China.

8. In 1995 a survey by *Zhongguo qingnianbao* showed 96.8 percent of Chinese still "angered by the tragic disaster inflicted by the Japanese imperialists"; a survey by the Japanese newspaper *Showa shinbun* found only slightly lower figures. See Jui-te Chang, "The Politics of Commemoration: A Comparative Analysis of the Fiftieth Anniversary Commemoration in Mainland China and Taiwan Regarding the Victory of the War of Resistance Against Japan" (unpublished paper), pp. 21, 31.

9. Primo Levi's eloquent reflections on the Holocaust in *The Drowned and the Saved* include an entire chapter (no. 3) on the "shame" that survivors may feel.

10. The retouching of photographs and the reworking of museum exhibits during the Mao years to make "incorrect" people disappear is one example. Another is the controversy in 1993 over the publication of Zheng Yi's book *Hongse jinianbei* (Red Memorial) (Taibei, Huashi wenhua gongsi, 1993), which shows how politically induced cannibalism had occurred in Guangxi in 1968. Those who opposed publication did not argue that the accounts were false; they held that it was wrong to publish to the world something that by Chinese standards should not have happened. The French Sinologist Jean Chesneaux has made the interesting—although tenuous—observation that the Chinese character *fei*, for "bandit"—or group outside the proper polity—resembles the character for *fei* meaning "is not."

11. In calling this story a "legend" I do not mean to suggest that it is a fiction. I do not believe that any sign read bluntly "No Dogs or Chinese Allowed," because photography arrived in Shanghai four decades before the alleged sign did, and anything so blatant would certainly have been photographed, if not by a Chinese then by some fair-minded Westerner. The only alleged photograph of such a sign that I have ever seen was in an old Shanghai guidebook the name of which now escapes me. The writing in the photograph was not legible, but the message on the sign was quite lengthy, consisting of about eight numbered items in English. To me it seems plausible that one of the items read "The Park Is for Europeans Only" or the like, and

another prohibited pets such as cats and dogs. To me it seems quite natural that the offensive implication would be simplified as it was passed along.

12. Iris Chang, *The Rape of Nanking: The Forgotten Holocaust of World War II* (New York: Penguin Books, 1997).

13. Of course, from our daily-life assumptions about physical similarities among human beings, we understand that the two very different kinds of impression are both evidence for the same basic thing—a rotting or infected tooth—and not reports of differing phenomena.

14. Ian Buruma, "The Joys and Perils of Victimhood," *New York Review of Books*, vol. XLVI, no. 7, (April 1999) p. 4.

15. Ian Buruma, *The Wages of Guilt*: *Memories of War in Germany and Japan* (New York: Meridian Books, 1994).

16. Chang, *Rape of Nanking*, "Introduction," p. 4.

17. Ibid., p. 1.

Acknowledgments

First and foremost, the editors would like to thank our three academic advisers, without whose assistance this book would never have been possible. Perry Link, Professor of Chinese Language and Literature at Princeton University, has provided us with unconditional support from the very first day of the conception of the Nanking 1937 Conference idea until this very moment. He has lent us his expertise, professionalism, and extraordinary insights, and has devoted hours of labor reviewing each paper, correcting each grammatical mistake and listening to our thoughts and debates. Sheldon Garon, Professor of History at Princeton University, has inspired us tremendously with his uncanny sense of honesty and sincerity. He has selflessly put aside tons of his own work to critique the papers and provided invaluable suggestions. Last but certainly not least is Professor Richard Falk, Albert G. Milbank Professor of International Laws and Practice at Princeton University. Professor Falk's warm-hearted support has encouraged us since the very beginning of our conference organization. His unparalleled perspective and rich experience have been an endless resource for our understanding of the subject and how to treat it from an objective, scholarly viewpoint.

We would also like to thank all the students who were core committee members of the Princeton University Nanking 1937 Conference for uncountable hours of dedication and inspiration that made the conference a memorable experience that will remain with all of us for a lifetime: Ying Zhou, class of 1999, our tireless cochair; I-Shin Chow, 2000, the amazingly talented publicity chair; Sulene Liu Chi, 1999, our dedicated and imaginative exhibition chair; Katherine Lam, 2000, the always energetic treasurer; Heather Yang, 2000, our cheerful film chair; and Haiyin Chen, 1998, our multitasking-but-always-on-top-of-things core member. We sincerely wish all of them the best of luck in the future, whether in further study or in other areas to which their hearts may lead them, and we hope our paths cross again soon in life.

We are also very grateful to all the people who willingly gave their time and energy to a bunch of students with grandiose dreams. Without their assistance the conference could not possibly have been as successful as it was, and the book would remain an empty dream. Thanks especially to Professor Ying-shih Yu of Princeton for an amazing amount of encouragement and advice; Rutgers Chinese Students and Scholars Association, and especially its coordinator Lu Wang, for the long hours they spent on conference publicity as well as Lu's critical reading of our manuscripts; Professor John Dower of MIT, who from the very beginning gave us tremendous support and provided us with a long list of initial contacts we could not possibly have compiled otherwise; Martha Smalley, Research Services Librarian and Curator of Special Collections at the Yale Divinity Library, who was a tremendously enjoyable collaborator on the photograph and document exhibition of the Nanking Massacre; President Harold Shapiro of Princeton University for both encouragement and monetary support; History Professor Ruth Rogaski of Princeton University, who has remained a faithful supporter of the conference and ensuing work; Professor Norman Itzkowitz of the Department of Near East Asian Studies of Princeton University, who was an enthusiastic participant in our conference and continued his support for our book; Paula Chow, director of Princeton's International Center, for an incredible amount of logistical support and invaluable publicity; Shi Young, coauthor of *The Rape of Nanking: An Undeniable History in Photographs,* for his advice and support for our photograph and document exhibition; Harry Bone for his tireless assistance in writing and editing the Introduction; Iris Chang, author of *The Rape of Nanking: The Forgotten Holocaust of World War II*, an active supporter of both our conference and our book; and Carol Gluck, whose advice and participation were key factors in the book's being published.

We would also like to thank our forever special friend Ōe Kenzaburō, Nobel laureate in literature and former visiting professor at Princeton University, not only for being one of the first people to take the conference seriously but also for the moral support that helped give us the encouragement necessary to carry it out.

Finally, a sincere thank you to all the participants in the conference and contributors to this book for helping making our dream a reality. Last but not least, we could not possibly have accomplished this much without our families and friends having put up with us whenever we became victims of the inadequate time and uncontrollable stress that occasionally made us less than totally pleasant to live with.

Introduction

In December 1937, Japan launched a massive attack on the Chinese capital of Nanking. The city fell on December 13, and over the next six weeks the Japanese military forces committed mass executions, raping and looting. The Nanking Massacre, or the Rape of Nanking, remains the single most important symbol of Japanese militarism in World War II in the minds of East Asians.

Various political factors have contributed to the delayed recognition of the Nanking Massacre in Western nations, however. The Japanese government downplayed the degree of its militaristic advances during World War II immediately after the war, while both Chinese governments purposefully neglected the incident as they focused on establishing their political and economic strength, which required a sound relationship with Japan. The U.S. government valued Japan's position as a strategic ally during the Cold War more than the need for justice. Such political complications led each country to circumvent the issues of Nanking.

Events in recent years have led to the internationalization of the Nanking Massacre though. The end of the Cold War has occurred simultaneously with China achieving a higher status within the international community. As China has tried to assert its political power, Japan has remained reluctant to bow to China for fear of losing its leadership position in the region. Meanwhile China has renewed contact with the West, allowing more Chinese citizens to emigrate to Western nations, bringing with them knowledge of Chinese culture and history that have heretofore been unknown in America.

Perhaps influenced by America's history of free speech, many recent Chinese immigrants are standing up and unleashing memories that have been suppressed for sixty years. They are demanding apologies and reparations that other victims of World War II atrocities have received but which have been denied them.

Partly as a result of all these factors, in recent years the international community has finally begun to scrutinize and, in many cases, condemn the atrocities at Nanking. The U.S. Congress has introduced two resolutions aimed at extracting an admission of wartime responsibility and restitution for the families of survivors. Japan itself has faced lawsuits from Japanese historians demanding an end to textbook censorship and from Chinese survivors demanding reparations. Public interest in Nanking has been fueled by the discovery and publications of eyewitness accounts such as the diary of John Rabe, a Nazi official stationed in Nanking, and the journals and photographs taken by American missionaries inside the Nanking Safety Zone.

Much of this information has been incorporated into Iris Chang's *The Rape of Nanking*, which was an international bestseller for two years, selling more than a half-million copies and causing a major controversy in Japan. It has raised the consciousness of many Westerners about this dark chapter in twentieth-century history and has accelerated the process of disclosure and investigation that had been proceeding slowly but steadily prior to the book's publication.

All this recent interest in Nanking is one aspect of a larger worldwide movement in which both nations and multinational groups are attempting to reach closure regarding past atrocities and inhumanities. These activities have an importance reaching far beyond aggressors or victims, beyond admission or vindication, but rather as a search for the common causes of all human atrocities and for solutions that would set humanity on a path toward a more peaceful and harmonious international community.

* * *

It is with all of this in mind that *Nanking 1937: Memory and Healing* was conceived. Other recently published books have considered the Nanking Massacre from a single point of view. However, the multiplicity of perspectives from which people have viewed the Nanking Massacre has frustrated those who aim for postwar reconciliation in East Asia. In order for discussions of the Nanking Massacre and other related atrocities to move beyond accusations and condemnations, all perspectives must be given fair exposure so as to provide a clearer lens through which this important event can be examined.

Thus *Nanking 1937: Memory and Healing* is the first attempt to consider all aspects of the debate. It contains articles from American, Chinese, European, and Japanese scholars, including both progressive and revisionist points of view. The book is subdivided into four sections, each of which examines a different aspect of the over sixty-year controversy.

The book's first section examines Nanking's role in twentieth-century history and discusses the importance of continuing the debate until resolution is reached. In the second section Chinese and Japanese scholars present their views of what actually took place in the winter of 1937–1938. The third section examines the historiography of Nanking, particularly how it has been remembered in Asia and in the West, and what factors have influenced that remembrance. In the final section, three scholars discuss the future of the Nanking debate.

By treating the Nanking Massacre from such a variety of perspectives, and by taking the position that all atrocities in human history have common features, we hope to reach a broader and deeper understanding of the issue than has heretofore taken place in any international forum and to dig deep into the very soul of a humanity that would not only commit such an atrocity but also allow its memory to linger without closure for more than sixty years.

* * *

Nanking 1937: Memory and Healing is an outgrowth of the Princeton University Nanking 1937 Conference, held on November 22, 1997, one of the first events in the United States to deal with that atrocity. The conference brought together speakers who represented a wide range of viewpoints similar to that in the subsequent book. The audience ranged from Chinese immigrants who bore a lifetime of memories about the event to college students who had never even heard of the Nanking Massacre before.

What occurred was an experience that was both educational and highly emotional. Aging survivors and children of victims stood up and unleashed long-pent-up emotions and tears in a public and, in many cases, shared catharsis. Students struggled to understand how such a tragedy could be virtually unknown in the West and how so many governments could allow it to remain unresolved after sixty years.

The trauma of that event encouraged the editors and most of the contributors of the conference to expand that moment into this broader-based book, which includes scholars not included in the November 1997 conference. But neither the Princeton University Nanking 1937 Conference nor *Nanking 1937: Memory and Healing* alone can heal the sixty-year-old wounds. They are only a beginning. Our hope is that the conference and the book will be effective steps in sparking discussions that will contribute to peace and understanding in East Asia and perhaps help to prevent such inhumanities from reoccurring by promoting a common understanding and forgiveness. Following the advice of Richard Falk, "The mere passage of time often does not by itself achieve healing. It requires a deliberate visible effort."

Fei Fei Li
Robert Sabella
David T. Liu
June 1, 1999
Princeton, N.J.

Part One
Nanking in a Global Context

1

The Nanking Massacre
as a Historical Symbol

Ian Buruma

While it is conventional to begin the discussion of a historical topic by presenting the historical background of the event itself, we chose a different route. Since its occurrence, the Nanking Massacre has become known equally for its atrocity and for its controversial aftermath, and has been a central topic in many political, economic, legal, and intellectual debates since the end of World War II. Discussions of the event often raise more issues than are settled. Moreover, the debate itself is subject to a broad scope of influences, ranging from pure denial to utter outrage.

With these concerns in mind, we start our discussion with Ian Buruma, whose logic and sharp insights constantly shake the existing order of analysis and arguments, a famous example being his widely acclaimed book The Wages of Guilt. *This follow-up essay to Buruma's Princeton University Nanking 1937 Conference keynote speech warns against the usage of the Nanking Massacre as a "negative badge" and questions many contemporary efforts concerning the postwar treatments of the Nanking Massacre. Buruma also alerts both sides of the debate to perspectives they may have overlooked or neglected. —Eds.*

Reading over what some of the Japanese revisionists have been saying about the Nanking Massacre, I marveled once again at the sheer childishness of their reasoning. In his introduction to Tanaka Masaaki's *Nanking Gyakusatsu no Kyoko* (The fabrication of the Nanking Massacre, 1984), Watanabe Shoichi wrote that people in Japan had not known about the Massacre during the war, and Japanese newspapers hadn't mentioned it, so it cannot really have happened. It must have been a fabrication, concocted by the victorious Allies during the Tokyo Trials to demonize Japan. Unfortunately, the revisionists claim, some Japanese persist in spreading the fabrication abroad, blackening the name not only of the Japanese wartime generation, but of their children and grandchildren too. Especially guilty in their eyes are the *Asahi Shimbun* and most especially its reporter Honda Katsuichi who simply parroted Chinese propaganda in his books on China. These reports are a "criminal insult" to Japan.

Tanaka himself harps on the same point, about the Massacre never having been reported in the wartime Japanese press, as though this constitutes a serious argument. He also has a peculiar observation about Japanese swords not being up to the job of mass executions. But he has an even stranger argument up his sleeve. Unlike Westerners and Chinese, he says, the Japanese have no history of planned massacres. To perpetrate a systematically executed massacre is un-Japanese. It is something foreigners do. Japanese soldiers may have killed Chinese during the war, but they were all soldiers in the heat of battle. When civilians got killed in the crossfire, it was unintentional. In any case, he maintains, it was physically impossible to kill hundreds of thousands of people in a matter of weeks.

In a notorious interview with *Playboy* magazine, the former Liberal-Democratic Party politician and current Tokyo mayor Ishihara Shintaro also denied that a massacre had ever taken place. It was just Chinese propaganda, he said. In any case, what about Hiroshima? Wasn't that many times worse? This is, in fact, a common variation of Tanaka's point: Hiroshima was a crime planned in cold blood. Nanking was the kind of thing that happens in any war.

From a historical point of view, these views are, of course, silly. But to look at the so-called *Nankin Ronso* (Nanking debate), which took place in the 1980s, a few years before the German *Historikerstreit* (historian's debate), as a debate about history is to miss the point. The *Historikerstreit* involved several eminent historians. The *Nankin Ronso* was dominated by nonhistorians. Tanaka was an ex-journalist; Honda is still a journalist; Yamamoto Shichihei was a writer; and Watanabe Shoichi is a *hyoronka* (publicist). The issue was not historical, in the sense of attempting to find out what actually happened and interpreting the data. The issue was political.

Since 1945 the Nanking Massacre has been used as a symbol of evil in the Tokyo Trials and in Japanese political discourse. The Nanking Massacre was, in a phrase that crops up quite often in current U.S. writing, the "Japanese Holocaust." "Nanking" was shorthand for the unique barbarity of Japanese militarism. Because of Nanking, Japanese cannot be trusted ever again with the sovereign right to wage war. The revisionists want to topple that symbol, or at least revise it, because they wish Japan to regain that right. To topple the symbol, they must negate the history behind it. This is the problem with historical events that became political symbols: They invite revisionists with political programs.

The Nanking Massacre was an atrocity on a huge scale. At least tens of thousands of Chinese civilians and soldiers were killed. Women of all ages were raped and humiliated. There was a large amount of looting and destruction. Houses were burnt down to provide Japanese soldiers with a bit of warmth. Men were killed for fun. In sheer inventiveness, the cruelty of Japanese troops was on a par with the worst twentieth-century barbarities, of which, as we know, there have been many.

It is easy to get indignant about the absurd attempts of the revisionists to deny basic facts. We can ridicule them and feel morally superior for doing so. We can repeat the official Chinese figures—300,000 dead, and 20,000 rapes—and feel outraged that this atrocity has not had the attention it surely deserves. Yet, I think the revisionists may be onto something, for the wrong motives, perhaps, and drawing the wrong conclusions, but onto a legitimate problem nonetheless. The history of the Nanking Massacre has indeed been obscured by political propaganda, and by its symbolic use. It is encrusted with mythology of one kind or another. If the revisionists encourage us to act as proper historians and start sifting facts from myths, they will have done us all a service.

What are some of the myths that have grown around the reception of the Nanking Massacre, in Japan and elsewhere? One of the most common accusations is that the facts of the massacre have been systematically suppressed after the war, not just in Japan, but also in China and in the United States. This is contrasted to the constant attention being paid to the Jewish Holocaust. If you search for "Nanking" on the Internet, you will find a Web site set up by the New Jersey Hong Kong Network. *Nanking Massacre: The Forgotten Holocaust* is the title. "The awful atrocities," it says, "committed during the Nanking Massacre have been ignored and scarcely mentioned."

In fact, this is not entirely true. It wasn't reported much in the Japanese wartime press, naturally. However, even there, there was something. Boastful stories about individual soldiers engaging in contests to see how many heads they could chop off were reported in the *Nichi Nichi Shimbun*. I was told by a Japanese veteran that soldiers often deliberately exaggerated these tales to Japanese reporters to show what tough guys they were.

If the heavily censored Japanese press failed to report the massive killing, the world's press did not. The *London Times*, for example, gave bigger headlines to the Japanese bombing of U.S. and British gunboats in December 1937, but the robbing, arson, and mass executions in Nanking are given space, too, under the headline "The Conquerors' Brutality." According to the newspaper reports, most of the victims were Chinese soldiers, or civilians assumed by the Japanese to be Chinese soldiers. The bulk of Chiang Kai-shek's army, including most senior officers, had left Nanking to its own devices before the Japanese broke through the city walls. The troops who couldn't get away changed into civilian clothes. The Japanese were ordered to kill all remaining Chinese troops. They did so, with great brutality and without much discrimination. It is impossible to tell from these reports how many people were killed. It is doubtful whether we will ever know with any precision.

What happened at Nanking happened on a smaller scale in many Chinese villages and towns. One of the most important questions to ponder is to what extent the Nanking Massacre was a deliberate policy of terror to force Chiang Kai-shek to give up his resistance to Japan. This would not be unique. We only need to think of Bosnia. But it could also have been a matter of brutalized and badly disciplined troops running amuck. Were superior officers incompetent, indifferent, or simply ruthless? Did they perhaps encourage the troops to run wild, as a payoff for their deprivations during a long and nasty campaign? These are important questions, especially if one is going to make comparisons with the Nazi Holocaust. It remains a horrific event, whatever our interpretation. But it was hardly unique. The mixture of paranoia and racism in Japanese wartime propaganda is a common way to encourage inhumanity against defenseless people. Again, we have seen this in Bosnia. But genocide is a specific category of war crime. It is not as clear as some might think whether Nanking fits it.

It is interesting that Ienaga Saburo, in his book *The Pacific War*, believes that the Nanking Massacre was a horrible consequence of battlefield brutality, the sort of thing that happens in any large-scale war. He contrasts this to the bombing of Hiroshima and the systematic murder of Jews, which, in his view, were clear examples of planned genocide. The linking of Hiroshima with Auschwitz has become commonplace, and is, in my view, wrong. But this, too, is an example of using symbols of evil politically. Left-wing opponents of so-called American imperialism, such as Ienaga, tend to make this link. He certainly can't be classified as a revisionist or a right-wing chauvinist.

The Nanking Massacre was considered to be crucially important for the Tokyo Trials. Genocide, or crimes against humanity, had been defined as a new category during the Nuremberg Trials. The Holocaust did not fit any previously known act of war. The idea that people of a given race or religion had no right to be alive, and had to be exterminated like vermin, was novel. However brutal they were, there had been nothing quite like this in the Japanese war in Asia. Even the most ferocious Japanese ideologue wanted Japan to subjugate China, not kill every last Chinese man, woman, and child. Indeed, the Serbian effort to exterminate Muslims might have been a closer parallel to the Nazi enterprise than the Japanese massacres in China.

Since this new law for crimes against humanity was to be applied at the Tokyo Trials, a parallel to the Holocaust had to be found, and the Nanking Massacre seemed to be the closest thing. Far from being ignored, then, it was given great prominence, and General Matsui Iwane, who was in overall charge of the troops in Nanking, was hanged for it.

Without wishing to diminish the horror of what happened in 1937, one wonders how wise it was in retrospect to equate Japanese atrocities with the Nazi Holocaust. You don't have to follow the Japanese revisionist example and deny the facts to have these doubts. A too-hasty equation of Japanese military brutality and the Nazi extermination program can warp our interpretation of the facts. It also had a great effect on the political conclusions that were drawn from these facts after the war. Which brings us to another myth.

It is not true that the Japanese uniformly ignored or suppressed the history of the Massacre. Officials did, to be sure. The Ministry of Education continues to do its best to do so. But writers, journalists, and political activists have paid attention to it. Many books have been published on the subject, even though school textbooks skirted it. Not all these books are obscure or scholarly. The *Mainichi Shimbun*, for instance, published a magazine in 1975 that contained photographs of Japanese atrocities, including pictures taken in Nanking.

This is hardly enough, to be sure, but the Massacre was never ignored. The reason pacifists kept the issue alive in Japan was precisely the reason the revisionists tried to deny it. Here a comparison with Auschwitz is useful. Auschwitz was the symbol of German evil, and the evils of racism. Racial laws, indeed any form of racial discrimination, have become associated with Auschwitz. The Anne Frank Foundation in Amsterdam gets involved with all matters of discrimination in Holland. Attacks on Turks and other foreigners in Germany are usually followed by reminders of Auschwitz. Gunter Grass even argued against the reunification of Germany on the grounds that a unified Germany was responsible for Auschwitz. This seems an odd conclusion to draw. Still, most people will agree that you cannot have a civilized, democratic society with racial laws on its books.

The Nanking Massacre was the symbol of Japanese evil. But the conclusions drawn were different. Since there was no Japanese ideology that propagated genocide, Nanking stands for something else, something more specific: Japanese militarism. Instead of arguing that aggressive wars unleashed by dictatorial regimes are bound to result in atrocities, which is difficult to deny, the Allies concluded from the Tokyo Trials that Japan could not be trusted with warfare under any circumstances. Japan was denied the right to wage war, even if it became a democracy. Most Japanese, who were sick to death of war, went along with this. Whenever there is any talk about changing the constitution, peace activists will bring up Nanking to warn against it. As long as this is the case, we will have people like Watanabe, or Ishihara Shintaro, who will deny that anything untoward happened in Nanking at all.

China is, of course, another matter. In the People's Republic the Nanking Massacre was not really an issue until 1982. Indeed, it was hardly mentioned at all. This had little to do with appeasing Japan. If anything, China under Mao was paranoid about the potential resurgence of Japanese militarism, but Nanking was the Guomindang (Kuomintang) capital. There were no Communist heroes there, and Mao was not sentimental about civilian victims. Nanking suddenly became an issue in China as an indirect result of Deng Xiaoping's Open Door policy. He was vulnerable to accusations of being soft on the United States and Taiwan. He wanted to make favorable trade deals with Japan, and just before the Japanese prime minister was to visit Beijing, a Japanese trade delegation had gone to Taipei. It was an opportune moment for Deng to twist the knife.

In 1982, Japanese newspapers reported that the Ministry of Education had insisted on changing the word "invasion" of China to the phrase "advance into" China in school textbooks. In fact, this change had already been made some years before. Deng took the opportunity to warn against Japanese militarism, and decided to commemorate the Nanking Massacre with a museum. Suddenly survivors were encouraged to talk to journalists, including Japanese journalists.

Their stories are horrific, and there is no reason to doubt their veracity, but the pursuit of truth is not encouraged in China under the current regime, and the Nanking museum does not invite critical debate. Instead, it demands piety from the Japanese and patriotism from the Chinese. Japanese visitors are encouraged to bow their heads in sincere repentance and help to cement the undying friendship between the Chinese and Japanese peoples. Chinese are told to glory in the antifascist struggle and, as a slogan on the museum wall puts it, "redouble their efforts to strengthen China and support its foreign policy of peace and independence." This is not an atmosphere in which dispassionate historical inquiry can thrive.

There is one other problem that hinders our inquiries into the Nanking Massacre. It has become more and more common for minorities, not only in the United States, to build their identities around symbols of collective suffering. As religious habits dwindle, languages fade away and cultural habits are narrowed down to eating bagels or dim sum, symbols of terrible collective suffering become a kind of badge of common identity. This is a sad development, for instead of celebrating a rich tradition, it tends to lead to resentment and collective self-pity.

Chinese history and culture are extraordinarily rich. It would be grotesque if a Japanese atrocity should become a negative badge of Chinese identity. History should never be used in this way. Once a historical event becomes a political symbol of collective identity, it becomes impossible to question it, challenge accepted opinions about it, discuss it rationally, in short, to act as a responsible historian. To question the number of dead in Nanking, say, would be construed as being anti-Chinese or, worse, as justifying Japanese militarism. It would surely be better for us to back off from symbolism, and get down to the more mundane business of finding out what actually went on.

2

Redressing Grievances: Assessing the Nanking Massacre

Richard Falk

*Why study the Nanking Massacre? And why so many years after its oc-
currence? Though heated debate of the Nanking Massacre has never
ceased in the decades since World War II, interest in the issue has increased dramatically in recent years among ordinary people in the West
as well as among scholars around the world. Richard Falk raises questions that have been in the minds of many other scholars as well. How
do we remember the war? How can we heal?*

*As an expert in international relations and law, Falk provides us with
an overview of the trend toward globalization that has nurtured the re-
dressing of human grievances such as war atrocities. Both acute and
expansive, this general background presents a perspective for the more
detailed analyses of the Nanking Massacre to follow. —Eds.*

I. Grounding the Inquiry: Why Nanking 1937?

In recent years, there have been many efforts to redress past grievances,
at least symbolically, but in some instances substantively as well. Among
the more prominent examples are efforts by survivors and heirs to recover Holocaust gold and art; arguments mounted under the auspices of
the Organization of African Unity and calling upon Western governments to pay reparations as atonement for slavery; and, less assertively,
measures taken by several governments to acknowledge the wrongs done
in the past to indigenous peoples and to offer resources designed to enable such peoples to improve their present and future. These initiatives,
along with others, represent essentially voluntary moves that seek to
soften the harsher aspects of remembered wrongs.

An inquiry into the Nanking Massacre of 1937–1938 fits within this
wider setting of clarifying and rectifying past wrongs at the initiative of

representatives of the still aggrieved community. There are also more particular explanations for the inquiry: recently discovered evidence of what happened during those fateful weeks in Nanking, widely read and discussed books reconstructing the events, and a mutual interest on the part of the governments in Japan and China to move forward into the next century free from the darker shadows of their interplay, especially the period 1930–1945.

Beyond this, however, reconsidering Nanking represents an example of a still broader feature of the present: responsiveness to the acceleration of history—the sheer speed of change—that seems to be making our political consciousness more sensitive to various aspects of the dimension of time. As we seek to grasp a future spiraling so rapidly out of the present, we are also becoming more aware of what preceded, particularly the wounding events left behind without being sufficiently addressed to allow for healing to take place. The mere passage of time often does not by itself achieve this healing. Healing requires a deliberate and visible effort.

Some action was taken in the immediate aftermath of World War II that appeared to acknowledge the wrongs committed at Nanking. Above all, the Japanese commanding general at Nanking, General Iwane Matsui, was sentenced to death by the Tokyo Tribunal for his role in the Nanking atrocities committed by Japanese soldiers, specifically for his failure to take effective preventive action during those weeks of atrocity against the inhabitants of the city.[1] But such an initiative did not achieve healing. For one thing, it was an acknowledgment imposed by the victors in the war, and not by the Japanese government or the Japanese people. For another, unlike the apparent impact of the Nuremberg Trials on world public opinion, the parallel Tokyo Trials were not widely noted and remained controversial in Japanese society as the outcome of "a kangaroo court."

Perhaps most important of all of these background considerations is the conviction that past and present crimes against humanity are becoming occurrences of universal relevance, not to be confined to the political and moral imagination of the countries and their peoples who experienced the horrific events. As such, the activation of historical memory is both cathartic and potentially risky. It can be risky if the side of the perpetrator is seen as minimizing, or even denying or somehow refusing to admit, the gravity of the past crimes. Such an outcome marred the November 1998 visit of China's head of state, Jiang Zemin, to Japan on which occasion Japanese Prime Minister Keizo Obuchi refused to issue an apology in *written* form for Japan's wartime atrocities in China. Evidently, an *oral* apology was perceived by the Chinese government as being too ephemeral and ambiguous, especially as compared to Japan's willingness to provide Korea with just such a written apology previously. On the Japanese side, Hiromu Nonaka, the chief cabinet secretary, confirmed the problematic character of the Japanese acknowledgment with respect to China when he ineptly declared publicly in apparent exasperation, "Isn't this a finished problem?"[2]

These concerns form a complex tapestry that is very much part of the contemporary scene. This article seeks to examine some of these general international developments as a context for the better appreciation of what is the significance of this complex matter of delving anew into the human and historical reality of Nanking. Such a presupposition opposes the view that because the inquiry is taking place under academic auspices, its proper scope of concerns should be confined to setting the historical record straight. In this view, scholarly efforts should be *exclusively* devoted to providing as objective and accurate an account of the events that transpired as possible, as well as unearthing what is known about the participants and their motivation as part of an exercise in historical reconstruction. Of course, such objectivity is important as an expression of sincerity, and it is an appropriate academic task to improve the accuracy of our interpretation and presentation of past events. Such professionalism should always guide a scholarly investigation of past events by specialists. In my view there can be further and, more important, legitimate contributions arising from an academic investigation by way of deriving lessons for the future and through expressions of meaningful solidarity with the victims. This latter may include suggesting one or more forms of redress for past grievances, especially if they have not been sufficiently acknowledged in various critical sectors of public and official opinion.

As suggested above, the dynamics of official acknowledgement at an intergovernmental level apparently are not presently satisfactory for either side. China's leaders evidently feel disappointed, if not dismayed, by Japan's unwillingness at this point to formalize an apology as a way of closing the intergovernmental book on the past. Japan's current leaders, perhaps fearing an agitation of their own unrepentant ultranationalists, appear reluctant to go further than to offer a casual and abstract oral acknowledgement of the wrongs committed, and would obviously much prefer that the matter be dropped altogether. In view of this apparent stalemate at intergovernmental levels, transnational initiatives under-taken by members of civil society may be more fruitful, possibly creat-ing a better climate of appreciation, even creating movement toward reconciliation at a people-to-people level. Eventually, in an altered soci-etal climate, the leaders of the two dominant countries in the Asia-Pacific region may be able to respond by adopting a common position that wipes away misunderstandings on both sides, acknowledges the past ordeal in its various dimensions, and expresses remorse in a form that seems credible.

There is one further factor in the background of this revival of con-cern about the unresolved grievances of the Chinese people and nation in relation to their experience in the 1930s and 1940s. It involves the relative lack of attention given in Western, and specifically American, circles to the suffering endured by Asian societies that were the main victims during the several decades of Japanese expansionist militarism. Such inattention contrasts with the high-profiled attention devoted to the suffering caused European peoples, and especially Jews, by Nazi-ism. Also, post-1945 Japan was not made to repudiate its past to nearly the same extent as was Germany. Japan was allowed to keep the Em-peror system intact. The list of Japanese war criminals was consider-ably abridged for Cold War reasons. The comparative superficiality of political reconstruction in Japan during the American years of occupa-tion undoubtedly makes the activation of unpleasant facets of historical memory more difficult in the Japanese case, and yet more necessary. Unlike Germany when it resorted to aggression against its neighbors, Japan was genuinely confronted by a security challenge taking the form of economic encirclement that endangered its viability as a resource-poor state. This interpretation of its recourse to military expansion was endorsed by neutral analysts, and was expressed in the celebrated dis-sent by the Indian member of the Tokyo War Crimes Tribunal, Judge Radhabinod Pal.[3] Further, the use of atomic bombs against Hiroshima and Nagasaki at the end of World War II evoked widespread sympathy for Japan as itself the victim of an international crime of the greatest magnitude, a victimization that has never been the subject of apology or regret by its perpetrator.

Arguably, as well, the West bears some responsibility for not being more sensitive all along to the suffering experienced by the Chinese people during the course of the Japanese invasion and occupation. This tendency to overlook the Chinese ordeal was reinforced by political developments, especially the Communist triumph in China in 1949, which tended to preclude any positive feelings in the West toward the country and its people for what had been endured earlier at the hands of Japan. Of course, this pattern of refusal was further reinforced by Cold War alignments that created a strong alliance relationship with Japan and a very hostile and adversarial relationship with China that erupted into a direct military encounter in the course of the Korean War (1950–1952).

With these several considerations in mind, the illumination of such events as the Nanking Massacre at this point is a way also of suggesting that Western leadership and public opinion has been morally complacent due to its failure to take more seriously the Japanese record of atrocity in China.[4] In the new setting of international relations, with the Cold War over and China now an important trading partner and a more assertive global presence, the atmosphere has become receptive to looking backward in time to allow an assessment of just how awful was the Chinese experience of Japanese militarism. It is notable, in this regard, although hardly surprising, that much more attention was given by the popular media in the West to the sixtieth anniversary of Nanking than to any earlier anniversary. It is natural to ask, "Why?" As indicated above, there is no categorical answer, but reference to several overlapping aspects of the current context seems to add up to a satisfactory explanation: a changing strategic equation relating China and Japan to the West on a more equal basis, along with the aforementioned global tendency to pursue more actively grievances associated with past grievances. The publication of Iris Chang's book and the documentary materials on which her research relied also generated interest and controversy, motivating a clarification of the events at Nanking and their interpretation.

Evoking these memories in an American setting may subtly reopen another unresolved chapter from the same era, namely the dropping of atomic bombs on Japanese cities. It is relevant to recall the controversy of several years back when the respected Smithsonian Institution was induced to cut back drastically its plans for a full-scale exhibition on the fiftieth anniversary of the horrors experienced by the peoples of Hiroshima and Nagasaki in 1945. The very prospect of evoking such memories, and their alleged effect of casting the Japanese in the role of victim, was then deeply resented by veterans groups and the political right in America, which managed to mobilize an effective opposition.[5] From this perspective there may be somewhat greater receptivity to the post–Cold War possibilities for Americans to examine the shadow sides of its relation to Japan's past. But we should not exaggerate these possibilities. The issues remain extremely sensitive. American leaders are not at all ready to accept moral and legal responsibility for the manner in which World War II was waged. The two main issues present involved strategic bombing and reliance on weapons of mass destruction. Both of these tactics of war remain deeply embedded in American military doctrine and practice, and are not being widely challenged even in their current applications. It is virtually impossible to know whether greater attentiveness to Japan's victimization in the past would encourage a corresponding willingness by Japan to be more forthcoming in acknowledging its own past wrongdoing.

As earlier suggested, the international climate is fostering multifaceted concerns on many fronts these days in relation to unresolved grievances of earlier eras. Previously claims deriving from such grievances had been dismissed as irrelevant, being scorned as laments in the wilderness. The prevailing view hitherto has been to view the injustices of the past as finished episodes for which an insistence on redress would serve no useful purpose except to evoke angry feelings of resentment and frustration, an alleged reopening of wounds that were otherwise slowly healing by the mere passage of time. Although general trends are evident, attentiveness to the distinctive features of each object of inquiry is essential. It is useful to consider contextual factors that help determine whether a past grievance is likely to be constructively raised and, if so, what can most usefully be done to ensure that such a reexamination nurtures a spirit of resolution and reconciliation rather than engendering a renewed cycle of hostility and bitterness.

This introductory discussion has tried to contextualize a reevaluation of the Nanking Massacre. The next section discusses the recent emergence of a normative dimension in international relations that is expressed partly through the quest for intertemporal justice. A final section contends that the Nanking Massacre as a particular occurrence situated in time and space warrants this increased attention that it is receiving both because of its intrinsic character and as an example of this trend toward recognizing and seeking to rectify unresolved intertemporal grievances.

II. A Newly Supportive Global Setting

A number of conjectures can be offered to explain this wider phenomenon of which the revived interest in the Nanking Massacre is but a small, yet telling, illustration. It may be clarifying to first review briefly the ideological and structural obstacles that have long stood in the way of all transnational actors who rest their claims on grievances of an *international* character whether arising from war or in a period of peace. My contention is that the evident weakening of some of these obstacles already represents a sea change in the international status of moral concerns, and that this weakening may be most generally understood as expressive of stronger normative impulses in an increasingly integrated world.

Sovereignty and the Realist Tradition

The background of global politics contains many instances of devastating behavior that violates minimal standards of morality and, more recently, of positive rules of international law. The system of sovereign states that has been the foundation of world order since at least the middle of the seventeenth century contains two properties that are peculiarly relevant to this traditional framework: first, the territorial supremacy of governments representing sovereign states; and second, the affirmation of "military necessity" as the governing principle for the conduct of war. On this basis, the role of moral and legal restraints has been minimal in wartime (and even more so in relation to excesses committed by rulers against their own people). As such, there have been no international procedures to assess accountability beyond what the victor could exact from the vanquished as a result of power relations, and the highly hegemonic practice of strong countries in the north claiming the right to protect their national interests against abuses allegedly committed by the territorial government.[6]

This condition has been reinforced intellectually over many years by a series of influential thinkers who stress the primacy of state power as the basis for minimal order in the relations among states, and counsel against a sentimental and allegedly self-destructive entrapment in the enticements of law and morality. Machiavelli, Hobbes, and Clausewitz are among the writers of the past whose realist assessments of international society have exerted an extraordinary influence on the thought and action of states. In our own time, Hans Morgenthau, Reinhold Niebuhr, George Kennan, and Henry Kissinger have in various ways applied this tradition of thought to contemporary circumstances, particularly since the end of World War II. A dominating consensus in support of realist orientations toward policy issues has been guiding U.S. foreign policy. A valuable softening of the realist outlook can be found in the work of Hedley Bull, who conceived of a modest form of international society in which territorial sovereignty of weaker states was generally respected (non-intervention norms), while dominant states, often self-styled "Great Powers," assume additional roles in sustaining overall moderation and stability.[7]

This ideological strength of realism has also been reinforced by an accompanying mainstream construction of the history of this century. Great stress in this regard has been placed on the supposed failures of idealist approaches to world order in the period after World War I either to provide stability in international relations or to meet the challenge posed by aggressive, expansive powers in Europe and Asia. The complacency of the liberal democracies after 1918, relying on a phantom League of Nations; on misleading moves toward disarmament; and, most of all, on a diplomacy of appeasement in the face of the Axis challenge shaped the most generally accepted understanding of the reasons for the onset of World War II. Such experience was summarized in the West as the "lessons of Munich," the highwater mark of the failed diplomacy of appeasement.

As a result, realist thinking based on countervailing power, continuous war preparations, and a vigilant diplomacy of containment toward potential adversaries became a widely endorsed foundation for world order after 1945, hardening into geopolitical doctrine in the course of and subsequent to the Cold War. As this period between 1945 and 1989 is perceived, the approach taken by the West is generally regarded as a success story. World War III was avoided in the face of the intense bipolar rivalry between opposed power blocs led by the two superpowers. Warfare occurred with frequency and intensity, but it was "safely" confined throughout the Cold War to interventionary uses of force in various "peripheral" countries of the south. The realist path is thus credited, although with monumental insensitivity considering the incidence and magnitude of violence during this period in the south, with maintaining world peace, achieving a generally bloodless victory for the West in the Cold War. John Lewis Gaddis has misleadingly, yet understandably, prominently labeled this achievement as the "long peace," assessing "peace" from a Eurocentric perspective. The persistent warfare in Asia, Africa, and Latin America in the aftermath of colonialism was thus treated as providing "acceptable" arenas for geopolitical competition although the consequence of this pattern was to magnify political violence in a large number of Third World countries.

Ever since the founding of the modern state, there have been present various countertraditions to realism, especially associated with the moral edge of political thought about foreign policy in the United States, perhaps best articulated early in its independent history by Thomas Jefferson. Jefferson's basic antirealist formulation contended that a state should respect moral guidelines as fully in its international relations as individuals should in their personal relations. This orientation was initially the dominant American view as it emerged from its own revolution as an independent state that was determined, above all else, not to emulate the European powers in their external relations that seemed driven by great power rivalry and geopolitical calculations. In contrast, the United States as a matter of fixed principle would remain aloof from "entangling alliances," avoid the seemingly continuous cycle of war among the European states, and seek to exemplify its claimed moral exceptionalism. In this way the new nation, the first victor in an anticolonial war, could exert a positive moral influence on the conduct of international relations, which at the time—the late eighteenth century—meant the avoidance of international warfare.

There is no doubt that a large part of this early quest for a distinctive American identity on the global stage involved distancing itself from its European forebears whose approach to international relations was perceived to be decadent, cynical, and needlessly war prone. Of course, a more "realist" reading of American exceptionalism would stress the special security benefits enjoyed by the United States from its beginning. The United States had the great geopolitical advantages of weak neighbors, two vast oceans separating its territory from the stronger states of the world, and a weakly defended continental expanse within which to realize its Great-Power destiny. Revealingly, the United States broke with isolationism and joined fully the European system of "internationalism" only after its sense of peacetime invulnerability was shattered by the attack on Pearl Harbor in 1941.[8]

Nevertheless, the idea of exerting a benign influence has never entirely disappeared in American thinking about world order. It reached the climax of its influence in the last years of the presidency of Woodrow Wilson at the end of World War I with the failed effort to supplant balance of power conceptions of global security. As suggested above, to the extent that such moralistic and legalist views were projected outwardly, they became later discredited especially among policy elites and within academic circles due to their alleged baneful effects on statecraft during the 1930s, and the overall lead-up to World War II.[9] Whether this was a proper historical judgment about the causes of Nazi expansionism and World War II remains somewhat contested in scholarly circles to this day, but there is no doubt that a strong consensus supports the view that departures from the canons of realism contributed to the terrible failures of foreign policy in Europe during the 1930s.

The Normative Dimension of International Relations

There is a strange contradictory impact of World War II on thought and policy relating to international relations. Because of its role as global leader since the middle of the twentieth century, this dual impact is most clearly discerned in relation to the United States. As indicated, the events leading up to World War II, especially the appeasement of perceived expansionist powers, led the United States to abandon once and for all its historic stand of noninvolvement outside the Western Hemisphere. This abandonment was also prompted by the evolution of long-range military technology that nullified the benefits of geographic isolation. As a result of these factors, the United States conceived of itself from 1945 onward as a global power, as an alliance leader, and as a nation continuously prepared to engage in major warfare.

The picture is incomplete without also taking account of the ambiguous ending of World War II, especially the atomic bomb attacks on Hiroshima and Nagasaki. The scale of devastation, combined with the sense that any subsequent large-scale war would likely be fought with improved weaponry of mass destruction, led to a public outcry against "the war system," even while victory in what was generally regarded as a "just war" was being celebrated. In effect, despite the "lesson of Munich" there was also generated a new idealistic pressure to revive the work of Woodrow Wilson to construct a different kind of world order, one based less on the interaction and political will of sovereign states and more on the collective responsibility of these states to keep the peace to avoid disappearing in a final orgy of annihilation.

Thus, despite the emergence of a realist consensus, elements of the earlier moral orientation continued to function as a counterpoint to realism, and have periodically been significant. Such attitudes contributed strongly to the early American enthusiasm in the mid-1940s for the United Nations as a partial approach to global security. The United Nations as depicted in its constitutional document, the UN Charter, appeared premised on international law and the collective responsibilities of the organized international community. The UN Charter prohibited all uses of international force other than those that could be justified as self-defense against a prior armed attack and those that were authorized by an explicit UN Security Council decision. As such, the UN did seem to offer an alternative to statist ideas of global security that rested on calculations of countervailing power and alliance arrangements, although it was not seriously implemented by real transfers of sovereignty, or capabilities. Also expressive of a renewed normative approach to its relations with the world was the move to include human rights as an integral part of international law, which gradually exerted a behavioral influence through the activism of nongovernmental organizations (NGOs) and then during the early years of the Carter presidency as the foreign policy innovation of the world's most powerful and influential state. Perhaps most relevant for our particular interest, it was the U.S. government that most strongly advocated a war crimes approach toward the leadership of the defeated Axis countries in 1945. Without this American insistence, the likelihood is that the victorious powers would have organized mass summary executions of large numbers of high-ranking German and Japanese military officers and civilian officials without being troubled by the niceties of indictment, prosecution, and assessment of individual cases.

Despite these normative initiatives, realist thinking carried the day. The United States exercised its leadership role mainly by way of exerting military, diplomatic, economic, and ideological pressure. The UN was definitely subordinated, a result that was blamed during the Cold War years on the East-West stalemate that made the organization unusable in most international crises. But in the last decade, with no central rivalry among states present, the continuing marginality of the UN confirms the extent to which the realist world picture remains ascendant. Ironically, it is now the European countries that seem more inclined to weigh heavily normative concerns, and the United States that behaves as if international relations is reducible to power and interest calculations.

Beyond Realism and Global Reform

Throughout this history there has also been evident a more transformative view of world order that has enjoyed some support in civil society, but without ever achieving much resonance in leadership circles. As

civil society has increased its relevance to the policy agenda, this uto-
pian aspiration has been more manifest, and may be part of the explanation of why intertemporal justice has begun to engage the political
imagination of many societies. From time to time, prominent thinkers
have proposed some form of world government as the essential foundation for a peaceful world that effectively eliminates war as a social institution. Such advocacy peaked in the aftermath of each of·the two world
wars in this century, enjoying considerable backing in society. For some,
the advent of nuclear weaponry was a conclusive argument in favor of
drastic disarmament at the level of states, with security functions being
transferred to global institutions. Jonathan Schell's *Fate of the Earth*, a
worldwide best-seller, argued with great eloquence the thesis that human survival depended on making a profound adjustment to the challenge posed by nuclear weaponry.[10] Articulation of such perspectives in
civil society with respect to the future creates an inevitable recall of
unacknowledged grievances from the past.

Persisting Realism in an Era of Globalization

At present, with the end of the Cold War and the absence of strategic
confrontation, concerns about nuclear war have receded from public
consciousness, temporarily at least. The managerial effort in international relations of the nuclear weapons states is now focused on nonpro-
liferation rather than on either disarmament or war avoidance. Realistic
approaches to global security remain in control of policymaking for major
countries, and exhibit a refusal to renounce the nuclear option. The main
preoccupation internationally as the new century begins is how to adjust
realistic views to the heightened importance associated with economic in-
tegration at regional and global levels. This is a tendency that is elevated to
a central position by allowing this historical stage of world politics to be
described as the "era of globalization." This rise of global market forces
goes against the current of transnational civic activism, which is primarily driven by a range of concerns that involve ethics and values.

Despite this dominion of realist thinking and in the face of the
economistic orientation arising from globalization, it is particularly impressive and somewhat puzzling that this interest in intertemporal equity should appear so powerfully on the international scene during the
course of the last several years.

The speeding up of history as a result of the pace of change on the electronic frontier seems to have heightened our sense of the time dimension as it relates to perceived justice and injustice. In this sense, both time future and time past become more active in political consciousness. The recent scholarly efforts to extend the protection of international law to future generations exhibits the futurist side of intertemporal equity.[11] Especially in the context of environmental decay and resource depletion there arises the concern that the lifestyles of present generations, abetted by increasing demographic pressures, are creating a situation in which the life prospects of future generations will be deteriorated, possibly catastrophically. Given prospects for global warming and fears of ecological collapses in the global commons, such concerns seem entirely appropriate to an ethos of responsibility. Anticipatory redress seeks to restrain present activity by invoking what has come to be called in international environmental law the "precautionary principle." The idea here is that restraint should be imposed in a precautionary spirit without waiting for a judgment of scientific certainty about the risks posed, in effect imposing a note of caution with respect to long-range risk taking. It remains to be seen whether such guardianship of future generations is a genuine political project, or is only a matter of giving more lip service to an ethos of temporal responsibility. From the vantage point of the present, a skeptical appraisal seems in order. The forces that favor maximizing the benefits to present generations remain firmly in control of market and governmental outlooks.

There is a direct opposition between market pressures and any concerted effort to rectify by direct action relations between rich and poor countries. This trend is visible in the dramatic decline in direct foreign economic assistance. The idea of distributive justice with countries seems also to be less important to the extent that territorial boundaries are being eroded by globalization, and its backlash, in the form of fragmentation or localization. These opposed tendencies diminish the central importance of the state as both the defining unit in the existing world order and the principal guardian of human wellbeing. But to look back in time is to resurrect the relevance of identities associated with the state and with the ideology of nationalism.

The Challenge and Relevance of Global Civil Society

A further development is the activation of global civil society, especially in relation to a broad normative agenda. As states and markets are shaped primarily by ideas associated with self-interest, it is movements and initiatives organized by voluntary associations of people acting spontaneously that are primarily raising issues of moral significance and global scope. Whether it be matters of Holocaust gold and looted works of art, the suppressed grievances of indigenous peoples around the world, the sense of still anguished injustice associated with such exploiting institutions as slavery or colonialism, or an effort to raise in public consciousness the historical reality of Nanking or Hiroshima, the motive force for such activation and remembrance is situated in civil society.

What is more, this civic activism is encouraged by two further factors. The first factor is a global media that gives audiences everywhere many vivid examples of the potency of people power, and makes the struggles in one setting suggestive for others comparably situated. Such a global learning process is greatly aided by way of television and the Internet, conveying in real time to all parts of the world various struggles for justice. The second factor has to do with the interspersing of the peoples of the world through various forms of transnational migration, including the flow of students across national and civilizational boundaries. In these postmigration settings there may emerge a particularly strong motivation to communicate deeply felt grievances, including anguish associated with past injustices that have never come to closure.

Trends toward democratization and internationalization are also helpful. There exists an increasing availability of arenas within which to raise consciousness and pursue specific forms of redress, thereby creating practical outlets for suppressed feelings of hurt and resentment. On global levels in a number of settings, the UN system has provided suitable arenas that allow such claims for recognition and redress to be pursued. Women, indigenous people, and environmentally aggrieved groups have made particularly effective and creative use of such arenas. This process reached its high-water mark in the early 1990s at a series of UN conferences that provided "space" for transnational civic activists to press their claims, and combined democratizing and international features.[12] Other important arenas include a variety of educational sites around the world, including international academic meetings.

Another set of supportive tendencies involves the emergence of human rights as an important dimension of world politics. This emergence is a complex story that has been narrated many times in recent years, especially in relation to celebrations organized around the fiftieth anniversary of the Universal Declaration of Human Rights in 1998.[13] The idea that rights exist on an international level, and deserve protection by regional and global institutions, automatically casts light on abuses of rights, past and present. The human rights movement started a half-century ago as an exercise in exhortation, with assurances to governments that there would be no intention to seek enforcement mechanisms, and thus no implicit threat to territorial supremacy of the sovereign state. It was here that civil society initiatives cast such political expectations in a new light that have come indeed to threaten sovereign rights and to confront authoritarian rule with a legitimate basis of resistance. Transnational human rights NGOs took the norms seriously, gathered information on violations, and used the media to exert leverage on governments. As well, opposition movements were encouraged to believe that their goals were legitimate, and enjoyed international support. This dynamic converged with geopolitics in the latter stages of the Cold War as Western governments mounted pressures based on human rights norms that greatly strengthened the position of internal movements, especially in the countries of Eastern Europe during the 1980s. The global antiapartheid campaign lent historical weight to the claim that the denial of human rights could be successfully converted into an international project for transformation of a structure of deeply entrenched injustice.

This direction of thinking, based on what the political philosopher Richard Rorty has called "a human rights culture," is bolstered by complementary ideas. One of the most fertile, powerful, and germane of these was set forth by Ken Booth through his reference to "human wrongs" as a corollary to the focus on "human rights."[14] Booth criticized the whole tradition of thought and practice in international relations that had for centuries sanitized "human wrongs" behind the protective screens of "sovereignty" and "war." In effect, a legitimate world order must not provide such mechanisms for insulating human wrongs from accountability and, in due course, must provide the means to correct existing abuses. In this respect, the ongoing quest for the future redress of past grievances would no longer be necessary, as present modes of redress would be sufficient. Such sufficiency is part of the goal and achievement of a well-functioning constitutional democracy. Booth's perspective would reinforce this democratic process with mechanisms to ensure the responsible and humane exercise of sovereignty by states.

The War Crimes Experiment

Perhaps, the strongest strand of all in this series of normative developments involves the push toward accountability for crimes of state. As mentioned earlier, the Nuremberg and Tokyo breakthroughs were in the special circumstances of a major war in which the defeated countries surrendered unconditionally, and their surviving leaders were available for indictment and prosecution in criminal tribunals set up for such a purpose. Although the human wrongs being addressed were of the greatest severity, the enterprise remained controversial because of its one-sidedness (the exemption of legal scrutiny of the alleged crimes committed on the victorious side) and its retroactivity (the post-factum nature of the delimitation of the crimes and the contention of individual criminal liability). This negative impression was reinforced by the failure to transform the Nuremberg and Tokyo framework into a more enduring foundation for accountability by establishing a permanent criminal court and setting forth a code of international crimes and punishments that would in the future bind all governments. The Cold War decades precluded most forms of international cooperation that rested on shared normative commitments, especially if the nature of the cooperation might lead to legally mandated accusations across the ideological divide.

In the last twenty years the outlook for international accountability has been steadily improving. One reason for this has been the experience of a series of Latin American societies with impunity arrangements in which individual criminal liability has been exchanged for some procedure of inquiry into the past that expressed and documented "the truth." Such arrangements were never entirely satisfactory, especially to those who had been victimized most directly by past human wrongs in the form of unforgivable crimes, but the disclosure of the past was at least a symbolic form of redress. Such a compromise was justified by the slogan "rather peace than justice." The issues have assumed worldwide salience recently due to the reports in 1998 of the Truth and Reconciliation Commission in South Africa, which offered a wide amnesty on condition that the perpetrator of past human wrongs cooperated as a witness by way of full disclosure.

The political violence that accompanied the breakup of former Yugoslavia in the 1990s also created a special set of circumstances that prompted the revival of the Nuremberg idea. Accordingly, the UN Security Council established an ad hoc tribunal in The Hague for the prosecution of those indicted for war crimes, and due to other pressures added a second tribunal in the same location to address charges against those alleged responsible for genocide and crimes against humanity in Rwanda during the course of 1994.[15] This tribunal has made notable progress, despite initial skepticism, and despite an inability to arrest the most prominent of the Serbian wrongdoers, especially Radovan Karadzic and General Ratko Mladic, who were the architects of "ethnic cleansing" in Bosnia. The year 1997 saw the arrest of Major General Radislav, the commander responsible for the 1995 genocidal attack on civilians trapped in the Bosnian town of Srebrenica, a place of refuge that had been formally declared to be a "safe haven" by the United Nations.[16] A further dramatic development occurred in March 1999, when Slobadan Milosevic, a sitting head of state, was indicted by the Hague Tribunal for his alleged commission of crimes against the people of Kosovar.

The Yugoslav and Rwandan initiative has also stimulated widespread support among governments and in global civil society for the establishment of a permanent international criminal court. This transnational coalition, opposed in essential respects by the U.S. government, succeeded in organizing a 1998 intergovernmental conference in Rome that produced a treaty in support of establishing such a court in the near future. It remains to be seen whether the coalition that provisionally approved the treaty can now maintain enough pressure to obtain its widespread ratification and meaningful implementation. If such an institution is established, it will strongly reinforce efforts to invoke international law to pursue criminal remedies in an international global setting against those responsible for past human wrongs.

The most dramatic development along these lines has been the 1998 detention of General Auguste Pinochet, the former dictator of Chile, in Britain pending an extradition request from Spain where he would be subject to prosecution for crimes against humanity committed during his time in the 1970s as head of state in Chile. The central question posed is not whether Pinochet enjoys immunity due to his former status as governmental leader, but whether an agreement by which he gave up political power in exchange for certain assurances and arrangements should be respected on an *international* level if that is what the Chilean government formally requests. In this instance, the government of Chile has requested Pinochet's release from British detention and return to Chile, supposedly to face pending charges arising from cases in Chilean courts. There is an alternative to returning Pinochet to Chile and thus internationally respecting agreed arrangements for transitions from military rule. This alternative applies international legal standards based on the character of the crime as engaging the whole world, thereby conferring a universal jurisdiction to prosecute, as in the case of piracy. Even if Pinochet is eventually not prosecuted in Spain or elsewhere, his detention has generated a very important debate about the accountability of political leaders and redress of grievances within the world as we know it.[17]

For all the reasons summarized above, the theme of redress for past grievances has generated unprecedented interest at the present time. This prominence may recede due to some counterpressures that have been mounted in reaction. There are allegations being made that it is unnecessary for subsequent generations to be overly apologetic about past human wrongs, which should be morally and legally evaluated only in the temporal context of their occurrence, and not retrospectively, when other considerations can be brought to bear. Such a contention has been advanced in relation to holding banks in Europe accountable for standards of moral responsibility during the 1940s that run counter to prevailing practice at the time that the illicit deposits were made. Another argument is that certain forms of redress, assuming a mercenary character, cheapen the historical memory by giving a cash value to past injustices.[18]

On a different level, many governments, despite their endorsement of democracy on a state or societal level, are very threatened by the democratization of transnational arenas of authority, as was occurring in the global conferences on world issues held under UN auspices. A backlash has ensued such that this UN conference format is unlikely to be available in the near future. Its disappearance, or reduced scope, will probably be explained as a result of bureaucratic downsizing and cost efficiency. The real reason for such a retreat is that these conferences were a mechanism of empowerment for those seeking redress through the availability of a series of arenas that provided ready access to the global media. Such access created an opportunity for aggrieved groups to magnify their overall influence and mount a campaign for redress.

The real opposition to democratization on a global level was less motivated by the substantive issues at stake, and more by a feared power shift, a loss of control by the state. This prospect was especially troubling at a time when state capacity was already being redefined and diminished by the rise of global market forces. As matters now stand, there exist a series of unresolved tensions between the priorities of an emergent global civil society and the defensive, and still formidable, moves of the state to dominate world order in the face of intensifying globalization.

III. Redress in the Setting of the Nanking Massacre

The above discussion depicts the context in which the unresolved character of Nanking 1937 needs to be viewed. An awakening of political consciousness accompanied the sixtieth anniversary of the ordeal endured by the citizens of Nanking, and disclosed a lingering sense of grievance and misunderstanding. That Nanking remains contested terrain is evident at intergovernmental diplomatic levels. Leaders of Japan and China seem unable to close the book on the past in a mutually satisfactory manner. At the level of civil society, preliminary efforts to engage the Japanese scholarly community in the dynamics of shared inquiry into the historical reality has achieved only a preliminary and partial success, which has generated its own tensions. Some Japanese scholars still question the scale of the massacre and victimization being alleged by Chinese scholars. Such a controversy was about the meaning of the inquiry as much as it was about the accuracy of the historical narrative. On one side, focusing on the statistical reliability upon which the allegations were based seems to divert attention from a posture of remorse. On the other side, the perceived exaggeration of the occurrences in terms of the scale of victimization is seen as a way of deepening Japanese responsibility beyond its factual reality.

The minimum achievement resulting from films, books, and conferences of the last several years is to extend to Nanking the spirit of serious remembrance, included in which is valuable work of historical clarification.[19] Carolyn Forche has aptly said that "[t]he resistance to terror is what makes the world habitable." Certainly part of this resistance is activating the memory, even if belatedly, of past human wrongs, especially those that have been allowed to be forgotten, drained of their full meaning, or presented in a distorted fashion. There is in this setting the belief in many quarters that, especially in the United States, there have been far greater shows of compassionate concern for the survivors of Nazism and their descendants than for Asian victims of Japanese expansionist militarism. On one level this is understandable. Nothing done by Japan, including its predatory behavior at Nanking and elsewhere in the region, approaches the sheer horror of the Holocaust. But on another level each experience of acute victimization deserves our most sensitive concern. In this regard, the long passage of time without taking account of Japanese atrocities seems to be partly explained by a series of secondary factors: China moved soon after World War II into the camp of America's ideological and strategic adversary; racial, ethnic, religious, and cultural factors made most Americans feel more affinity with European victims than with Asian victims; postwar efforts to impose criminal accountability on surviving leaders were far more prominent in Europe through the Nuremberg trials than were the rather obscure parallel efforts in Tokyo; and finally, the American use of atomic bombs in its war against Japan appears to have made the U.S. government somewhat reluctant to press the Japanese too hard on the war crimes front, especially as the Japanese elite were solicited very soon as allies in the quickly developing conflict with the Soviet Union, and in view of the Communist successes in China.

Beyond the complexities of remembrance, and their embeddedness in subsequent politics and history, is the question of appropriate redress. Perhaps there is a natural division of labor in relation to such unresolved grievances. For the government representing the victims and their descendants, there is the search for formal recognition, whether by apology or through some kind of material restitution. For the victimized society, the work of memory involves a kind of collective psychotherapy that centers on rituals of acknowledgment by representatives of the perpetrator to the community that identifies with the victims. If that memory work can be genuinely shared with exemplary representatives of the perpetrator country, there ensues a collaboration that helps overcome the accusatory and defensive interaction and tone that will otherwise mar this work of excavating such a painful past. It seems that the inquiry into Nanking 1937 seeks to proceed on this basis, with the effort of those who pose the challenge being to engender reflection and remorse, but not to insist on some form of material restitution or public humiliation.

This effort also has transnational implications. Locating some of the Asian memory work within the United States is a way of seeking to offset the persisting Eurocentrism that somehow is seen as taking human wrongs more seriously if they occur in the West than if their locus is elsewhere, as in this instance in China. Similarly, a further intention is undoubtedly to awaken Japanese society from its official and societal forms of "denial," which have kept the shadow sides of the past in darkness for the Japanese generally, despite some brave and notable exceptions. There are several Japanese individuals of conscience who have taken steps on their own to verify the accusations and to give them currency in Japan. It remains doubtful that the minimal goals of redress for the crimes at Nanking have yet been realized, but at least a start has been made.

As again the American setting confirms, it is not only the victims and perpetrator societies that are related to this process of recalling painful past memories, and properly acknowledging past wrongs. It needs to engage people as people, exhibiting an ethos of human solidarity whose reality would help deter future crimes against humanity and organize timely global responses to such profound challenges. The world community's ineffectual and tepid responses to "ethnic cleansing" in Bosnia and to "genocide" in Rwanda suggests that much work needs to be done. The North Atlantic Treaty Organization (NATO) War over Kosovo, although responsive, also reveals the dangers of a vengeful form of "humanitarianism" that is far from encouraging.[20]

In conclusion, not only is an emphasis on redress of past wrongs needed, as in relation to Nanking 1937, but also a sense of shared human commitment to the pledge "Never again!" made in the wake of discovering the full extent of the Holocaust carried out by the Nazis, primarily against the Jewish people. The past has intrinsic importance, partly because it informs the present, but it also has relevance for what it can teach us to do to prevent future repetitions of criminal behavior by governments and by their militarist undertakings.

Notes

1. Richard H. Minear, in his important book on the legal proceedings, criticizes such a punishment because it rested on charges of "negative culpability," that is, on failures to act rather than on prohibited acts, and further because there was no evidence introduced by the prosecution to demonstrate that General Matsui had either knowledge of the atrocities or the capacity to prevent them. Richard H. Minear, *Victors' Justice: The Tokyo War Crimes Tribunal* (Princeton University Press, 1971), 69–72.

2. As quoted in Paul Abrahams, "Japan's Wartime Ghosts," *Financial Times,* 28–29 November 1998, 7.

3. Text of Judge Radhabinod Pal's opinion is available in a separate book: Radhabinod Pal, *International Military Tribunal for the Far East: Dissentient Judgement* (Calcutta, India: Sanyal, 1953); also see Minear, *Victors' Justice,* 213–214, where he notes the dramatic difference between the availability of the Nuremberg proceedings of forty-two volumes in an official U.S. government series and the in-

accessibility of the Tokyo proceedings, most of which are not even published, and can be obtained only with difficulty and, then, in microfilm form.

4. This failure is one of the themes of Iris Chang's important book, a concern signaled by the subtitle. Iris Chang, *The Rape of Nanking: The Forgotten Holocaust of World War II* (New York: Basic Books, 1997).

5. For interpretations of this backlash, see Edward T. Linenthal and Tom Engelhardt, eds., *History Wars: The Enola Gay and Other Battles for the American Past* (New York: Metropolitan Books, 1996); also, Robert Jay Lifton and Greg Mitchell, *Hiroshima in America: Fifty Years of Denial* (New York: Putnam, 1995).

6. In international law this practice is discussed under the somewhat misleading and self-serving doctrinal headings "diplomatic protection" and "state responsibility."

7. Hedley Bull, *The Anarchical Society: A Study of Order in World Politics* (New York: Columbia University, 1977).

8. In World War I the United States reluctantly abandoned isolationism to turn the tide of war in favor of the liberal democracies. Despite the efforts of Woodrow Wilson to construct a new architecture of global security, the United States refused to take part, resuming its diplomacy of noninvolvement with European conflict patterns. Even the rise of Hitler and Germany's expansionism did not rouse the United States to respond, and this despite the efforts of its popular leader, Franklin Delano Roosevelt, to nudge the country ever closer to participation. Isolationist sentiments remained predominant until America was attacked. It is also correct to note that isolationism was driven as much by self-interest as it was by a pacifist ethos. The elements of this self-interest included fiscal desires to keep military expenditures and human casualties as low as possible. Another aspect of the American orientation related to the conviction of many among its early leaders that military establishments and constitutional democracy did not mix. There was strong support, only narrowly circumvented, for including in the Constitution a total prohibition on "standing armies," that is, on a peacetime military.

9. For an important reappraisal of reformist initiatives in this period, see Cecelia Lynch, *Beyond Appeasement: Interpreting Interwar Peace Movements in World Politics* (Ithaca, NY: Cornell University Press, 1999).

10. Jonathan Schell, *Fate of the Earth* (New York: Alfred A. Knopf, 1982).

11. See, for example, the book by E.B. Weiss, *In Fairness to Future Generations: International Law, Common Patrimony, and Intergenerational Equity* (Dobbs Ferry, NY: Transnational Publishers, 1989); also *Future Generations Journal*, published in Malta.

12. Among these were the Rio Conference on Environment and Development (1992), the so-called earth summit (1992), the Vienna Conference on Human Rights and Development (1993), the Cairo Conference on Population and Development (1994), the Beijing Conference on Women and Development (1995), and the Copenhagen Social Summit (1995).

13. For my own version, see Richard Falk, "A Half-Century of Human Rights," *Australian Journal of International Affairs* 52 (1998), 255–272.

14. Ken Booth, "Human Wrongs and International Relations," *International Relations* 71 (1995), 103–126.

15. The scale and texture of the Rwandan genocide are graphically depicted in Philip Gourevitch, *We Wish to Inform You that Tomorrow We Will be Killed with Our Families—Stories from Rwanda* (New York: Farrar, Straus and Giroux, 1998).

16. See Steven Erlanger, "Bosnian Serb General Is Arrested by Allied Force in Genocide Case," *New York Times*, December 3, 1998; for a broad account of background and approach, see Roger S. Clark and Madeline Sann, eds., *The Prosecution of International Crimes* (New Brunswick, NJ: Transaction Publishers, 1996).

17. For an overall evaluation of the Pinochet detention in relation to wider issues of justice as an element of world order, see Richard Falk, "The Pursuit of International Justice: Present Dilemmas and an Imagined Future," *Journal of International Affairs* 52 (1999), 409–441.

18. See Abraham H. Foxman, "The Dangers of Holocaust Restitution," *Wall Street Journal*, December 4, 1998, A18, which includes the phrase "There is no place for ambulance chasers in this sacred undertaking."

19. A wonderfully realized expression of this spirit is found in the introductory essay by Carolyn Forche to her anthology of poetry collected under the title *Against Forgetting: Twentieth-Century Poetry of Witness* (New York: W.W. Norton, 1993), 27–47.

20. For interpretation see Richard Falk, "Reflections on the War," *Nation*, June 28, 1999, 11–15.

Part Two
Revisiting Nanking:
Views from China and Japan

3

Causes of the Nanking Massacre

Sun Zhaiwei

Translated by Kurt Beidler

*There has been much discussion of the Nanking Massacre since its oc-
currence, but, quite strangely, there has been very little discussion by
the actual victims. There are many reasons for this silence, such as the
political complications and isolation during the postwar period of China
on both sides of the Taiwan Strait. In order for the process of healing to
be all-inclusive, we must consider memories of the event from all possible angles. Hence this book would not be complete without views of
the event from Chinese scholars, who offer years of their own research
as well as decades of memories of the World War II era.*

Sun Zaiwei, editor-in-chief of the book The Nanking Massacre, *which
was published in China, here analyzes both the direct and the indirect
causes of the Nanking Massacre. Sun's arguments are representative of
the voices of the mainland Chinese scholarly community. —Eds.*

1. Historical Background

The invasion of China by Japan started long before the Nanking Massacre. At the earliest it can be traced back to shortly after the Meiji Restoration, when Japanese forces invaded Taiwan in 1874. This was followed
by the Sino-Japanese War (1894–1895), the Jinan Incident (1928), and
the September 18 Incident (1931). Finally, on July 7, 1937, Japan began
its large-scale invasion of China, from Pingjin to Songhu and ultimately
to the capital, Nanking.

In the Sino-Japanese War, after the Japanese Army seized Lüshun
they killed 18,000 Chinese during three days and three nights of butchery. Fifty years earlier, invading Japanese troops killed more than 2,000
civilians in Jijia Zhuang, a village in the suburbs of Tianjin. In the Pingjin
region they pilfered 3.67 million liang of silver. In the tragic May 30

Incident of 1928 in Jinan, Japanese killed 3,945 Chinese soldiers and civilians, wounding 1,537 and resulting in a loss of Chinese personal property totaling nearly 30 million yuan. From the September 18 Incident until the end of 1932, a total of 23,662 Chinese soldiers and civilians were killed by various methods, resulting in a loss of public and private property totaling 20 billion yuan. After the July 7 Incident, Japanese troops killed 4,000 each in Shuo County and Ningwu, nearly 6,000 in Chengan, and more than 11,000 in Baoshan. Throughout these massacres all kinds of cruel means were used, including killing contests, bayonets, decapitation, burying alive, and burning.

The resistance of Chinese military and civilians to the Japanese invaders never ceased. Some instances of spontaneous and conscious resistance were related to the attitude of the government and some were not. When the government upheld policies of resistance, military and civilians were encouraged to carry out organized, well-led resistance. When the government upheld policies of nonresistance, Chinese military and civilians nonetheless undertook unyielding struggles of resistance.

Within the broad historical context outlined above, the Nanking Massacre was directly related to the battle in defense of Nanking. After the fall of Shanghai, the vanguard of the invading Japanese troops headed straight for China's capital. The Japanese killed all the way to Nanking, from Songhu to the Hangjia Lake region, hoping to force China to surrender in her own capital. Chinese troops, under the direction of General Tang Shengzhi, staged a heroic resistance in the outlying areas of Nanking. When the Chinese defenders received the order to retreat, they were unable to carry it out in an effective, organized manner, resulting in nearly 100,000 troops being detained by the river or dispersed into civilian society. These events compose the specific background and environment in which the Nanking Massacre took place, and the occurrence and scale of the massacre were directly related to this background.

In general, the massacre itself can be divided into two types of killings: mass killing and sporadic killing. Incidents of mass killing ranged from the murder of ten and twenty to the slaughter of tens of thousands of people, with the greatest number in any one incident reaching more than 50,000. Sporadic killing included varying numbers of three to eight people. Among the mass killings, in addition to those who died by the sword and firing squad, others were burned, buried alive, or drowned. Several, after being soaked with gasoline, were set on fire by gunshot, causing the wounded person to lie covered in flames, rolling and writhing on the ground, until finally dying a miserable death. Individual, sporadic acts of torture and killing included splitting, gutting, slicing, piercing alive, and dog biting. Some were even burned with acid and then left, burning all over. Others were tortured to death. Two Japanese lieutenants amused themselves by having a killing contest. The first one to reach 100 killed won the "game." Then they raised the limit to 150.

In addition to killing, the Nanking Massacre also involved rape, arson, theft, and other violent crimes. The Japanese troops who attacked Nanking raped tens of thousands of Chinese women, many of whom were then murdered. From Zhonghua Gate all along the Xiaguan River there were great fires everywhere, emitting flames that reached the sky and reducing a third of the city's buildings to ashes. Property from many residences and stores was stolen. Focusing on the Japanese troops' barbaric pillaging of valuable Chinese literary and cultural objects, the scholarly community has suggested using the term "Cultural Massacre." Here, the words "Nanking Massacre" have surpassed the narrow meaning of "massacre" and taken on a more general meaning, one that includes all atrocities committed by the Japanese troops.

The time frame of the Nanking Massacre is generally understood to be the six-week period following December 13, 1937, the day Nanking fell to the Japanese. That represents only the most concentrated period of atrocities committed by the Japanese troops, however; it is not the time period in which all atrocities were committed. Actually the Massacre began before Nanking fell to the Japanese. It started as the attacking soldiers approached Nanking, where they committed murderous acts of violence in the suburbs of the city. The horrifying "killing contests" actually began in late November, along the path of attack from Wuxi to Changzhou.

It is difficult to say when the atrocities finally ended. In the famous *Anquanqu Dangan* (Safety Zone file), the number of recorded atrocities committed by Japanese soldiers totals 444, and the time frame lasts until February 7, 1938. In a statement made after the war, Nanking resident Peng Xiangsong reported that Japanese troops killed Han Decheng and more than 230 others on Tang Mountain between December 1937 and February 1938.[1] That same year Gong Yukun, gatekeeper at the Yangzi Flour Factory on Sancha River, told in his written testimony the bitter story of how in March 1938 he was hacked with a knife by a Japanese soldier and then set upon with dogs.[2] Zhou Changrong, a young farmer from Shifo Temple in Jiangpu County, was labeled a "Chinese soldier," after which his spine was broken during a brutal beating with a rifle butt, leaving him handicapped for life.[3] The German diplomat Munson, who was stationed in Nanking, said in a March 4, 1938, report to the Foreign Ministry, "Atrocities committed by the Japanese have decreased in number, but the nature of them has not changed."[4] Therefore, it is appropriate to include February and March 1938 as part of the span of concentrated killings and atrocities committed by the Japanese.

The geographical scope of the Nanking Massacre was generally limited to the regions under the jurisdiction of the Nanking municipal government. Before Nanking fell to the Japanese, there were seven inner-city regions (including Xiaguan) under the jurisdiction of the Nanking municipal government, plus the five suburban areas of Pukou, Xiaoling Wei, Yanzi Ji, Shangxin He, and Lingyuan, a total of twelve districts. The murders and atrocities committed in these twelve districts should be considered part of the Nanking Massacre. If we consider atrocities committed during the same time, by the same troops, in places of close proximity, then counties surrounding Nanking, such as Jiangning, Jurong, Lishui, Jiangpu, and Liuhe, should also be included in the geographical area of the Nanking Massacre. In fact, people around the world have always taken into consideration the extensive materials from the suburban districts and counties listed above in their writings on the Nanking Massacre. Li Kehen, in his *Lunjing Wuyue Ji* (Record of the capital's fallen five months), mentions the atrocities committed by Japanese soldiers at Liulang Bridge in Jiangning County. The Chongshan Hall statistical table of buried corpses lists all the corpses buried from outside Tongji Gate all the way to Fang Mountain of Jiangning County. Guo Qi, in his *Xiandu Xielei Ji* (Record of blood and tears of the fallen capital), includes accounts of people struggling to resist the Japanese in Mao and the Baohua Mountains of Liuhe and Jurong counties. Professor Lewis Smythe of the United States, in his investigative report entitled "Portrait of the Disaster of War in Nanjing," makes the five counties Jiangning, Jurong, Lishui, Jiangpu, and Liuhe the focus of his rural investigation. The reason for including the surrounding counties in the geographic scope of the Nanking Massacre is merely to examine and understand this event more completely and scientifically.

In the haze surrounding the War of Resistance against Japan during the early days of the People's Republic of China, there was some discrepancy regarding the number of people who were victims of the Nanking Massacre. Chinese books and periodicals published conflicting reports with the number killed ranging from as few as 100,000 to as many as 500,000. Under the conditions of war before systematic research had begun, it is not surprising that such conflicting reports existed. Because of restrictions of various records, the conditions prevailing at that time, and particularly the population just before Nanking fell to the Japanese, either underestimates or overestimates of the death toll would lead to logical confusion and contradictions. The important requirement is to respect historical truth. We must admit, first, that the Japanese troops who invaded China indiscriminately massacred Nanking citizens, and, second, that they did so on a large-scale basis. Under this premise, the exact number, whether more or less than 300,000, will continue to be debated until we compile a complete "detailed list" of the Massacre.

In recent years, people in Chinese political and academic circles have gradually come to agree that the death toll of the Nanking Massacre was "more than 300,000." This figure first appeared in March 1947 in the written verdict of the "Chinese Military Court for Trying War Criminals" against war criminal Tani Hisao. The affirmation of this number reflects the mutual recognition of the Nationalist (Guomindang) and Communist parties, as well as people and scholars on both sides of the Taiwan Strait. Having undergone the gradual statistical analysis of every case relating to the Nanking Massacre, research on buried corpses, repeated analysis, and debate over the population of Nanking at the time, most scholars believe that this estimate is scientific and in line with the actual situation at that time.

2. Causes of the Massacre

In the history of research on the Nanking Massacre there is one question that occurs repeatedly: Why did the Nanking Massacre occur?

The first fundamental cause was the barbaric nature of Japanese militarism. Starting with the Meiji Restoration of the 1860s, Japan embarked on a path of militarism that continued until the end of World War II, when Japanese militarism came to an enforced end as part of the country's unconditional surrender. Japanese militarism was unique in its unceasing outward expansion. This ideology was closely related to the feudalistic, religious system of emperor worship and the spirit of *Bushido* (samurai moral code). The Japanese educated their soldiers to be absolute in their loyalty to the emperor and in carrying out his orders. Soldiers cultivated and educated under this militarism became barbarous and cruel. Japanese war criminal Yamaoka Shigeru once described the militaristic education that he received and the horrific spiritual attitude that it formed:

> At that time we harbored an ingrained sense of superiority about the Japanese race, and we adopted a condescending attitude toward other races. We also had a kind of cruel Bushido spirit, which considered killing a heroic act. Furthermore, from the extremism of worshipping the emperor came an inhumane ideology, which was to submit to the strong and powerful and force into submission anyone weak or not powerful. . . . It was precisely because we had this ideology that we viewed a war of invasion as a war of righteousness, committing cruel and inhumane acts as if they were nothing at all.[5]

One soldier of the Tenth Regiment who participated in the attack on Nanking believed that the war set off by Japan's militarism caused soldiers to become brutal and mad. He said, "The war turned them into people who thought only about their own loss or gain. Throughout day after day and night after night on the bloody battlefield, their so-called 'self-control' and 'upbringing' were forgotten immediately. Everyone got this horrific look in his eyes and started speaking roughly and acting crazily."[6] The famous Japanese historian Hora Tomio accurately explains the complex state of mind of Japanese soldiers during the war. He writes:

> I believe that Japanese farmers were originally simple and good. After the Restoration there was a kind of ideology and a set of feudalistic customs that I'm afraid brought with them a violent martial society. These were called "National Morals" and were forced into people's heads. The Japanese farmers became the ferocious soldiers of a fascist army. This is the way we must understand it. The commander of the Allied Forces occupying Japan believed that "the inhumane, horrific crimes against humanity committed by the Japanese were the certain and inevitable outcome of Japan's past fifty years of propagating "Kodo" (Way of the Emperor) and "Yamato Damashii" (Soul of Japan).[7]

After the Japanese troops occupied the outskirts of Nanking, the defending Chinese troops there rejected Matsui Iwane's letter urging them to surrender. They replied instead with a stubborn defense. This frustrated the hopes of the invading Japanese troops for a quick end to the resistance in Nanking. Later, during the brutal battle to take the walls of Nanking, Japanese troops described the war scene at the time as an "illustration of Hell." In battles at places like Chunhua Village, Zijin Mountain, Yuhua Tai, Guanghua Gate, Zhonghua Gate, and Yangfang Mountain, Japanese troops incurred heavy losses. The Japanese said of the battle at Guanghua Gate, "After fighting a bloody, ferocious battle for three days, we have suffered many dead and wounded and are absolutely exhausted."[8] Upon receiving his sentence for the Nanking Massacre, the Japanese commander Matsui Iwane said, "Ever since we came ashore at Shanghai, a deep hatred of the enemy built up inside my troops because we fought so bitterly and paid such a heavy sacrifice."[9] In early 1938, Major Amadani, garrison commander of the western area of Nanking, believed the atrocities of the Japanese in Nanking were a result of "the long, tense battle and the unexpected stubborn resistance of the Chinese troops."[10] Japanese Air Force lieutenant Ide Junji once saw a "forty-year-old long-bearded recruit" slashing into Chinese prisoners with his sword and shouting, "Revenge for my dead comrade-in-arms XXX! Taste my wrath!"[11] One foreign professor staying in Nanking reported that the invading Japanese troops "have long since put aside the standards of international law and openly admit that they are fighting out of revenge for their compatriots killed taking Nanking."[12] While we cannot accept the excuses made by people like Matsui and Amadani for the atrocities in Nanking, we can certainly use the above accounts of the war scene and the soldiers' state of mind as references during our probe into the causes of the Nanking Massacre. It is conceivable that a collective Japanese psychology of frustration and anger, fueled by a desire for revenge, which in turn was induced by an unexpectedly strong Chinese resistance, constitutes a fundamental cause for the atrocities at Nanking.

The second cause, which is the direct cause, was the special importance of the city of Nanking. At that time Nanking was the capital of China, and it was a political, economic, and cultural center. Japanese troops attempted to use large-scale killing of people in the capital to force the Chinese people to stop resisting.

The fundamental cause referred to above is only a universal, root reason that atrocities occurred during the whole war between China and Japan. Without the violence of the aggressors and the resistance of the defenders, large-scale atrocities would have lacked the necessary conditions for their existence. Regardless of the unique importance of a particular area or city, whether atrocities were committed at all was determined by the conditions of the fundamental cause mentioned earlier. But the fundamental cause does not explain why cities such as Beijing,

Tianjing, and Taiyuan, which also resisted the Japanese troops vigorously, and Shanghai, where fierce resistance lasted for three months
during which the Japanese troops suffered heavy losses, did not incur
atrocities on the same scale as Nanking. This suggests that Nanking was
different in some way from Beijing, Tianjing, and Shanghai.

As far as the significance of Nanking is concerned, and the attitude of
people like Matsui Iwane with respect to this question, there is a bril-
liant account in the written verdict of the Far East International Military
Tribunal that reads:

> When Matsui was appointed Commanding Officer of Shanghai, while
> still en route from Tokyo to the battlefield, he had already decided to
> invade Nanking after taking Shanghai. Before he left Tokyo he demanded
> five divisions of "Shanghai dispatch troops." He had long since investi-
> gated the geography of the areas around Shanghai and Nanking, so he
> was fully prepared to carry out an attack on Nanking. On July 8, 1937,
> Matsui declared, "My demon-defeating sword has left its scabbard and is
> about to unleash its awesome force!" Because they planned to enlarge
> the war zone in the area surrounding Shanghai, they appointed Matsui as
> Commanding Officer of Japan's Shanghai dispatch forces.
>
> In late October 1937, Matsui appointed Muto Akira as his chief strat-
> egist. After occupying Shanghai for a month, Japanese troops reached
> the outskirts of Nanking. Matsui sent out an order, the essence of which
> was, "Nanking is the capital of China, and taking Nanking will be an
> international incident, so we must research thoroughly how to maximize
> Japan's military might and force China into submission." China com-
> pletely ignored Japan's summons to surrender, so Japan started to attack.
> On December 13, 1937, Nanking fell. Although the Japanese troops that
> entered Nanking were newly formed, they were formed of experienced
> soldiers. On December 17, 1937, Matsui proudly entered the city. From
> December 13 what is commonly known as the Nanking Massacre began.[13]

Under the above conditions, when the Japanese troops under Matsui
Iwane's command were first maneuvering in the area around Suzhou
and Jiaxing, a telegram was sent to Intelligence Headquarters on November 22. It read, "In order to resolve the incident, attacking the capital Nanking will have the greatest value." The response from Intelligence
Headquarters instructed Iwane to "use [his] current forces and spare no
sacrifice" to accomplish this goal.

While the fall of a nation's capital does not always play the decisive
role in the outcome of a war, the defeat or defense of a nation's capital

does have an unusual effect on people's psychology, spirit, and
quent conduct. Thus there exist plenty of examples of countries th
wars after losing their capitals. To further develop Japan's "military
might," to force the Chinese people into "submission," and to add greater
"value" to their occupancy of Nanking all became extensions of the war
of invasion. So it is not difficult to see how the strategic importance of
Nanking served as a direct cause for the Nanking Massacre.

After discussing the fundamental and direct causes behind the Nanking
Massacre, our research into its causes is still not complete. The fundamental cause is only a cause of a general or root nature, thus it was
applicable to any related area or city in China or throughout the world.
The direct cause only emphasized the particular ways in which Nanking
was especially important or valuable. Other cities that fought fierce battles
of resistance against the invading Japanese troops could be said to equal
Nanking in importance or value. One example is Shanghai, the financial
and economic center in China. The invading Japanese surely wanted to
destroy the will of resistance of the people of Shanghai as well. Therefore, there must be other distinguishing factors besides the fact that
Nanking was China's capital that explain why this shocking massacre
occurred in Nanking and not in other cities. The third cause, which is
the indirect cause, for the Nanking Massacre was the unsuccessful retreat of the Chinese troops under the command of Tang Shengzhi, resulting in nearly 100,000 Chinese soldiers being detained in the city or
hiding among the civilian population.

On December 12, Tang Shengzhi, in accordance with Jiang Jieshi's
(Chiang Kai-Chek) orders, issued an order for a complete military withdrawal from Nanking. His retreat lacked sufficient organization and
turned into a grave mistake. In the beginning of the retreat, Tang Shengzhi
did take into account such objective factors as the pressure of time and
the small number of boats for the large number of people. He confirmed
the principle of sending "a larger percentage to break through the surrounding enemy lines and a smaller percentage across the river by boat."
He ordered only the Thirty-Sixth Division and the members of the Defense Command Division to cross the river from the dock at Xiaguan;
the other divisions were to go straight at the enemy and break through
the line. This principle was realistic and appropriate given the situation.
Considering the ratio of Chinese to Japanese troops and the hurried long-
range attacks by the Japanese, it was impossible for the Japanese to
suddenly seal off their lines so tightly that Chinese troops would have

had no way to break through. But when Tang Shengzhi gave the official order to retreat, he added at the last minute that the Eighty-Seventh Division, the Eighty-Eighth Division, and the Seventy-Fourth Division should instruct their troops, "If you can't all break through the enemy, take turns crossing the river and regroup on the other side in Chuzhou." Immediately the number of troops being transported across the river jumped by more than five divisions, resulting in a situation of "a larger percentage crossing the river and a smaller percentage breaking through the surrounding enemy lines." This was simply more than the transportation facilities were able to accommodate. As soon as Teng Shengzhi's order was given, a large number of troops—nine divisions in all—who were supposed to break through the line swarmed instead to the edge of the river. There were more people than boats to hold them. Discipline was lost, causing a large number of troops to be detained in the city and by the river, some to become Japanese prisoners, and others to merge into the civilian population.

According to statistics, there were thirteen divisions and fifteen regiments—approximately 150,000 soldiers—defending Nanking. About 10,000 were killed or wounded, 50,000 withdrew safely from Nanking, and more than 90,000 were detained in the city.[14] Of the 90,000 detained in Nanking, except for a few who were lucky enough to escape, or at least to avoid immediate death, the majority either became Japanese prisoners, or became "civilians" who were eventually discovered and massacred. This number accounts for almost 30 percent of the total 300,000 Chinese victims of the massacre and had a significant effect on the size and scale of the Nanking Massacre.

Throughout the course of the Sino-Japanese War, there was no other city that after falling to the enemy detained 90,000 soldiers in the city, unable to escape yet also unable to organize into military units capable of engaging in battle. The soldiers detained in Nanking were like a headless dragon or a plate of loose grains of sand, and those who became prisoners numbered in the tens of thousands.

The predefined goal of the Japanese invaders was to use terrorist tactics to force China to submit. In September of that year, Japan's foreign secretary Hirota Koki raised the cry, "The only alternative for the Japanese Empire is to cause the Chinese troops to lose all will to fight." Matsui Iwane personally gave the order to "correct and discipline" Chinese prisoners of war, which gave permission to kill them. The commander of the Shanghai Dispatch Troops, Prince Asaka Yasuhiko, also personally gave the order to "kill all prisoners." The Far East International Military Tribunal points out in its written verdict, "A large number of Chinese soldiers put down their weapons and surrendered outside the city. Within 72 hours of their surrender, they were lined up on the bank of the Yangtze River and killed with machine guns. More than 30,000 prisoners were killed in this way."[15]

The large numbers of soldiers who put down their weapons and merged into the civilian population gave the Japanese troops an excu
capture, and kill. After the invading Japanese troops entered
was precisely under the pretext of looking for "Chinese
they wantonly captured innocent civilians, killing or wou
will. In many cases they murdered indiscriminately, kil
regardless of age or sex. In some cases they decided whe
a young man on the basis of certain typical military chara
as helmet marks on the forehead and calluses on the hands
H.J. Timperley, a reporter for Britain's *Manchester Gua*
his *What War Means: Japanese Terror in China*, "Anyone
his hands could be labeled a soldier, in which case he would most ce
be killed."[16] Zhang Daofu, a witness, says in his statement, "Japanese troops came to the refugee camps to catch people. As soon as they found a man they would examine his head for helmet marks and his hands for calluses. If they found any they would assume he was a soldier and take him off to be killed."[17] Therefore, the large number of soldiers who hid among civilians gave an excuse for the Japanese troops to further harm Chinese civilians and enlarged the scale of atrocities considerably.

If we look at the situation from another angle, we can see the serious consequences caused by large numbers of soldiers hiding among civilians and the effects this had on the Nanking Massacre. If the Chinese army at Nanking had been able to retreat completely, as did the troops at Xuzhou five months later, along with those at many other cities, then both the form and the severity of the Japanese atrocities in Nanking might have been much different.

Notes

1. "Peng Xiangsong Chenshushu" (Witness account of Peng Xiangsong). Nanking City Archive, May 15, 1946.

2. "Gong Yukun Zhengyan" (Testimony of Gong Yukun). *Qin Hua Rijun Nanjing datusha shiliao* (Historical materials of Nanking Massacre under the invading Japanese military). Jiangsu guji chubanshe, 1985, p. 432.

3. "Zhou Changrong Zhengyan" (Testimony of Zhou Changrong). *Qin Hua Rijun Nanjing datusha shiliao* (Historical materials of Nanking Massacre under the invading Japanese military). Jiangsu guji chubanshe, 1985, p. 429.

4. "Deguo danganguan zhong you guan qin Hua Rijun Nanjing datusha de dangan ziliao" (Archival materials relating to the Nanking Massacre under the invading Japanese military in German archive). *Kang Ji Zhanzheng Yanjiu*, vol. 2, 1991.

5. Yamaoka Shigeru. *My Experience: Accusing War of Invasion*, taken from Hora Tomio. *Nanjing Datusha*, transl. Shanghai yiwen chubanshe, 1987, p. 265.

6. *Nacuidang buzhichi de yemanxingwei*, taken from Hora Tomio. *Nanjing Datusha*, transl. Shanghai yiwen chubanshe, 1987, p. 240.

7. Hora Tomio. *Nanjing Datusha*, transl. Shanghai yiwen chubanshe, 1987, p. 269.

8. Nankin Nihon Shyōkō kaigi, ed. *Nankin kōryaku shi* (History of the invasion of Nanking). August 1941.

9. Tanaka Masaaki. *Nanjing Datusha zhi Xugou* (The fabrication of Nanking Massacre). Shijie zhishi chubanshe, 1985, p. 150.

10. Hora Tomio. *Nanjing Datusha. trans.* Shanghai yiwen chubanshe, 1987, p. 238.

11. Li Xiushi, ed. and transl. *Riben guonei guanyu "Nanjing Datusha" de Xinzhenglun* (The new data over Nanking Massacre in Japan). *Shijieshi yanjiu dongtai*, vol. 5, 1988.

12. *Qin Hua Rijun Nanjing datusha shiliao* (Historical materials of Nanking Massacre under the invading Japanese military). Jiangsu guji chubanshe, 1985, p. 193.

13. Zhang Xiaolin, transl. *Yuandong guoji junshi fating panjueshu* (The verdict of the Far Eastern military tribunal). Wushi niandai chubanshe, 1953, Chinese edition.

14. Sun Zhaiwei. *Nanjing Datusha yu Nanjing Renkou* (Nanking massacre and the population of Nanking). *Nanjing shehui kexue*, vol. 3, 1990.

15. Zhang Xiaolin, transl. *Yuandong guoji junshi fating panjueshu* (*The verdict of the Far Eastern military tribunal*). Wushi niandai chubanshe, 1953, Chinese edition.

16. *Qin Hua Rijun Nanjing datusha shiliao* (Historical materials of Nanking Massacre under the invading Japanese military). Jiangsu guji chubanshe, 1985, p. 181.

17. *Qin Hua Rijun Nanjing datusha shiliao* (Historical materials of Nanking Massacre under the invading Japanese military). Jiangsu guji chubanshe, 1985, p. 467.

4

The Nanking Massacre Reassessed: A Study of the Sino-Japanese Controversy over the Factual Number of Massacred Victims

Lee En-Han

One of the most bitter controversies in the debate over the Nanking Massacre is the argument about the actual numbers of victims. One's position in the "numbers" argument tends to reflect one's position on the spectrum in the overall debate. Often, the lines between various groups of revisionists and progressives are drawn according to their levels of acknowledgment of the numbers massacred. Though many scholars have advocated the need to look beyond numbers and into humanity itself, to truly understand the full scope of debate over the Nanking Massacre, it is important as well to consider the "numbers" controversy.

A researcher at the Academica Sinaca in Taiwan, Lee En-Han is one of Taiwan's leading scholars on Asian atrocities in World War II, including the Nanking Massacre. In this chapter he attempts a comprehensive study of the "numbers" issue. —Eds.

1. The Sino-Japanese War

Generally speaking, there has been, and still is, a strong and deep-rooted sense of mutual animosity and mistrust between the Chinese and Japanese peoples. As described tersely but obliquely by Akira Iriye, although there has developed a kind of commonality, interdependence, mutual respect, and attraction between them, there simultaneously coexists an emotional sense of disparity, autonomy, repulsion, and condescension between them.[1] Historically, the two peoples have been mutually influenced by the "export" of their cultural achievements, but intermittent clashes and conflicts have often occurred, which have easily developed from petty bickering to limited or large-scale warfare. This has been especially true since the 1920s and 1930s when an imperialistic Japan began its plan of aggression against China, aimed at an eventual dismemberment of that old, tradition-burdened, and weak country into various regions, intended purposefully to reduce that once great empire to a secondary status under Japanese hegemony. The clashes and conflicts between a nationalistic China, which struggled bitterly for a resurgence of the nation, and an expansive and high-handed Japan ensued. It culminated in a full-fledged but initially undeclared war between the two countries on July 7, 1937, extending for more than eight years. Eventually Japan was defeated in August 1945 through the collaboration of China, the United States, the Soviet Union, and other states.

However, during the prolonged eight-year (1937–1945) war between China and Japan, the Imperial Japanese Army (IJA) had committed numerous atrocities in a well-planned, large-scale manner in the occupied regions of China, aimed at terrorizing the Chinese into submission. Present research shows Chinese casualties were put at 21 million persons (dead and wounded), more than the casualties of the Soviet Union inflicted by Nazi Germany,[2] and a preliminarily partial calculation of the nation's materialist loss was set at a total of US$62 billion (price value in 1945).[3] The war atrocities committed by the IJA included, most notably, the Rape of Nanking (starting on December 13, 1937, and extending until mid-February or mid-May 1938) in which a minimum of 300,000 prisoners of war (POWs) and civilians were massacred; the *Sanko Seisaku* (or *San guang,* in Chinese, meaning kill-all, burn-all, destroy-all) military campaigns against Chinese Communist guerrillas in North China, killing mercilessly more than a reported total of 3,180,000 civilians and Communist cadets; the germ and biological warfare experiments conducted by the IJA's Unit 731 (and other units) on at least 3,000 prisoners (Chinese, Korean, and Russian, but mostly Chinese) who were still alive; the recurrent, indiscriminate bombing of civilian areas of Chong Qing, Sichuan, the wartime capital; and the large-scale and systematic trafficking of narcotic drugs involving a yearly, startling volume of US$300 million (in 1939).[4] Although Japanese spoke idealistically of proposing such schemes as the "New Order for East Asia," "A Combined Coordination Between Japan, Manchukuo and China," and "Co-prosperity in East Asia," these "slogans" never became real policies. As refuted pointedly by Generalissimo Jiang Jieshi (Chiang Kaishek) in December 1938, "To speak frankly, when we Chinese mention the name of Japan, we would immediately remember the omnipresence of the Japanese infamous, troublemaking, special agents, the notorious, vulgarized *ronins* (rascals). They usually engage in trafficking and manufacturing opium, morphine, and heroin, opening those sordid businesses of prostitution and gambling dens, smuggling military weapons and ammunition into China, sponsoring the subsistence of Chinese thugs and traitors. The Japanese in China are actually conspiring to disturb our order and laws, decaying our social, moral standard and poisoning our physical forces."[5] The Japanese wartime atrocities in China were also reaffirmed by the late prominent historian Lloyd E. Eastman, who concluded that "the Japanese maltreatment of Chinese civilians was also part of a conscious policy to terrorize the Chinese into submission. In areas they could not occupy, the Japanese sometimes applied a scorched-earth policy. To combat Chinese guerrilla operations, they often wrought fearful retributions against innocent civilians."[6] Thus, after a thorough investigation of the available multilanguage sources, Professor Eastman concluded that "the record of Japanese military in China forms an ineradicable stain on the history of the Japanese nation."[7] All these Japanese major criminal cases, except the Unit 731 case, and all the senior Japanese war criminals, except Emperor Hirohito, had been investigated and tried in the Tokyo War Crimes Trials organized by the twelve Allied nations and conducted by the International Military Tribunal for the Far East from May 1946 to November 1948. All these war criminals were convicted and punished according to international laws.[8]

2. The Nanking Massacre

In the case of the Nanking Massacre, the International Military Tribunal for the Far East spent three weeks in Tokyo on a thorough investigation and verification of the facts, while its prosecution section labored many months in summoning for testimony more than ten American eyewitnesses who were on the scene in Nanking when the massacre happened. There were more than 100 written testimonies and supporting documents collected for the case.[9] Under oath before the court, the witnesses all reconfirmed the occurrence of the Massacre, and collectively described the event as having started on December 13, 1937, when the Imperial Japanese Army occupied the city, and continued for at least six weeks until mid-February 1938 (recent research shows that the IJA's rampage actually continued until May 1938). The Japanese soldiers were

described as like "loosened barbarians" and "human beasts" in committing savage depraved acts upon these disarmed Chinese troops and helpless civilian noncombatants.[10] The city of Nanking was depicted by
journalist Harold J. Timperley as a living hell. He wrote that the Japanese atrocities "unquestionably represent the darkest days of the modern [world] history."[11] Others commented that the city was surely a "hell
on earth."[12] Tillman Durdin, a *New York Times* reporter in Nanking,
wrote that "the Japanese army's barbarity and savagery can be comparable to the brutal and savage behavior in the dark age of medieval European and Asian conquerors."[13] The Chinese POWs and unarmed
captives were not treated according to international laws, but rather were
grouped together, marched forcibly to the outskirts of the city or suburban areas, and machine-gunned to death. Dr. Miner Searle Bates, an
American professor of history at Nanking University, testified that within
two days of the city's fall to Japanese occupation there were approximately 12,000 noncombatant men, women, and children murdered, and
the raping of women was so rampant that within the first month there
occurred more than 20,000 cases.[14] Recent research shows that during
that entire period about 80,000 women were raped.[15]

Simultaneously, systematic destruction of the urban areas began and
all the major government buildings and private houses were set ablaze,
starting from the main streets and proceeding to the minor avenues. It is
estimated that over 30,000 soldiers were slaughtered in cold blood within
the first three days of the city's capture.[16] Dr. Louis S.C. Smythe, a professor of sociology at the same university, estimated through an incomplete sampling that the massacred civilians within the city and the
outskirts were numbered at 12,000 and the forced "laborers" at 4,200.[17]

Both Bates and Smythe confined their estimations to civilians, and,
in addition, they limited their discussion of the Massacre to its early
period. They did not know or could not imagine the sad situation suffered by the POWs, the disarmed soldiers, and the mixed-in refugees
who were massacred wholesale in various suburban areas. Their under-
estimated figures for the event, however, were soon verified by an American military expert, Colonel Frank Dorn, who had calculated that "over
200,000 [Chinese] civilians and possibly as many as 300,000 had been
senselessly massacred."[18] Furthermore, Dr. Xu Chuanyin, who served
as a deputy head of the Red Cross Society in Nanking, presented his
estimate of killed civilians and POWs as more than 200,000 persons.[19]
The scale and intensity of the Nanking Massacre was witnessed in full

view by a score of neutral Western observers who compiled court testimonials, diaries, reminiscences, and personal correspondences, together with newspaper reports, editorials, and commentaries in contemporaneous Western journals, most of which remain available to the present day.[20] This made it hard for the Japanese authorities to cover up the event with twisted facts and interpretations and also difficult for the present Japanese conservative government, along with some diehard neorightists and apologists, to deny.

3. The Tokyo War Crimes Trial

During the Tokyo Trials the Chinese Nationalist government at Nanking made careful, thorough, and extensive on-the-spot investigations of the Nanking Massacre. The preliminary figure reached and submitted to the International Military Tribunal was about 430,000 victims, composed of 230,000 civilians and 200,000 soldiers, including those who fought to the death, POWs, and refugees.[21] The Chinese prosecutor at the Tribunal, Dr. Xiang Zhechun, charged that in the eight-year period of war the Japanese committed a reported 75,000–odd criminal acts in China, including massacres and killings, mistreatments, rapes, and lootings and plunderings. Among them, the Rape of Nanking stood as the greatest and the most ferocious.[22] The chief prosecutor of the Nanking District Court, Chen Guangyu, with the assistance of the capital city's fourteen government and private institutions, made a strenuous, exhaustive search of the related facts. Eventually he determined that the massacres actually consisted of two categories: collective massacres and individual and wanton massacres. Most of the collective massacres happened in different areas of suburban Nanking, which were mostly unknown to residents of the city. Four notable cases in the category are particularly mentioned and elaborated in his report:

(1) At Yu Hua Tai, an outskirt just near the city's major south gate Zhong Hua Men, roughly 20,000–30,000 soldiers and civilians were killed;
(2) On the sand-fluid bar in the middle of the Yangzi river, tens of thousands of POWs and civilians were machine-gunned to death;
(3) In the hill-side villages of Cao Xia Gorge at the Front of Mu Fu Mountain in the northeastern suburb of Nanking, 50,000–60,000 POWs were mercilessly massacred en masse (later sources gave a concrete figure of 57,418 persons);
(4) Other considerably large mass-killings included a massacre of 2,873

persons near Shangxin River, on the western outskirt of the city; a massacre of about 7,000 persons in the southern outskirt near the Nanking Arsenal and Hua Shen Miao compounds; a killing of 3,000 persons near the Han Chong Gate of the western city; and a slaying of about 3,000 persons in and near the Ling Gu Temple in the eastern suburb.[23]

Chief Prosecutor Chen's report in September 1946 also included unquestionably reliable records of two local philanthropic societies that had actively engaged in burying the corpses within and outside the city after the massacres. Chung Shan Tang, a traditional social welfare organization, which had existed for several hundred years since the Ming Dynasty, and the Red Swastika Society of Nanking, which was a semimodern, voluntary association organized by the local gentry and rich businessmen for social relief work, faithfully recorded their services in their books. The combined figure in their burying services was more than 155,000 corpses in areas within and outside the city.[24] The number of massacred victims was collectively set at 279,586 persons.[25] In addition, there were numerous individual and wanton slaughters in the city—42,000 persons according to Dr. Miner Searle Bates. Thus, the accumulated massacred victims was definitely set at more than 300,000 persons. This round figure, however, did not include an additional, unverified number of 200,000 victims that were reported to Chen individually and needed to be further corroborated.[26] Chen Guangyu's report gave vivid narration of the Japanese savagery during the six to eight weeks of the Nanking Massacre. The early breakdown of the Chinese defenses along the city wall was made along the southern gates by the IJA. The victorious Japanese soldiers broke into Chinese houses along the path of their march, killing men they met in the streets and raping women who remained at home. The houses were then set on fire and wanton atrocities occurred. The formerly prosperous, commercial areas of the city, with large traditional or modernized shops, department stores, and restaurants, were burned down one by one. The burning black smoke curled into the sky over the city, continuing unabated for many days and nights, and one-third of the city was thus changed to ashes and ruins. Within and outside the city, the destruction was similarly thorough. From the eastern outskirts to the suburban Cao Xia Gorge and Yan Zi Ji (Swallow's Rock), and from the northern city to the river harbor of Xia Guan, blood was shed far and wide. The corpses of deceased fighters,

POWs, and civilians were lying around everywhere, creating a pungent smell. Ponds large and small, as well as scenic Muo Chou Lake, were full of human corpses that had colored the water red. Victims' corpses, both men and women, were heaped on the corners of the streets. It was estimated that in the first eight days, from December 13 to December 20, 1937, the Japanese had slaughtered approximately 200,000 Chinese civilians and POW's.[27]

After September 1946, Chief Prosecutor Chen made a continuous effort to verify and intensify his field investigations. He distributed an information sheet to the concerned institutions and individuals and used the collected materials as additional evidence. Thus, he slightly revised his total figure for the collective massacres from 279,586 to 295,886. He was extremely careful in his calculation and was very serious in finding correct figures. At that time the Nationalist government's National Relief and Rehabilitation Agency also made separate and independent examinations of the number of massacred victims, and an additional 96,260 persons were added to the list, bringing the final total number of victims to 391,785 persons.[28] In Chen's new checklist of collective and individual massacres, he elaborated notable cases as follows (some were new cases that he discovered, while others were old cases that were reconfirmed):

1. The Chung Shan Tang buried 112,267 corpses;
2. The Red Swastika Society buried 43,071 corpses (the total burials of the two societies totaled 155,338 corpses, a figure unchanged from their earlier investigations);
3. Massacred POWs and civilians (refugees) totaled 57,818 in the Cao Xia Gorge near the Mu Fu Mountain and Xia Guan. This figure was reaffirmed from the former findings;
4. The Japanese buried alive about 3,000 POWs and refugees on the hillside of the Zi Jin Mountain in the eastern suburb of Nanking (this was a new finding after September 1946);
5. 28,730 POWs and civilians were massacred near the Shangxin River in the western outskirts of the city (this figure represents more killings than that found in the original total of 2,877 persons in the first survey);
6. Approximately 100,000 POWs and civilian refugees were massacred in Yan Zi Ji (Swallow Rock), the sand bar Ba Gua Zhou in the Yangzi River and Xia Guan areas. (This newly calculated figure was more precise than the originally designated "tens of thousand" in the first survey);

7. Roughly 2,000 civilians were killed near the Han Zheng Gate in the western city (the figure was less by 1,000 persons than in the first survey);

8. More than 10,000 "disarmed soldiers" were arbitrarily captured (so called "plain-clothed soldiers" fetched from the foreign-controlled "Safety Zone") and marched to Xia Guan near the Yangtze River, to be machine-gunned to death;

9. Five hundred refugees were burned alive in the Judiciary Hall;

10. About 5,000 civilian refugees were captured in the Overseas Chinese Building in downtown Nanking and compelled to march to Xia Guan to be machine-gunned to death;

11. More than 10,000 refugees escaped to the compound of the British Ho Chi Company in Xia Guan, where they were caught by the IJA and massacred on the riverside;

12. In an area near the Guan Yin Gate and the Big-Forest Field, 30,000 people were slaughtered;

13. In the outskirts of the Han Xi Gate in western Nanking, 6,000–7,000 POWs and civilians were massacred;

14. Near the Shang Yuan Gate of the eastern city, more than 9,000 POWs were machine-gunned and bayoneted to death.[29]

All the above-mentioned old and new findings combined give a new casualty total of over 410,000 souls. Even if the first two items of the above list were deleted from the combined total on account of possible repetitions, the grand total was still 260,000 souls. This figure, however, must be added to the massacred total through individual and wanton slaughters, which was at least a minimum of 42,000 or possibly 80,000 souls. So, the grand total would be 302,000 or 342,000 victims.[30] It is noted that one of the salient features found in these two sources is that the great majority of the Japanese massacres were conducted in the outskirts and the suburban areas of Nanking rather than within the city wall.

In February 1947 the Chinese Ministry of Defense began to bring some second-ranked Japanese war criminals, such as Lieutenant General Hisao Tani, former commander of the IJA's crack Sixth Division, to a military tribunal in Nanking.[31] The Ministry's prosecutors made every effort to recheck and verify all Chinese casualties, military and civilian, during the Nanking Massacre period. Their penetrating investigations uncovered some obscure cases of collective killings and a total of eighteen cases in that category were reconfirmed, rather than the former fourteen cases registered by Chief Prosecutor Chen in 1946.[32] The new findings were, however, rather minor instances involving some hundreds of POWs or civilians slain, but the largest case also covered about

10,000 monks, nuns, and Buddhist laymen who were slaughtered in various temples and shrines outside the city proper.[33] The Ministry's verdict sentenced Lieutenant General Hisao Tani to death, and he was shot by Chinese gendarmes. It reconfirmed the actual number of massacred victims including POWs and civilians at more than 300,000 persons composed of 150,00 corpses buried by the two welfare societies as well as those corpses thrown into the Yangtze River, other streams and ponds possibly accounting for more than 190,000 persons.[34]

In November 1948 the International Military Tribunal in Tokyo authenticated that the occurrence of the Nanking Massacre lasted for a prolonged period of at least six weeks in and outside the city. The event's large-scale nature was also reaffirmed, and the well-planned and concerted action followed the policy of the Japanese government. Thus, the massacres in Nanking were unquestionably true and most of the collective massacres were made under the order of high-ranking commanders. In some cases, these high-ranking officers even joined the killings themselves.[35]

The International Military Tribunal was rather conservative in its judgment of the factual number of Chinese victims and put its estimate at "more than 200,000 persons," roughly based on the testimonials of Dr. Xu Chuanyin at the court. The Tribunal reasoned that since the combined burial records by the two philanthropic societies and others had already totaled more than 150,000 persons, if this figure was added to the number of corpses buried or disposed of by other methods by the IJA units themselves, the figure of "more than 200,000 persons" was certainly a reasonable sum. The Tribunal further concluded that the Japanese savagery in Nanking could not be excused on the pretext that there were highly stimulated emotions in the fierce fighting on the battlefield, since most of the collective massacres, rapes, plunderings, and depredations happened after the fall of the city and these unlawful activities proceeded in a large-scale way within a period of at least six weeks.[36]

The Tribunal thus set the death penalty for General Matsui Iwane since, as the highest ranking commander in the field, he should bear the responsibility for the occurrence of the tragic massacres. He had the power to control his troops' discipline and should have provided basic safeguards for the helpless, innocent and unarmed people in occupied Nanking. The atrocities committed by his troops meant that he failed to perform his duties.[37]

The Japanese foreign minister, Hirota Kōbi, was also sentenced to death because, (together with two other crime counts), as a member of the Japanese Cabinet, he did not take action to prevent the incident, which was contrary to international laws, and "his inaction amounted to criminal negligence."[38] However, the Tribunal's estimated figure of the massacred victims was considered by the Chinese judge, Dr. Mei Yuao, to be very conservative. Mei firmly believed that the correct number should be a figure between 300,000 and 400,000.[39] This means that the figure amounting to "more than 300,000 victims" (or between 300,000 and 400,000 victims) as counted by the Chinese Ministry of Defense in 1948, could be feasible and authoritative.

Indeed, this Chinese official figure of more than 300,000 victims has been reconfirmed by Hirota Kōbi, the above-mentioned convicted Japanese foreign minister himself. In his recently declassified extra-confidential telegram to the Japanese Embassy in Washington, D.C., on January 17, 1938, he said that the "verbal account [of] reliable eye-witnesses and letters from individuals whose credibility [is] beyond question afford convincing proof [that the] Japanese army behaved and [is] continuing [to] behave in a fashion reminiscent [of] Attila and his Huns. [Not] less than three hundred thousand Chinese civilians slaughtered, many cases [in] cold blood." His telegram also gave a moderately detailed narration of the incident, saying that "robbery, rape, including children [of] under tender years and insensate brutality towards civilians continues [to] be reported from areas where actual hostilities ceased weeks ago. Deep shame which better type [of] Japanese here feel reprehensible conduct [of] Japanese troops elsewhere heightened by series [of] local incidents where Japanese soldiers run amuck in Shanghai itself."[40] It is noted that on January 17, 1938, when the massacres in Nanking were still in progress, the Japanese foreign minister had already put the figure of massacred victims at 300,000. Since the massacres were generally drawing to an end in mid-February 1938, Chief Prosecutor Chen's second figure of 391,785 or up to a possible 500,000 victims becomes true. Recent research on this topic by James Yin and Shi Young, which puts the figure at 350,000, is also roughly comparable to the above-mentioned Chinese Defense Ministry's statistics in 1947.[41]

4. Japanese Postwar Debate Through 1982

Immediately after World War II, Japan as a defeated country never really relinquished its old expansive and aggressive ambition, although it experienced a seven-year occupation by the United States. Its military machine was nominally demolished, but its financial and manpower resources remained intact. Its first batch of twenty-eight (or twenty-five) of the highest-level war criminals, except Emperor Hirohito and some biological warfare criminals, had been punished by the International Military Tribunal for the Far East before November 1948, but the nation's second and third batches of twenty-three and nineteen war criminals, respectively, included some important political leaders: Kishi Nobusuke, Kaya Okinori, Sasagawa Ryoichi, and others who had never been formally prosecuted at the international court.[42] As the Cold War between the United States and Soviet Union worsened and a Communist victory in China appeared imminent, these war criminals were all released by the United States before the end of 1948.[43] The outbreak of the Korean War in June 1950 further pushed Japan toward an economic rejuvenation as well as a preliminary military revival in the form of a police force acting as quasi-military troops, which was established in the 1950s and 1960s.[44] When the San Francisco Peace Treaty was signed in September 1951 and Japan resumed its sovereignty from the American occupation in 1952, all the above-mentioned war criminals and other lower-level wartime officials resumed their influential positions under the Yoshida government. The people who controlled the postwar government of Japan were basically the same people as during the war period, although they now were organized into the Liberal-Democratic Party (LDP) in competition with the Socialist Party, the Communist Party, and others in a democratic framework.[45]

However, the Japanese scholars and journalists in the 1950s and 1960s generally accepted the figures derived from the Chinese investigations or those from the verdict made at the International Tribunal. Hata Ikuhiko originally served in the War History Department of the Japanese Self-Defense Agency. He is the author of *A History of Japanese-Chinese War* (1961), in which he gives a detailed discussion on the Nanking Massacre, elaborating on the earliest Chinese statistics of 430,000 victims, including soldiers who died in battle, POWs, the "dispersed," and "plain-clothed" soldiers (unarmed, without any intention of fighting), as well as civilians massacred amounting to 12,000–42,000 (a figure presented by Dr. Miner Searle Bates for the first month or a combined number including the slaughtered soldiers in the first three days only). He also mentioned the rough figures from Chinese sources indicating that the Imperial Japanese Army's (IJA's) Sixth Division killed about 230,000 persons and the Sixteenth Division murdered about 140,000.[46] Professor Hora Tomio of Yaseda University wrote *Myths in Warfare of the Modern History* (1967). In this book he mentioned the figure of 430,000 victims and the established figure of over 200,000 victims set by the Tokyo Military Tribunal in 1948. Hora further reiterated Chief Prosecutor Chen's first figure of 279,586 victims, as well as Chen's second, corroborated, figure of over 450,000 (392,146 victims by collective massacres and 60,000 victims by individual and wanton killings), but he concluded that the Military Tribunal's verdict setting the number at over 200,000 persons was more probable.[47]

In the summer of 1971, Honda Katsuichi, a correspondent from the *Asahi Shimbun* in Tokyo, began touring Communist China. His daily reports on the Nanking Massacre were printed serially in his newspaper. The liberal left in Japan, by reading these reports, began to realize the facts. Although the Japanese leftists were victims of American atomic bombs, they were also victimizers in China. Their fellow Japanese had actually killed more Chinese in Nanking than the combined number of victims in Hiroshima and Nagasaki by Americans.[48] Many ex-soldiers who fought the war in China published their personal wartime experiences, confessing to the atrocities committed by them and their comrades-in-arms. Professor Hora therefore rewrote and expanded his former book, calling it *The Nanking Massacre* and publishing it in 1972. In addition, he compiled all the available documents in Chinese, Japanese, and English relating to the incident into a two-volume collection and printed them in 1973.[49] Kuroda Toshihide, in *Nanking, Hiroshima and Auschwitz* (1974), indicates clearly this Japanese victimizer-victim status in the past war. He makes an objective and conscientious stand for the Tokyo Trials over the Rape of Nanking and reaffirms the stated number of victims there at over 200,000.[50]

The Japanese government and the mainstream of Japanese society were firmly controlled by conservative elements, which emphasized their role as victims. While they remain militarily protected by the U.S. nuclear umbrella, Japanese are ungrateful for the American protection. Numerous books and articles have been published with respect to the atomic bombings in Hiroshima and Nagasaki, indirectly charging the United States with "atrocities." Starting in the mid-1960s, these nonrepentant, conservative apologists began to implicitly attack the United States, forgetting completely their own atrocities in Nanking and elsewhere in wartime China. On February 27, 1963, a judge at the Tokyo District Court ruled

that the American bombing of the two cities, which it said were unforti-
fied and undefended districts (a false statement), were unlawful.[51] On
May 13, 1992, the Association of Societies of Victims of Atomic Bombs
passed a resolution demanding the United States pay reparations for
their sufferings.[52] Professor John W. Dower countercharged that "the
nuclear destruction of the two cities is easily turned into victimization
narrative in which [it seems] the bombs fall from the heaven without
historical content—as if the [Pacific] war was begun on August 6, 1945
and innocent Japan bore the cross of bearing witness to the horrendous
birth of the nuclear age."[53] He calls American public attention to the
Japanese double-standard attitude toward this event and their historical
amnesia, saying that "they (Japanese) cannot honestly confront their
World War II past and these [Japanese evasion to face their criminal
atrocities] range from sanitized textbooks to virtually routinized public
denials of Japanese aggression and atrocities by conservative politicians
(usually associated with LDP) to the government's failure, until recently,
to offer an unequivocal apology to Asians and all victims of Imperial
Japanese wartime conduct."[54] Thus Professor Dower presents a "motion
of retribution" for the nonrepentant Japanese, asserting that "the Japanese reaped what they sowed [and] that having tried to flourish the sword,
they deservedly perished by it."[55] The nonrepentant Japanese elements
of the social mainstream directed their major renunciations toward a
weaker China, a poor performance of their samurai spirit. They began to
whitewash their savage record in Nanking. In January 1972, Yamamoto
Shichihei, a column writer who used a pseudonym and presented himself as a Jew, published an article denying the occurrence of the Nanking
Massacre, and refused to admit that Japan had ever committed any war
crimes during the last war. His second article repeated the former points
and strongly argued that Japan should not offer an apology for the
Nanking incident.[56] These initiations were quickly echoed by Suzuki Akira,
a reporter at a local broadcasting corporation, who wrote a series of
articles charging the exaggeration of the Nanking Massacre by Chinese,
American, and other wartime enemies. He presented the examples of two
Japanese junior officers sentenced to death by the Chinese Nationalist government in Nanking for their killing of more than a hundred innocent Chinese civilians each as a myth. Suzuki further pushed his argument by
attacking the "exaggerated" reports of the event by H.J. Timperley, saying
that he was not a personal witness to the event (an inaccurate charge without factual basis). Suzuki also criticized Professor Hora Tomio's book,

The Nanking Incident, as not a good book and said it did not consult primary sources of documents.[57] These arguments were quickly followed by conservative, right-wing writers who enthusiastically attacked the actual occurence of the Nanking Massacre as well as condemning Professor Hora's scholarship. Suzuki's ensuing articles in 1973 sustained his charges on the so-called insubstantial evidence and exaggerated nature of the Nanking Massacre because there were "few eyewitnesses" (a completely false statement).[58] Eventually, his articles were collected and printed in a book in 1982. The book even won a nationally known nonfiction literary prize in the same year.[59] However, all Suzuki's accusations were countered by the late Professor Lloyd E. Eastman as groundless since Suzuki himself "discounts a mountain of evidences that there was a massive atrocity in Nanking and that what occurred there was probably of little significance [for him]. But he adduces virtually no positive evidence to support his view."[60] Suzuki's work is representative of that of Japanese revisionists of the Nanking Incident in the early phase.

The theory of total denial of the Massacre was effectively rebuked by the progressive-minded liberal and left scholars as well as by objective-minded journalists. Honda Katsuichi of the *Asahi* wrote another book, *The Japanese Army in China,* elaborating upon all of the savage atrocities committed by the Japanese troops in different regions of China.[61] Hora Tomio also revised his *Nanking Massacre,* including in the new edition additional evidence for the event. His compilation of two volumes of documents from Japanese, Chinese, and English sources was also further expanded to include new documents. In addition, Professor Hora wrote a series of articles that were printed in the prestigious scholarly journal the *Historical Review,* criticizing Suzuki's theory as subjective and not factual persuasion. He also answered Suzuki's and Yamamoto's criticism of his book as unreasonable and groundless. Hora's articles were reprinted in a book entitled *The Nanking Massacre: A Critique of the "Exaggeration" Theory* (1975).[62] Honda compiled an additional book, collecting all the articles that criticized Suzuki's and Yamamoto's points, together with a strong reconfirmation of the facts of the Nanking Massacre.[63]

In the autumn of 1982, the conservative LDP government in Tokyo began to circulate its revised historical textbooks for primary and secondary school students in which it barred the original narration of the Nanking Massacre and changed the term "invasion of Korea and China" to "moving into Korea and China." This aroused strong, wrathful protests from China and South Korea. Unrepentant ex-officers of the IJA and conservative politicians and writers were adamant in maintaining their complete denial of the Massacre's occurrence. They refused to accept the fact of Japan being aggressors at all.[64] The Japanese LDP government, which tacitly supported these diehards, took an evasive, intentionally ignorant, and nonreflective stance, although it occasionally expresses some insincere quasi-remorseful murmurings. The second and third generations of the postwar political and social leaders in Japan usually assume the same viewpoint, intending to shy away from the Massacre as if those worst atrocities done by their fathers and grandfathers have no connection with them.[65] The Japanese government and the mainstream of Japanese society hope to forget that their predecessors and forefathers were victimizers in China and other countries, while continuing to reproach the American conscience for bombing them with two atomic weapons.

5. Japanese Postwar Debate Since 1982

With this general political and social background in the 1980s, Tanaka Masaasi—a retired journalist and an ex-secretary to General Matsui Iwane, who was hanged for his role in the Nanking Massacre—published his book *Fabrication of the Nanking Massacre* in 1984. He completely denied the occurrence of that event. The book is composed of many reminiscent articles written and published by him in various influential journals. He maintains his nonrepentant stand in denying the occurrence of the Massacre, dismissing all available multilingual evidence and documents as unbelievable and "faked." He even refuses to admit Japan had any war responsibility to China, intending to transfer the responsibility of the Sino-Japanese War to the Chinese.[66] Tanaka's popular fame as a writer in this respect became besmirched due to the fact that for his compilation of Matsui Iwane's diary, he had been found guilty of rewriting and arbitrarily replacing over 900 sentences and words.[67] Most important of all, the diary printed in November 1984 by the late Lieutenant General Nakajima Kesago, who was one of the major military commanders in charge of the Nanking Massacre, presents vivid, detailed day-to-day accounts of his and his troops' atrocities. The diary directly destroyed the scheme of the "total denial" group's credibility such as that of Suzuki, Tanaka, and many others. They and their fellow apologists quickly changed tactics to partial denial, stressing that neither the over 200,000 victims established by the Tokyo International Military Tribunal nor the more than 300,000 victims repeatedly confirmed by the Chinese is an acceptable number.[68]

Unemoto Masami, an ex-officer and an editor of the monthly *Walking Partnerly*, which is published by the graduates of imperial Japanese military schools, was especially enthusiastic in following Tanaka's revised strategy. He maintained that the illegal massacres in the Rape of Nanking should be only 3,000–6,000 victims. He organized a symposium that was attended by many IJA ex-officers who took part in the capture of Nanking in December 1937, and their collective conclusion was that the above figure should be slightly revised to 3,000–13,000 persons.[69] The Society of Graduates of Imperial Japan's Military Schools published a book entitled *Records of the Battle of Nanking* in two volumes in November 1989, collecting portions of the battle reports, memoranda, command orders, together with some partially selected incomplete reports by foreign witnesses to the Massacre. The book presents an accumulated account showing that the number of Chinese POWs massacred was roughly 16,000 persons, that Chinese soldiers who died in battle numbered about 30,000, that the number of civilians killed was 2,400, and that 4,200 civilians were captured as "laborers" and later put to death. In addition to these casualties, 31,760 civilians were killed in the adjacent countryside of Nanking.[70] However, the above-cited figures were calculated from limited sources drawn from an incomplete list of regiments and brigades that had participated in the battle.

Another writer, Idakura Yauhensi, based upon so-called research in limited, arbitrarily selected sources, concluded that the massacred civilians stand at slightly more than 10,000 persons, while 30,000 Chinese soldiers and POWs died. Although the total figure killed should be about 50,000 persons, only 12,000–13,000 should be considered as an "illegal massacre."[71] This means that Chinese POWs can be "legally" massacred without a court martial and without consideration of the provisions of the international laws on land warfare. Among all the figures for victims presented by these conservatives and revisionists are those of a supposed authority on the Sino-Japanese War of 1937–1945 in general and on the Nanking Massacre in particular; this is Professor Hata Ikuhiko, who gives various totally unacceptable figures. He is said to be a stepson of Colonel Morozumi Gyosaku, a regimental commander who had captured 14,777 Chinese POWs in the Battle of Nanking. Colonel Morozumi ordered them all killed without a trial.[72] Hata, in *The Nanking*

Incident: the Structure of the Massacre (1986), gives a detailed study of the origin, process, result, and consequences of the incident. He divides the massacre into two categories of killing: one relating to Chinese soldiers and the other to local residents (civilians). The former category includes the massacre of the defeated, remnant soldiers (1A), the surrendered soldiers (1B), the POWs (1C), and the plainclothes ex-soldiers (1D, meaning the soldiers who escaped to the International Safety Zone in Nanking wearing civilian clothes rather than military uniform). The latter category includes depredations (2A), setting fires (2B), rapes and murders following rape (2C), wanton killings (2D), and killings during the course of fighting or of people who involved themselves to be killed in fighting (2E).[73] Hata's classification of the atrocities is very similar to that of Unemoto, who, as a former IJA officer, forthrightly considered that all the Chinese soldiers in Nanking, whether "defeated, remnant soldiers" (1A) or the "plain-clothes ex-soldiers" (1D), who were caught by the Japanese troops should be considered as "legal killings," while all the "[individually] surrendered soldiers" (1B), and those "involving themselves in fighting (2E) as well as those plain-clothes soldiers" (1D) should be considered as "quasi-fighting-to-death" (meaning died in the act of fighting, so that their massacre is considered a "legal" action).[74] Hata admits that the Massacre did happen, but he considers that only the people who were actually civilians but were wrongly identified as ex-soldiers and put to death, as well as the wanton killings (2D), should be considered "illegally massacred." All the killings of 1A (defeated, remnant soldiers), 1B (the surrendered soldiers), 1C (POWs), 1D (actual plainclothes ex-soldiers), and civilians killed in 2E are implied by him as generally "admissible" in certain cases, since Hata does not definitely place any blame for their killing (he just describes these killings in detail without condemning them.)[75] He mentions many cases of killing "surrendered soldiers" (1B), POWs (1C), and "plain-clothed soldiers" (1D), but he has never reminded his readers that these actions were illegal; he just says that the Japanese general policy toward the POWs did not follow international laws. He even says that both the Americans and the Australians had practiced similar precedents of killing POWs (the historical sources cited in this respect are not clearly indicated by him).[76] Thus, the "illegal massacre" of Chinese soldiers is only counted at about 30,000 persons and the total, combined number of "illegal massacres" of military and civilian victims is only 38,000–42,000. Hata even justifies the fact without any reprimand of Lieutenant General Nakajima, the IJA's Sixteenth Division commander (who testified to the quality of his sword by killing several captured Chinese POWs) by saying that it is a "bad habit" of the Japanese Army, without mentioning that the act was contrary to the Fourth Hague Convention of 1907 (the Convention Respecting the Laws and Customs of War on Land). [77] Apparently Hata is not an objective-minded historian and his ambiguous evaluation of the Nanking Incident is really not just. His narrowly defined "illegal killings" of wrongly identified soldiers and 2D, without clearly mentioning 1A, 1B, 1C, 1D, and 2C, are contrary to the spirit of the preface and Articles 1 and 2 of the above-mentioned convention.

All publications in this new wave of "partial denials" of the Nanking Massacre in the 1980s had been duly rebuked again by conscientious, enlightened-minded professors such as Hora Tomio, Fujiwara Akira, Yoshida Herube, and Kimijima Kazuhiko. Hora's book *To Prove the Nanking Massacre* (1986) is a particularly impressive work. He thoroughly collected all the available IJA daily fighting reports and fighting records of the Battle of Nanking, and found that the accumulated number of deaths was approximately 114,300. This figure includes massacres of about 87,000 Chinese POWs and "plain-clothes soldiers" as well as an additional 27,000 POWs. Thus, Professor Hora concludes that the number massacred inside and outside Nanking is about 200,000, a figure established by the International Military Tribunal in 1948. Later, after reading more credible sources, Hora revised his figure to 250,000–300,000. He considers the number of massacred victims in Nanking and its outskirts to be about 200,000, but adding killings from the adjacent countryside regions would bring the number to nearly 300,000. [78] Professor Fujiwara, an authority on Japanese military history, also accepts the figure of 200,000–300,000. [79] Professor Yoshida Herube, an assistant professor of the Hitotsubashi University (at thirty-one years of age in 1985) also implicitly agreed with the figure of 200,000 as reasonable, although he does not mention any concrete figure in his well-researched and well-written book, *The Emperor's Army and the Nanking Incident*. [80]

6. Contemporary Chinese Research

Stimulated by the challenge of the Japanese nonrepentant conservatives in the 1970s and 1980s, especially after the textbook revision controversy, Chinese scholars on both sides of the Taiwan Straits began their intensive studies on Japanese aggression in China in general and the

Nanking Massacre in particular. Professor Gao Xunzu of Nanking University led a group of professors in writing *The Massive Massacre of Japanese Imperialists in Nanking* (1979). This book was not published for overseas circulation but was limited to internal purchase within China. The brief 128-page work elaborates upon the investigated figures of more than 340,000 and more than 390,000 victims, respectively, as proposed by Chief Prosecutor Chen's first and second surveys.

Gao Xunzu and his colleagues concluded that the actual number of victims was about 400,000. Professor Gao stressed that a series of large-scale massacres occurred in the city's outskirts and suburban regions, especially the areas along the southern bank of the Yangtzu River.[81] Later the Nanking city government organized the Compilation Committee on Documents Relating to the Nanking Massacre, composed of scholars from Nanking University, Nanking Normal University, the Second Historical Archives Bureau, and other institutions. The committee started an oral history project, interviewing and recording the testimonials of all survivors of the Massacre. The oral records were eventually published in a book in 1994 under the editorship of Zhu Chengshan.[82] The People's Republic of China (PRC) government built the Victims of Nanking Massacre Memorial Museum, which was opened to the public in August 1985. Deng Xiaoping, the paramount leader of China, handwrote the museum's name on a large, bronze-plated inscription at the main gate, memorializing the Japanese aggressors' atrocities.[83] In addition, the Compilation Committee under the leadership of Professor Gao published *Drafted History of the Nanking Massacre* (a 246-page book) in 1987. It lists all collective, individual, and wanton massacres one by one in a detailed narrative of the cases with all available evidences. The book's authors reaffirm the Chinese Defense Ministry military court's figure of over 300,000 victims in 1937.[84] In 1995 Gao published another book, *The Nanking Massacre: A Japanese Aggressors' Atrocity*, which gave the massacred figure as "over 300,000."[85] A 1997 book by a group of scholars in Nanking under the editorship of Professor Sun Zhaiwei of the Jiang Su Social Science Academy cites a figure of over 300,000, based on various recently discovered sources.[86] The Nanking Compilation Committee also engages in publishing various important collections of primary documents, such as the 708-page *Archives of the Nanking Massacre of the Invading Japanese Army* with appendixes relating to the city's population prior to and after the Massacre. *The Photographs Relating to the Nanking Massacre* was printed in 1995.[87] These primary sources clearly indicate the great horror of the Japanese aggressors in Nanking. They also make available to general readers archival documents regarding the repeated Chinese investigations of the Massacre and the figures calculated by the Chinese Nationalist government in 1946–1948.

In Taiwan, the people in general and the historians in the field of Chinese modern history in particular were shocked by the Japanese textbooks issued in 1982. Concerned historians intensified their research on the Sino-Japanese War. In 1984 Academia Sinica's Modern History Institute held the Symposium on the History of National Reconstruction before the War, 1927–1937, selecting about twenty research papers for publication. The Kuomintang's (KMT) Party History Commission organized three large-scale international conferences, to be held in 1985, 1986, and 1987, assembling local and international scholars (including Japanese scholars) in the field to present and criticize each other's papers. Among the 120-odd research papers presented during these three conferences, only one, written by Professor Lee Yun-han in 1987, was about the Nanking Massacre. Its emphasis was on a critical elaboration of all related historical sources concerning the Massacre in Chinese, Japanese, and English languages but refrained from pushing deeper into the Massacre itself. However, the paper estimated that the number of massacred victims should be about 300,000.[88] The commission published an important collection of photographs entitled *Ironclad Proof: The Veritable Record of the Japanese Army's Atrocities in the Aggression Against China* (1982), including many rare and formerly unprinted photographs of Japanese atrocities.[89] The late Professor Hong Guiji of Academia Historica translated and compiled the invaluable 1,024-page *Record of Japanese Atrocities in China* (1985), in which a special chapter was devoted to the narration of the Rape of Nanking. It is an annotated collection of translated Japanese memoirs, testimonials, the IJA's "daily fighting reports," memoranda and fighting records, and so on, but the author's emphasis is not on doing a critical study of the incident but on collecting all materials in one place for further research.[90] Professor Chi Jingde published a book relating to the Nationalist government's efforts to claim reparation from Japan before 1948, basing his discussions on the official archives.[91] I began my own research on the Nanking Massacre after 1966 while at the National University of Singapore. I published three research papers before 1993 relating to the incident, reconfirming the figure of approximately 300,000 persons presented by the Chinese investigations in 1946–1947.

In the United States and other Western countries, the Nanking Massacre had not been the subject of serious research by professional historians until the publication of two recent works: the eye-stinging *The Rape of Nanking: An Undeniable History in Photographs* (Chicago, 1996), written and compiled by James Yin and Shi Young, and the best-selling book, *The Rape of Nanking: The Forgotten Holocaust of World War II* (New York, 1997), written by Iris Chang.[92] But the topic of Japanese wartime atrocities in China and elsewhere has long been well exposed by various scholars and nonscholars. Notable works include *Crimes Against International Law* (Washington, DC, 1950), by Joseph Keenan (the chief prosecutor at the Tokyo International Military Tribunal) and Brendan Brown; *The Knights of Bushido: A Short History of Japanese War Crimes* (London, 1958), by Lord Russell of Liverpool; *Japan's Imperial Conspiracy,* by David Bergamini (the book provides invaluable and generally reliable information although it was written by a journalist; it has long been "slandered" by some Japanophiles); *Judgements of International Military Tribunal for the Far East* (2 vols., Amsterdam, 1977), by B.V.A. Rölling (a judge from Holland at the Tokyo International Military Tribunal); *The Japanese on Trial: Allied War Crimes Operations in the East, 1945–1951* (Austin, 1979), by Philip R. Piccigallo; *War Without Mercy: Race and Power of the Pacific War* (New York, 1986), by John W. Dower; and *The Other Nuremberg: The Untold Story of the Tokyo War Crimes Trials* (New York, 1987). Emeritus Professor Wu Tienwei of the University of Southern Illinois organized the Society for Studies of Japanese Aggression Against China in 1989 and single-handedly published in that year the *Journal of Studies of Japanese Aggression Against China,* which was issued regularly from then until June 1997. His research on the Nanking Massacre indicated that the massacre figure should be about 340,000, a figure that had been proposed through careful verification by scholars in Nanking in the early 1980's.[93] The above-cited telegram from Hirota Kōbi, which unequivocally proves the massacre figure of over 300,000 victims, was actually discovered in the National Archives in Washington by Professor Wu.

7. Conclusion

Although the actual number of massacred victims has been repeatedly and thoroughly investigated and corroborated by Chinese scholars in the PRC and Taiwan, as well as by various progressive-minded Japanese historians, confirming and reconfirming the figures as at least over 200,000 victims, and possibly over 300,000, conservative scholars in Japan still use every possible tactic to resist the figures. In May 1983, an international symposium on the Tokyo War Crimes Trials was held in Tokyo and attended by scholars from the United States, the Soviet Union, China, West Germany, Holland, and Japan.[94] The Japanese scholars apparently intended to use this opportunity to repudiate the verdict of the Allied trials. They attacked the trials as "victor's judgment" (a phrase coined by Richard Minear) as well as charging that the trials' assignment of war responsibility to the individual Japanese "war criminals" was contrary to the international laws in effect at that time.[95] In addition, the Japanese charged that the Allied judges for the Tribunal were not duly appointed since few Asian judges were included in the group.[96] Actually, the Japanese accusations at the symposium are misleading repetitions, since all their charges had been duly rejected by judges at the trials. First of all, the victorious Allied countries had the authority to punish the war criminals, who were mostly Japanese wartime leaders, and those leaders who represented the Japanese nation were punished according to the Declaration of Cairo, the Declaration of Potsdam, and the "Instrument of [Japanese] surrender," all of which had been duly accepted and presented by Japan. Thus, a surrendered Japan had the obligation to submit all suspected war criminals under the orders of Allied supreme commander, and they would be tried at an international military tribunal. The conviction of those war criminals was also a victors' right. The Japanese scholars' "attack" on the U.S. atomic bombing of Hiroshima and Nagasaki had also been duly replied to by an American judge at the military court, who ruled that the bombings were based on "right of reprisal," meaning a reprisal against the Japanese surprise bombing of Pearl Harbor without a declaration of war.[97] Furthermore, the Japanese scholars' presentations at the symposium "attacking" the verdicts of the Tokyo International Military Tribunal in 1948 were in reality illegal, since they violated Article 11 of the Japan Peace Treaty signed in San Francisco in September 1951. Article 11 reads, in part, "Japan accepts the judgement of the International Military Tribunal for the Far East and of other Allied war courts both within and outside Japan, and will carry out the sentences imposed thereby upon Japanese nationals imprisoned in Japan."[98]

In confronting persistent challenges made by the nonrepentant conservatives in Japan in a fresh wave of denial regarding the Nanking

Massacre in explicit or implicit ways, Chinese survivors from the Massacre—who are now in their eighties or nineties, and who were seriously wounded and left with clear scars on their bodies (e.g., Li Xiuying)—came to Tokyo to sue the Japanese government for civil compensation.[99] In the meantime, representative survivors of the Japanese germ bombings in Ning Bo and Changshan (Zhe Jiang province) as well as those from Changde (Hunan province), plus surviving relatives of Chinese victims in the IJA's 731 unit's cruel biological experiments, and surviving descendants of Chinese victims from Ping Ding Shan village of Liaoning province—where a savage massacre had been conducted by the IJA in 1932—have all come to Tokyo to sue the Japanese government for civil reparations.[100] These lawsuits have not been openly supported by the PRC government but are wholeheartedly supported by the people of China and by progressive-minded Japanese lawyers and academicians. However, this kind of news is not widely circulated in China. Legally, although the PRC abandoned her right to claim war reparations from Japan in 1972, Chinese civilians still retain their right to claim civil reparations.[101] The Chinese actions initiated by the people to punish the Japanese government for Japan's wartime atrocities in China through Japanese legal processes is probably a first step toward healing the past wounds between the two countries. Their appeals are a test of the Japanese conscience and sense of international justice.

World opinion, especially that of the United States, has to recognize that Japan as an economic and technological superpower is not a responsible and reliable one in this ever-shrinking world. A militarily and politically resurgent Japan and its mainstream elites in society take an increasingly dangerous attitude toward their notorious record in World War II, which is emphatically different from that of the reunited Germany. Japan refused to apologize to the United States on the fiftieth-anniversary commemoration of Pearl Harbor in 1991 but demanded an American apology for the atomic bombings (the demand was made by an organization of survivors).[102] It seems the Japanese elites as a whole have a very strange logic, different from that of the responsible people of other countries. As clearly warned by the highly respected and highly conscious Ōe Kenzaburō, a Japanese Nobel Laureate in Literature, "Japan was a great danger to the world" and "the Japanese had never faced up to their crimes. Japan was a racist country."[103]

Since the Nanking Massacre's occurrence and its objectively investigated and researched figures have been repeatedly rejected by many elites of Japan, there is a proposal for an international scholarly conference, attended by all concerned and qualified scholars, to engage in rational argument and reach a general conclusion. For those Chinese civilian survivors of the Japanese wartime atrocities who are now suing the Japanese government in Tokyo, there probably should be a symposium of international jurists to be held concerning the issue. The war responsibilities and obligations of the Japanese government have to be fully discussed and argued according to the international laws effective in 1932–1945 as well as to the provisions of present-day international law.

Notes

A version of this chapter was read at the Nanking Incident Conference held at the Institute of East Asian Studies of the University of California, Berkeley, on April 17–18, 1998. The author expresses his indebtedness to the constructive criticism of Professor Irwin Scheiner, Professor Frederick Wakeman, Jr., Professor Wen-hsin Yeh, and Professor Tien-wei Wu at the conference. Other assistance, given by his colleagues at the Institute of Modern History, Professor Chen Tsu-yu and Thomas McGrath of Cornell University, is also greatly appreciated.

1. Akira Iriye, ed., *The Chinese and Japanese: Essays in Political and Cultural Interaction* (Princeton, NJ: Princeton University Press, 1980), p. 3.

2. Meng Qingxiang et al., "China's Military and Civilian Death and the Wounded in the War of Resistance Against Japan," 3 (August 25, 1995), p. 107.

3. Chi Jingde, "China's Efforts to Claim Reparations from Japan After 1945" (paper presented in 1995), p. 529.

4. Lee En-Han, *Studies on Japan's War Atrocities* (Taipei: Taiwan shangwu yinshuguan, 1994), pp. 104–105, 171.

5. *The Chronological Major Events, July–December 1938* (1993), p. 813; *Documents on Japan's Opium Policy as Centered on the Japanese-Controlled Inner Mongolian Regime* (1985), pp. 111–112.

6. Lloyd E. Eastman, "Facts of an Ambivalent Relationship: Smuggling, Puppets and Atrocities During the War, 1937–1945," in Akira Iriye, ed., *The Chinese and Japanese*, pp. 298–301.

7. Ibid., p. 298.

8. Richard H. Minear, *Victor's Judgement: The Tokyo War Crimes Trial* (Princeton, NJ: Princeton University Press, 1971), pp. 5–6; R. John Pritchard and Sonia Magbanna Zaide, eds., *The Tokyo War Crimes Trials* (New York and London: Garland Publishing, 1981), "Historical Introduction" by Professor D.C. Watt, p. xx.

9. Documents Compilation Committee, *Drafted History of the Nanking Massacre* (1987), pp. 207–208; Yu Xianyu et al., *History of the Tokyo Trials* (1986), pp. 212, 214–215, 218–219.

10. Leon Friedman, ed., *The Laws of War: A Documentary History* (New York: Random House, 1972), vol. II, pp. 1061–1062.

11. Lee Yun-han, *A Critique of the Chinese and Foreign Materials Relating to the Rape of Nanking* (1985), p. 38, cites H.J. Timperley, pp. 10–11.

12. Martha Lund Smalley, ed., Tien-wei Wu (Preface), and Beatrice S. Bartlett (Introduction), *American Missionary Eyewitnesses to the Nanking Massacre, 1937–1938* (New Haven: Yale Divinity School Library, 1997), Occasional Publication No. 9, p. vi.

13. Hora Tomio, ed., *Documents on the Sino-Japanese War: The Nanking Incident* (Tokyo: Aoki shoten, 1973), vol. I, pp. 385–391.

14. Friedman, *Laws of War*, pp. 1061–1062.

15. Lee En-Han, "The Nanking Massacre and the International Laws on Land Warfare," *Bulletin of IMH*, 20 (June 1991), p. 335.

16. Eastman, "Facts of an Ambivalent Relationship," p. 295.

17. Lewis S.C. Smythe, *War Damages in the Nanking Area, December 1937–March 1938* (Shanghai: Commercial Press, 1938).

18. Eastman, "Facts of an Ambivalent Relationship," p. 295, note 75.

19. Friedman, *Laws of War*, p. 1062.

20. Lee En-Han, "The Number of Massacred Victims of the Rape of Nanking," *Bulletin of Historical Research* (Taiwan Normal University), vol. 18 (June 1990), pp. 457–458.

21. Tienjin Political Consultative Council Committee (trans.), *The Nanking Massacre and the San-kuang Military Campaigns*, 1954, p. 27.

22. Hora, *Documents on the Sino-Japanese War*, vol. I, p. 85.

23. Ibid., pp. 143–145; *Transcripts of Proceedings of the International Military Tribunal for the Far East* (April 29–May 4, 1946, through April 1948), vols. 1–113 (Tokyo, 1946–1948, mimeographed copy; Exhibits Nos. 1–3,915, deposited at the Government Documents Department, Doe Library, University of California, Berkeley), pp. 4541–4547.

24. Ibid.

25. Ibid.

26. Ibid.

27. Lee En-Han, "The Number of Massacred Victims," p. 460.

28. Ibid, p. 462.

29. Ibid.

30. Ibid., p. 463.

31. Chinese Military Academy, *The Atrocities of Japanese Aggressive Army in China* (1986), p. 128.

32. Lee En-Han, "The Number of Massacred Victims," p. 463.

33. Chinese Military Academy, *The Atrocities of Japanese Aggressive Army in China*, pp. 130–131.

34. Shi Mei-yu, *Memoirs on My Trials of Japanese War Criminals: The Biographical Literature*, vol. 2, 2.

35. Friedman, *Laws of War*, p. 1062; *Testimonials of the Nanking Massacre* (1984), pp. 118–119.

36. Lee En-Han, "The Number of Massacred Victims," pp. 472, 475–476; Friedman, *Laws of War*, p. 1064.

37. Friedman, *Laws of War*, p. 1142.

38. Ibid., pp. 1133–1134; Minear, *Victor's Judgement*, p. 72.

39. Mei Yuao, "The Trial of the Nanking Massacre in the International Military Tribunal for the Far East," *The Defensive Battle of Nanking* (1987), pp. 307–308.

40. National Archives (Washington, DC) no. 1257.

41. Lee En-Han, "The Number of Massacred Victims," p. 462, 164.

42. Wu Tienwei, "The Trials of the War Criminals in Nuremberg and Tokyo: A Preliminary Comparison," *The Second Symposium on the Sino-Japanese Relations in the Past 100 Years*, 1995, pp. 440–442.

43. John W. Dower, *Empire and Aftermath: Yoshida, Shigeru and the Japanese Experience, 1878–1954* (Cambridge, MA: Harvard University Press, 1979), pp. 7–12, 490–492.

44. John Dower, *Japan in War and Peace: Essays on History, Culture and Race* (London: HarperCollins, 1996), pp. 23–28.

45. Wu Tienwei, "Trials of the War Criminals," p. 442.

46. Hata Ikuhiko, *The Japanese-Chinese War* (1961), pp. 280–286, 283.

47. Hora Tomio, *Myths in Warfare of the Modern History* (1967), pp. 55–168.

48. Lee En-Han, "The Number of Massacred Victims," pp. 451, 453.

49. Ibid., p. 453, cites p. vii.

50. Ibid., p. 465, cites Kuroda Toshide, *Nanking, Hiroshima and Auschwitz* (1974), p. 15–22.

51. Saburo Ienaga, *The Pacific War: World War II and the Japanese, 1931–1945* (transl. from Japanese). New York: Pantheon Books, 1978), pp. 201–202.

52. *United Daily News*, Taipei, May 5, 1992, p. 9.

53. John W. Dower, "Triumphal and Tragic Narratives of the War in Asia," in Laura Hein and Mark Selden, eds., *Living with the Bomb: American and Japanese Cultural Conflicts in the Nuclear Age* (New York: M.E. Sharpe, 1997), p. 44.

54. Ibid.

55. Ibid.

56. Lee En-Han, "The Number of Massacred Victims," pp. 451–452.

57. *Gentlemen Magazine*, April 1972, pp. 177–191.

58. Lee En-Han, "The Number of Massacred Victims," p. 52 cites Hora Tomio, *To Prove the Nanking Massacre* (1986), p. 2.

59. Fugiwara Akira, *The Nanking Massacre: A New Edition* (1975), pp. 21, vii.

60. Eastman, "Facts of an Ambivalent Relationship," p. 295, note 75.

61. Fugiwara, *The Nanking Massacre*, p. 22.

62. *Testimonials Relating to the Nanking Massacre*, p. vii.

63. Hora Tomio, *The Nanking Massacre* (1987), p. 2.

64. Lee En-Han, "The Number of Massacred Victims," pp. 453–454.

65. Ian Buruma, *The Wages of Guilt: Memories of War in Germany and Japan* (New York: Farrar Straus Giroux, 1994), pp. 115–116.

66. Lee En-Han, "The Number of Massacred Victims," pp. 453–454; p. 13; p. 266.

67. Itakura Yauhensi, "Surprised to Find the Fighting Diary of General Matsui Iwane Revised," *History and Famous Men* (Tokyo) (Winter 1985).

68. Ibid.

69. Hora Tomio, *Myths in Warfare of the Modern History*, pp. 155–156; Hora Tomio et al., eds., *Researches on the Nanking Massacre*, 1987, pp. 20, 109, 116, 127–128.

70. Lee En-Han, "The Number of Massacred Victims," pp. 467–468.

71. Hora Tomio, *To Prove the Nanking Massacre*, (Tokyo: Asahi shinbunsha, 1986), p. 190, cites "A Research on the Massacred Number of the Nanking Massacre," *The Overall Perspectives* (Tokyo) (March 1984), (October 1984).

72. Hora's *To Prove the Nanking Massacre*, pp. 131–132, 129–140.

73. Hata Ikuhiko, *The Nanking Incident: The Structure of the Massacre* (Tokyo: Chūō Kōronsha, 1986), pp. 188–204, 205–206, 214.

74. Kimijima Kazuhiko, "A New Point of Dispute Concerning the Nanking Incident" in *Researches on the Nanking Incident* (1987), pp. 125–127.

75. Hata, *The Nanking Incident*, pp. 189, 190, 192, 193, 196–198, 214.

76. Ibid., pp. 190, 214.

77. Ibid., p. 192.

78. Hora Tomio, *To Prove the Nanking Massacre*, pp. 150–152, 153, 154; Hora Tomio, *The Nanking Massacre: An Authorized Edition* (1982), pp. 150–152, 3.

79. Fugiwara, *The Nanking Massacre: A New Edition*, p. 20; *Researches on the Nanking Incident*, p. 28.

80. Yoshida Herube, *The Emperor's Imperial Army and the Nanking Incident* (1985), p. 103–159, 162–163.

81. See *Selected Literary and History Materials of Kiangsu Province*, vol. 12 (1983), p. 45.

82. *Testimonials of the Surviving Victims of the Nanking Massacre* (1994).

83. Lee En-Han, "The Number of Massacred Victims," p. 473.

84. *Drafted History of the Nanking Massacre Made by the Aggression of Japanese Army* (1987).

85. *The Nanking Massacre: A Japanese Aggressors' Atrocity* (1985), p. 66.

86. Sun Zhaiwei, ed., *The Nanking Massacre* (1997), p. 440.

87. Second Historical Archives Bureau et al., eds., *Archives of the Nanking Massacre of the Invading Japanese Troops* (1987); *Photographs Relating to the Nanking Massacre* (1995).

88. Lee Yun-han, "Materials and Works Relating to the War with Japan," in *Studies on Modern Chinese History in the Past Sixty Years* (1988), vol. 1, p. 424.

89. Lee En-Han, "The Number of Massacred Victims," p. 474.

90. Ibid.

91. Chi Jingde, *History of the Investigations of China's Loss in the War with Japan* (1987).

92. James Yin and Shi Young, *The Rape of Nanking: An Undeniable History in Photographs*, ed. Ron Dorfman (Chicago: Innovative Publishing Group, 1996); Iris Chang, *The Rape of Nanking: The Forgotten Holocaust of World War II* (New York: Basic Books, HarperCollins, 1997).

93. Lee En-Han, "The Number of Massacred Victims," pp. 478–479, note 3.

94. C. Hosoya, N. Ando, Y. Onuma, and R. Minear, eds., *The Tokyo War Crimes Trials: An International Symposium* (Tokyo: Kotansha, 1986).

95. Lee En-Han, "The Rape of Nanking Committed by the Japanese Troops and Its Implication to the International Laws on Land Warfare" in *Bulletin of the Institute of Modern History, Academia Sinica*, 20 (June 1991), pp. 48–49, 50, 58–59.

96. Y. Onuda, *Reflections on the Post-War Responsibility from the Viewpoint of the Tokyo Trials* (Tokyo, 1985), pp. 26, 30.

97. Asahi Shinbum Correspondences, comp., *The Tokyo Trials*, vol. 1 (1962), p. 52; Friedman, *Laws of War*, pp. 1035–1036.

98. *Handbook on the Tokyo Trials* (1989), p. 256; International Forum Implementation Committee, *Research on the Japanese Reparations in the Post-War Period* (1992), pp. 176–182.

99. Lee En-Han, "Japan Is Not Qualified to Be a Permanent Member of UN's Security Council," *United Daily* (Taipei), February 15, 1997.

100. Ibid.

101. *Hopes for a Network: Admit the Fact of Germ Warfare and Apologize to Victims to Compensate* (Tokyo: Hibiya Law Office, July 1996), pp. 3–8.

102. Buruma, *The Wages of Guilt*, pp. 8–9, 117, 118–119, 121; Yui Daizabura, "Between Pearl Harbor and Hiroshima/Nagasaki: Nationalism and Memory in Japan and the U. S.," in Laura Hein and Mark Seldon, eds., *Living with the Bomb*, p. 61.

103. Buruma, *The Wages of Guilt*, pp. 11–12.

5

Remembering the Nanking Mas~~~~~

Kasahara Tokushi

Many years into the debate over the Nanking Massacre, the views of the more vocal Japanese conservative groups have frequently overshadowed in the public eye those of the progressive community. But many scholars in Japan continue to strive for a less politically inspired and more objective picture of Japan's World War II history.

Tokushi Kasahara is one of the leaders of this group of progressive scholars. Not content with mere analysis of the causes and events of the Nanking Massacre, Kasahara strives to understand the formation and transmission of memories of World War II, particularly the Nanking Massacre. He is a native Japanese and his cultural understanding provides a valuable introduction to the question of postwar Japanese memory. —Eds.

Part I: Historical Causes of the Nanking Massacre

1. Definition and Scope of the Nanking Massacre

The term *Nanking Massacre* refers to the totality of atrocities committed by Japanese troops against Chinese soldiers and civilians during and after the attack on Nanking. These atrocities were illegal from the perspectives of both international law on combat behavior and international humanitarian law. The geographical scope of this incident applies to all areas under the jurisdiction of the Nanking Special Municipality, which included the city of Nanking as well as six counties in the vicinity. This is the Battle Zone of Nanking as well as the area occupied by the Japanese troops after the fall of the city.

The duration of this incident began approximately December 4, 1937, when Japan's General Headquarters (GHQ) ordered the attack on Nanking, and Japan's Central China Expedition Army (Central China Army) entered the above zone. Although the GHQ dissolved the Central

China Army on February 14, 1938, after the completion of the Nanking battle, Japanese atrocities in Nanking continued. Therefore, the establishment of the *weixin zhengfu* (Renovation Government) by the Central China Army on March 28 can be considered the conclusion of the Nanking Massacre. After that, order was restored in Nanking and atrocities by Japanese troops considerably lessened.

There are in general two types of atrocities and other illegal behavior. The first type of atrocity is killing and bodily injuries. Chinese soldiers, including those wounded, surrendered, and taken prisoner, as well as stragglers, were murdered either as a group or individually, in violation of international law. Residents who became victims of the encirclement of Japanese troops were murdered. Many adult men were murdered in groups or individually in the so-called mopping-up operations simply because they were thought to be former soldiers. Japanese soldiers also killed many residents and peasants at random.

During the Nanking Incident an extremely large number of women were raped or gang-raped and killed by the Japanese troops. Although it is difficult to get exact figures, the Nanking International Safety Zone Committee estimated that tens of thousands were raped. Rape did not only injure women physically but also left deep scars psychologically. Some women took their own lives; others became mentally ill. Still others were wasted due to severe venereal disease. Some tried abortion after becoming pregnant and further damaged their health. The tragedy goes on.

The second type of atrocity is violation of property rights. Japanese troops engaged in pillaging and arson that had nothing to do with the combat in Nanking. According to the Nanking International Safety Zone Committee, 73 percent of all buildings in Nanking were looted. Many business areas in the city center were looted several times by soldiers, followed by organized looting with military trucks, and finally were set on fire. Arson began after Japanese troops entered the city and lasted till early February, and 24 percent of the city was burnt down. Across the fields in Nanking's suburbs 40 percent of peasant houses were burnt, and their cattle, farming tools, stored goods, or crops were severely damaged. Crops in the field became the feed for military horses, and vegetables were taken freely by the soldiers. Almost half the vegetables in the Jiangnin and Jurong Counties were damaged. Large quantities of food and cattle were taken away under the name of requisition.

To correctly calculate the number of Chinese victims in the Nanking

Massacre is impossible today. It is possible, however, to present an approximate number based on available sources and current research. According to my research, out of a total of 150,000 defense troops, about 40,000 broke out from Nanking and reassembled. About 20,000 were killed or wounded in combat, and about 10,000 escaped or were missing in the retreat. The remaining 80,000 or so were killed by the Japanese troops as prisoners or stragglers, or after surrendering. What is difficult to count from the sources are civilian victims. If Nanking city is distinguished from the towns and countryside in the vicinity, more people died in the latter. John Rabe, chairman of the Nanking Safety Zone International Committee, estimated 50,000 to 60,000 civilian deaths inside the city alone. According to a survey by Professor Lewis Smythe, over 30,000 were estimated to have died outside the city in the vicinity.[1]

Based on present sources and circumstances, I estimate that over 100,000, perhaps nearly 200,000 or even more, Chinese soldiers and civilians perished in the Nanking Massacre. If more Japanese military sources are discovered and published, and if more surveys of the number of victims in the suburbs are conducted, it may be possible to reach a more definitive figure.

2. Why Japanese Troops Committed the Atrocities— Historical Background

During the battle of Nanking, Japanese soldiers did not feel much sense of guilt. Many soldiers had no sense of guilt at all. They even committed atrocities with a certain kind of pleasant sensation. The background of this is the discrimination and prejudice that had taken root among the Japanese troops and Japanese people since the Meiji period. This is a consciousness that took its roots historically among the Japanese through school education, social learning, and mass media in modern Japan. I would like to discuss three such factors in the Japanese background that enabled Japanese soldiers to commit the atrocities.

The first factor was the Japanese contempt for Asians and the Chinese people. After Japan gained victory in the First Sino-Japanese War (1894–95), the Russo-Japanese War, and World War I, and joined the ranks of world powers, the discriminatory consciousness permeated the Japanese public: Only the Japanese Empire with the emperor and the Japanese people were superior, and nearby Koreans, Chinese, and Mongols were inferior peoples. Japan should "part from Asia and join Europe."

In Japanese society at the time, the emperor was the sovereign of the state. The citizens were his subjects, and did not have any guarantee of human rights. Since the Japanese people lacked the concept of human rights at home, they came to think they could do anything they wanted against nearby Asian people whom they considered their inferiors. Japanese soldiers with such consciousness of racial discrimination therefore did not feel the stings of a guilty conscience even when they committed aggression, looting and destruction, and other atrocities in China, since the Chinese were considered subhuman.

The second factor was sexual discrimination against women. In Japanese society at the time women's rights were suppressed by a patriarchal family system and legal prostitution. Under the patriarchal family system, women, considered to be tools for childbearing who served to extend the family line, were required to maintain their chastity. Husbands, on the other hand, who had access to a legal prostitution system recognized and managed by the state, were allowed to indulge in sexual activity outside the home. In Japanese society, legal prostitution not only served as an outlet for the male's sexual indulgence, but the state also used it to screen prostitutes with venereal disease to protect men so that they could produce "healthy descendants."

In this male-dominated society, the husband's sexual indulgence outside the home was socially recognized and the wife could not interfere. In other words, no matter how men sexually victimized women outside the home, wives could not protest, and this was considered socially acceptable. Almost all Japanese soldiers were influenced by this sexual consciousness that did not recognize women's human rights and instead treated them only as tools for men's libido. Because of this, in addition to the racist consciousness, Japanese soldiers felt no guilt or remorse at all even if they raped and violated Chinese women.

The third factor was the inhumane nature of the Japanese Army. The Japanese Army was the emperor's army. It was an army to protect the "national policy," namely, the emperor system. It was not an army for the protection of the people. During the second Sino-Japanese War, (1937–45), soldiers and human lives were treated lightly, and were even compared to the "one-*sen,* five-*lin*" (roughly half a U.S. one-cent) stamp used on the conscription orders. Although Japan had signed on to the Treaty Concerning the Treatment of POWs, the treaty was not approved, due to the military's opposition. This was because the military feared that if such a law applied to Japan, Japanese soldiers would surrender and become prisoners of war (POWs). Japanese soldiers were forbidden to surrender and were compelled to commit suicide so as not to damage the army's reputation. As a result, the Japanese Army, which forbade its own soldiers to become POWs, lacked a consciousness of fair treatment for captured enemy soldiers and often killed those they should have taken as POWs. On the treatment of captives, Japanese troops dealt with European or Americans differently from the Chinese. With European and Americans, the above treaty applied even though it had not been approved. In contrast, as a 1933 study by the Army Infantry School indicated, "It wouldn't become a problem even if Chinese captives were killed, since they did not have clear census registers or addresses."[2] Therefore, they considered it acceptable not to apply the 1907 Hague Convention of Land Combat to Chinese soldiers.

Moreover, in a society with strict social hierarchy, Japanese troops demanded absolute obedience of superiors—even just by one rank—no matter how irrational their orders might be, since superiors' orders were the emperor's orders. Any opposition to this would be punished without mercy. Therefore, lower-ranking soldiers might harbor discontent or complaints. To release their anger or stress, they made use of the legal prostitution system and abused the women. Ultimately, this also contributed to the so-called comfort-women system during the war.

3. Why Japanese Troops Committed the Atrocities— Direct Causes

After the Marco Polo Bridge incident on July 7, 1937, Japan began a full-scale war of aggression against China, without a declaration of war. The Japanese slogan was "to punish a China that is resisting Japan." Those in the military and government favoring escalation sought to "subdue China at one strike," to carry out colonial domination of China by detaching north China, and expanding Japanese interests in Central and South China. Under the "punish China" slogan, Japan adopted a war of encirclement and annihilation in the battle of Nanking, in order to subdue China by striking thoroughly at its capital of Nanking. The idea of encircling and annihilating all Chinese troops and civilians who resisted Japan—in other words, killing them all—went hand in hand with the idea that it was acceptable to disregard the Hague Convention for Chinese captives, easily leading to the massacre of Chinese soldiers and civilians outside the realm of conventionally accepted combat behavior.

The Shanghai Expedition Army that engaged in the battle of Shanghai from August 13 to mid-November had been organized as a temporary unit for the battle in the limited areas of Shanghai. For this, Retired General Matsui Iwane was called back to active duty from reserve, as were many soldiers who were not currently in service and who were rather old, in their late twenties and their thirties. As a result, the morale was low and discipline was poor. Moreover, since a march over long distance was not expected, logistical support such as food and other military supplies were extremely limited.

The General Staff of the Army had considered recalling the Shanghai Expedition Army home to rest, since it had suffered heavy losses during the prolonged battle in Shanghai and its discipline had already deteriorated. However, both Commander Matsui and his vice chief of staff Colonel Muto Akira (both of whom were hanged as Class A war criminals at the Tokyo Trials) in charge of the Central China Area Army (a temporary force combining the Shanghai Expedition Army and the Tenth Army, which had landed in the Bay of Hangzhou) went against the Army General Staff and decided on their own to launch the attack on Nanking because of their own ambitions and desire for personal glory. The attempt to rush to Nanking by forced march is a direct cause of the Nanking Massacre.

The Japanese troops that rushed to Nanking adopted the policy of obtaining food for both men and horses almost entirely on the spot. This means they took food from the residents in areas they went through. According to Article 86 in the army's Penal Code, "Those who take property by force from local residents in battle or occupied areas shall be imprisoned for over one year." In spite of this, the command of the Central China Army had soldiers take part in the illegal looting of food and living materials as part of their combat behavior.

The looting of food as combat behavior easily contributed to the killing of civilians. When Japanese troops invaded the villages or towns in search of food, local residents who resisted or complained were considered to be fighting against Japan and were killed. Those who fled the Japanese were seen as suspicious and were shot. If the residents were hiding when Japanese soldiers broke into Chinese homes, they were often shot by the Japanese soldiers to protect themselves. Although many peasants died in the "village mopping-up operations," the Japanese soldiers considered it combat action and killed civilians without any sense of guilt.

When Japanese soldiers broke into Chinese houses for looting or mopping up and found women hiding, they raped them. When soldiers went scouting for food and found women hiding in the bushes, they raped or gang-raped these women. Although rape was an offense to be severely punished in the army's Penal Code, it required the victim to report the crime. To prevent the victims from reporting to the Military Police, Japanese soldiers often killed their rape victims.

Many soldiers of the Central China Army were reserve soldiers who had left their wives and children at home. Since they had expected to be able to return to Japan after the Shanghai battle, they were filled with pent-up frustration and anger when they were driven to fight in Nanking. The officers tended to condone sexual offenses as an outlet, a way "to give soldiers energy." Sexual violence such as "conquer the Chinese women" or "treat a woman as an object by sheer force" were treated as privileges of the battlefield and were condoned to propel soldiers forward in the attack on Nanking.

Troops that had to manage their own meals often took furniture from Chinese homes to burn for cooking, sometimes even burning the entire house. Moreover, since ordinary soldiers were equipped the same way as they went to Shanghai in the summer, in some cases they set the Chinese houses on fire to ward off the winter cold after November. Finally, some Japanese soldiers burned Chinese houses down out of sheer hatred, simply to cause destruction. or even just for fun.

In such ways, large portions of the Japanese troops on their way to Nanking committed atrocities such as looting, killing, rape, and arson, in part because the reckless attack on Nanking disregarded logistics, as well as due to both the mental and the physical conditions of the soldiers.

The Battle of Nanking, targeting the area of the Nanking Special Municipality, began in early December. Nearly 200,000 Japanese troops encircled Nanking in several waves. Within this encirclement were about 150,000 Chinese troops, who were "fighting to death." They included front-line and rear armies, miscellaneous forces, and laborers and porters. At this time there were over one million residents and refugees in the surrounding areas, and between 400,000 to 500,000 residents and refugees inside the city. (At its peak of the massacre, 250,000 people were inside the refugee zone.)

The final fierce fighting took place from December 10 to December 12 around Nanking, and Japanese troops fought a harder battle than they had expected. However, early on the evening of December 12, Chinese

Commander Tang Shengzhi ordered a retreat and his headquarters drove straight across the Yangtze first, causing the Chinese command system to break down completely. By midnight Nanking fell. Over 100,000 Chinese defense forces became stragglers, trapped by the Japanese troops. Japanese troops, which had completely occupied the outer perimeters, moved into the city on the morning of December 13 and began a thorough mopping-up operation in order to annihilate the Chinese troops. Many of the 50,000 to 100,000 residents who remained in their homes in the city were killed by the Japanese troops.

To publicize their victory, General Matsui and other commanders decided to hold a "formal triumphal entry" into Nanking on December 17. In order to ensure safety for the day, the mopping-up and "hunting-for-stragglers" operations were conducted with a renewed intensity. Large numbers of adult men suspected of being former soldiers were taken away from the Refugee Zone and massacred in groups. Large numbers of Chinese soldiers who had already surrendered to the Japanese troops were also killed by several Japanese units under the order of the commanders of the Central China Army. In these group massacres many refugees who had followed and mixed with retreating Chinese troops also became victims.

After the formal entry on the seventeenth, the Japanese commander gave their troops ten days of so-called rest. To relieve their frustration and anger after being thrown into an almost impossible Nanking battle, and as rewards for the victory, more than 70,000 Japanese troops entered Nanking at various times and exercised their so-called privileges as conquerors, by looting, killing, raping, and committing arson. The Japanese commander either condoned or simply refrained from interfering. After the formal entry, rape cases shot up, with an average of about 1,000 women raped each day for a week.

By Christmas most Japanese troops moved on to other areas after the so-called rest. The troops left by the Central China Army to maintain the military occupation of Nanking was the Sixteenth Division, known for its poor discipline. Therefore, although the rate of atrocities declined, killing, rapes, looting, and arson continued.

After early January 1938, the atrocities in Nanking became known to the Japanese military and government leaders in Tokyo through diplomatic channels and the foreign press. Because of this, General Matsui was relieved of his duty, recalled home, and returned to reserve status. However, while military leaders knew about the atrocities resulting from

Matsui's inaction, they did not pursue his responsibility and continued to conceal the truth from the Japanese public.

Part II. How the Japanese Have Remembered the Nanking Massacre

It is estimated that more than 20 million Chinese died in the second Sino-Japanese War (1937–1945), victims of various atrocities by the Japanese troops, including mass murder and random killings, chemical and biological warfare, live experiments on human bodies, selling of opium and other drugs, and forced labor. Despite this fact, many Japanese today do not have a conscious memory of these historical facts of victimization.

Nevertheless, in the past decade or so, much progress has been made in clarifying the historical facts of such atrocities as the Nanking Massacre, the 731 Unit, and the so-called comfort women. Many books have been published on these subjects, and they are often featured in the mass media, including newspapers, magazines, and television. The Nanking Massacre (also called the Nanking Incident) is perhaps the most extensively researched field among all Japanese atrocities during the Sino-Japanese War. For instance, there are at least six published document collections on the Nanking Massacre alone. Almost all historical dictionaries include separate entries on the Nanking Massacre, and offer a clear description. I have written articles on the Nanking Massacre for five such dictionaries. Monographic studies of the Nanking Massacre include those by Hora Tomio, Fujiwara Akira, Honda Katsuichi, Yoshida Yutaka, and myself.

Descriptions of the Nanking Massacre in school textbooks have also improved. It is now featured in many social science textbooks for elementary and middle schools, and in almost all high school textbooks for Japanese history. When Professor Fujioka Nobukatsu of Tokyo University organized the Liberal View of History Study Group, the first things he attacked were six different middle school textbooks that gave estimates of Nanking Massacre victims that ranged from over 100,000 to 300,000. His attack in one sense reveals that the coverage of the Nanking Massacre by Japanese textbooks has actually improved.

Concerning the question of whether or not the Nanking Massacre took place at all, the academic debate has come to a resolution, since no serious historian today denies the existence of the Nanking Massacre.

In spite of this, those of us who acknowledge the Nanking Massacre often seem overwhelmed by voices in the mass media calling it an "illusion" or a "fabrication"—scholars, critics, and journalists unrelated to the history profession, who for political reasons repeatedly make the denials that have already been proved bankrupt. Among Diet members of the ruling Liberal Democratic Party, there is a strong force that publicly denies the Nanking Massacre and propagates such denials.

Furthermore, in direct contrast to Germany's treatment of the Holocaust issue, in Japan those who attempt to minimize or outright deny the Nanking Massacre enjoy complete freedom of speech and activity, while people like us who study the Nanking Massacre face pressure, obstruction, and even threats from right-wing groups, unrepentant veterans, and right-wing journalists and scholars.

In the remainder of this chapter I shall discuss the following questions: Why have the facts of the Nanking Massacre, which have become evident in the fields of history and education, not occupied a place in the Japanese remembrance of war? Why is it that the Japanese cannot feel deep regret and cannot support compensation for the victims of the Nanking Massacre? Why haven't we Japanese recognized the Nanking Massacre as an issue of our war responsibility? By examining the history of how the Japanese have remembered the Nanking Massacre, I would like to examine the larger issue of how Japanese view the war.

1. The Lack of Direct Memory—1937–1945

Historical memories are made of both what we directly experience and what we come to know through historical studies without direct experience. The former is direct; the latter is indirect. Direct experience—the feelings, the shock, the strong impressions—take firm hold and cannot be forgotten. With regard to the Nanking Massacre, Western countries like the United States, Britain, and Germany reported the event through newspapers, magazines, and newsreels, shocking their people with its brutality and inhumanity. Through such reportage, many people around the world came to know and remember the Nanking Massacre at the time it happened.

In contrast, the Japanese people did not come to remember the Nanking Massacre directly. There was strict press censorship and limitation of free speech in Japan during the time of the war. Although major newspapers competed with each other by sending large numbers of reporters to cover the Nanking battle, and many reporters and cameramen witnessed the scene of the atrocities, no one faithfully reported the event. Moreover, the letters and diaries of Japanese soldiers who participated in the battle were also censored, and returning soldiers were given orders to keep silent so that people at home would not know of the atrocities. Finally, foreign newspapers and magazines that reported the incident were confiscated by the police in the Home Ministry so that they would not reach Japanese readers.

For Japanese people who did not learn about the truth of the Nanking Massacre at the time, the Nanking Massacre became an event that lacked direct recollections and was devoid of a real sense of history. This would become an obstacle to later Japanese comprehension of the Nanking Massacre, and would serve as the psychological basis for accepting denials.

Without direct remembrance based on historical experience, one has to experience the past intellectually through historical study, and imagine the past based on historical knowledge. Otherwise, what was not remembered becomes, in the end, the same as something that has never happened.

Nonetheless, this does not mean that no Japanese remembered the Nanking Massacre during the war. Army leaders received information about the Nanking Incident, and as an internal measure they relieved General Matsui from his duty in China in February 1938. However, they did not pursue his responsibility for the event and continued to hide the truth from the public. Top officials in the Foreign Ministry also knew about foreign reports of the incident and had direct memories of the event. Ishii Itarō, director of the East Asian Bureau in the Foreign Ministry, recorded in his diary on January 6, 1938:

> Reports from Shanghai detailed the atrocities of our troops in Nanjing. There are looting and rapes that one cannot bear to witness. Ah, is this the Imperial Army? Isn't this a revelation of the decay of Japanese morals? This is a big social problem.

In a strict sense, one cannot say that the Japanese public did not have any direct memory. One of the readers of my book *The Nanjing Incident* recalled that during 1938 or 1939, when he was still a child, a veteran who had fought in Nanking boasted that "in our unit it was common to stick a bottle inside the body of a young Chinese woman after she was gang-raped, and then kill her by cracking the bottle inside her." People of the older generation have often heard such "battlefield stories" about the brutal behavior of Japanese troops in Nanking from discharged soldiers, despite strict attempts by the government and the military to suppress "gossip that is harmful to the honor of the Imperial Army."

Moreover, some stories were reported in newspapers, magazines, and other war-related publications, such as reports of two Japanese officers engaging in a "killing contest" on the way to Nanking, the episode of an officer killing 300 Chinese with his sword, and news about executions of disarmed soldiers. Although Japanese people may have known fragments or heard rumors of the Japanese atrocities, they did not remember them as unlawful, inhumane events. Therefore, even today, many Japanese continue to lack such a consciousness.

In May 1994, then Justice Minister Nagano Shigeto made the statement, "I was in Nanjing immediately after the occupation as an officer, and did not hear anything about that sort of incident." He also called the Nanking Massacre "a fabrication," and in the end, was forced to resign from his office. There may be some truth to testimonies by a number of veterans who claim that they had participated in the battle or had been to Nanking immediately after its occupation yet did not witness the massacre or hear about it. Yet these veterans who deny the facts of Nanking Massacre based on their own experiences and recollections fail to recognize the limitations to their experiences and recollections.

First, there were several limitations to what soldiers could see in a battlefield where they could not move around freely. As the army was organized vertically, soldiers did not know what other units were doing. The massacre was carried out separately by troops, and rapes of women, which were in violation of the military code, did not always take place in broad view. Yet while it is possible that some soldiers did not witness the atrocities, this cannot be used to deny that the Nanking Massacre did not take place at all. Second, soldiers often did not recognize their own unlawful and inhumane behavior. As I have discussed in my books, Japanese soldiers were fighting a battle of encirclement and annihilation that was aimed to "punish the Chinese." They did not consider their killing of prisoners, surrendering soldiers and stragglers, and even civilians, to be part of the Nanking Massacre. Third, some presuppose an inaccurate and exaggerated picture of the Nanking Massacre and then deny the whole atrocity completely since such a picture does not coincide with their memory. Some journalists and soldiers, who were at the scene of the incident, presume a simplistic image of 200,000 civilian corpses scattered through Nanking, and then testify that they did not see such a scene. There is a saying "He can't see the forest for the trees." Soldiers and journalists who were in Nanking saw the "trees"—individual scenes of atrocities—but nobody was in a position to see the "forest"—the entire massacre over time and space.

2. The Tokyo War Crimes Trial—Cold War in Asia

A common reason given for calling the Nanking Massacre a "fabrication" or an "illusion" is that "it was fabricated by the Allied countries to make Japan the villain at the Tokyo War Crimes Trial[s]." Fujioka Nobukatsu argues that it is the "Tokyo Trial[s] view of history" to regard Japan's war as an unjust war of aggression, and calls the Nanking Massacre "American propaganda to instill a sense of guilt in the Japanese mind about Japan's war."[3] However, the opposite is true. It was because the governments and people of the Allied countries first remembered the Nanking Incident directly and were dealt a great shock by it that they made it an important case at the trial.

But it is also true that most Japanese first learned about the Nanking Massacre through reports about the Tokyo Trials: They were greatly shocked by the fact that Matsui Iwane was hanged only on account of "the responsibility of inaction." However, although the verdict on the Nanking Massacre dealt the Japanese a strong shock, its content, based on numerous testimonies given at the Tokyo Trials, did not form the basis of the Japanese image of the Nanking Incident; that is, it did not turn into their indirect memory of the Massacre. Rather, this verdict came to be perceived as an image of the Nanking Massacre separated from historical facts, and as such it became used by some deniers as an excuse that "such an indiscriminate massacre did not happen."

In his opening statement in 1946, chief prosecutor Keenan described the Nanking Incident as incomparably cruel, a total disregard of human lives, with no parallel in modern warfare. Around the same time, under the guidance of the Civil Information Bureau of the General Headquarters (GHQ), the NHK radio program "The Truth Box" gave the following broadcast with the purpose to "imbed among Japanese listeners" the facts of the Nanking Massacre:

The massacre in Nanjing is rare in modern history in its cruelty, with 20,000 women and children slaughtered. Streets inside Nanjing were stained with the blood of the victims, and covered with the corpses for several weeks. Blood-thirsty Japanese soldiers killed non-combatants they captured, looted at will, and committed other indescribable crimes.[4]

According to the historian Fujiwara Akira, many Japanese who heard this program thought it was Allied propaganda, not historical fact. Although the verdict of the Tokyo Trials based on the testimonies in court recognized that the massacre occurred, it did not make clear the entire picture. Yet, because the proceedings were not published immediately following the trials, and because Japanese scholars were not very interested in investigating the event through the examination of these materials, the truth of Nanking was not further clarified. Individual testimonies of a particular time and location were then understood as representing the whole picture, and it is this image of the Nanking Massacre that has been stressed and exaggerated by those who deny the Nanking Massacre. Thus, according to these people, since "that kind of massacre did not happen," it followed that the "Nanjing massacre was fabricated at the Tokyo Trial[s]."[5]

The Tokyo Trials distinguished between wartime leaders and ordinary citizens, and pursued only the national leaders, especially army officers. Because the court separated militaristic leaders and the people whom they had fooled, it ended the trials by holding only Matsui and Foreign Minister Hirota responsible. Originally it was necessary to interrogate many commanders involved in the battle to clarify the whole picture before responsibility could be confirmed. In the end the Tokyo Trials and its verdict failed to serve as an opportunity to elucidate a correct picture of the Nanking Massacre based on historical facts, and to have the Japanese people comprehend and acknowledge it.

Despite the fact that the Japanese government announced its acceptance of the Tokyo Trials verdict to the world in the 1951 San Francisco Treaty, and although the Tokyo Trials actually had left out many other inhumane war crimes against the Chinese people during the war, the Japanese people still did not make the Nanking Massacre part of their postwar collective memory.

As the Cold War began in East Asia in the late 1940s, the U.S. government quickly lost interest in trying Japanese war criminals, and gave up the second and third trials that had been previously planned. The Cold War further intensified after the founding of the People's Republic of China, and the U.S. government wanted Japan to join the Western camp. Therefore, the United States promoted the idea of a "generous peace" by urging major Allied countries to renounce their right to reparations and not to pursue Japan's war responsibility. When the San Francisco Treaty became effective in 1952, the postwar settlement by Allied Powers came to an end.

After the restoration of sovereignty to Japan, conservative forces, which inherited prewar politics in many aspects, continued to hold power in Japan during the Cold War period, as symbolized by the fact that released Class A war criminals and former military leaders served in the government cabinet. The Japanese government during the Cold War period adopted measures that in effect denied Japan's war responsibility and continued to deny the aggressive nature of Japan's war. During this time, the Asian countries that had been invaded by Japan were weak in political influence, and the questions of Japan's responsibility for war and aggression—both at the state and the individual levels—were shelved in an ambiguous way.

Immediately after the war, the Nanking Massacre was featured in history textbooks. The Democratic Party issued a pamphlet in 1955 attacking social science textbooks for advocating peace and democracy (this is known as the First Textbook Attack). In November of that year, the Democratic Party and the Liberal Party merged to become the Liberal Democratic Party (LDP), and under its rule the Ministry of Education strengthened its textbook screening. The Nanking Massacre thus disappeared from the textbooks. In the same way, Japanese people after the war avoided confronting the issue of war and aggression, and the Nanking Massacre was removed from the national memory. Thus, it took what is called "the debate over the Nanking Massacre" for most Japanese people to confront the Nanking Massacre once again.

3. The Debate over the Nanking Massacre—From the 1970s to the Present

In the beginning of the 1970s, thanks to the widespread movement against the Vietnam War, many ordinary Japanese began to recognize the aggressive nature of Japan's own war in the past. Many historians who had participated in the antiwar movement, myself included, published studies to clarify Japan's war of aggression and to raise questions about war responsibilities of the postwar generation. After the restoration of Sino-

Japanese diplomatic relations, gradually the voice of Chinese victims also began to be heard in Japan. It was then that the memory of the Nanking Massacre became the subject of a debate after being sealed off and frozen for decades. The debate was divided into three stages, with the verdict in the textbook trial as an appropriate conclusion.

The first stage occurred in the early 1970s, when Honda Katsuichi, a journalist of the *Asahi Shimbun*, went to China in 1971 to collect evidence from victims of Japanese aggression. This took place on the eve of the normalization of Sino-Japanese diplomatic relations. He completed a collection of oral history and published it in the book *A Journey to China*.[6] The book created a big sensation in Japan. Its influence was so great that it provoked counterattacks from the conservative camp. One member of this camp, Bungei Shinju, published a book called *The Illusion of the Nanjing Massacre,* by Suzuki Akira, in 1973. Since then, Bungei Shinju and the Sankei newspapers have taken a leading part in disseminating the view that the Nanking Massacre was an illusion or fiction.

The second stage took place in the early 1980s, when the unreasonable screening of history textbooks by the Ministry of Education (known as the Second Textbook Attack) was strongly condemned by neighboring Asian countries. This matter eventually became known as the "Textbook Controversy," which set off another round of conservative counterattacks. One of their leaders was Tanaka Akira, who had formerly been a secretary to Matsui. During this period, there were several other signals that Japanese politics was turning to the right, such as Prime Minister Nakasone's official visit to the Yasukuni Shrine.

The third stage, in the late 1980s, was the defeat of those who completely denied the Nanking Massacre. One of the most important developments during this time is that of the veterans' organization Kaikōsha, which had originally intended to prove with veterans' evidence that the Nanking Massacre was a fiction. Its efforts backfired, and in the face of mounting evidence it was forced to admit that the slaughter did happen.

The work that led to the recent Tokyo Court ruling is another important development. In the wake of the textbook controversy, some scholars, journalists, and attorneys, including myself, set up a study group to support Ienaga Saburo's trial against the government for censoring textbooks to remove all mention of Japanese aggression during World War II. We have published our research and attempted to make certain the truth will take hold in Japanese society. I myself took the witness stand in the Third Textbook Trial. I went to the United States and studied archives and newspapers of the wartime, and found that everyone but the Japanese knew the truth about the Nanking Massacre. I believe my testimony partly worked for the favorable judgment. With the breakdown of the Cold War structure in Asia today, many Asian countries have accelerated their democratization and their influence is increasing. With these developments in the background, they have instigated movements to demand that Japan account for its war responsibility. Related to this is the appearance of similar movements inside Japan by conscientious Japanese who pressed the government on the issue of war responsibility. Such a change in the social conditions must have been taken into consideration by the Tokyo court, which cannot help but judge the government position illegal. The Ministry of Education did not want to admit that the Nanking Massacre was a systematic crime of the Japanese military, and insisted that militaries all over the world have committed rapes. On October 20, 1993, the Tokyo court issued a ruling that considered the government positions on these two issues illegal. When the deadline of appeal passed on May 10, 1994, the government took no action, and in effect, admitted defeat. This decision, in my opinion, has pronounced the defeat of the deniers.

4. The Present and Problems of Nanking Massacre Remembrance

Except for those who deny it out of a political agenda, the majority of Japanese today have come to acknowledge the fact of the Nanking Massacre. However, because the scale and the whole picture of the Nanking Massacre have not been grasped and understood, those who insist that "only a small massacre happened" still have considerable influence among the Japanese. Many argue that although the Nanking Massacre did happen, the Chinese claim of 300,000 is an exaggeration, and in fact there were at most several tens of thousands of victims. In addition to the fact that most Japanese at the time did not remember the Nanking Massacre directly, today over 70 percent of the population was born after the war. While this situation calls for historical studies both in and outside schools, such efforts are often obstructed and resisted in Japan.

The active obstruction to remembrance of the Nanking Massacre is related to the fact that, refusing to declare its role in World War II as a war of aggression, the Japanese government has avoided formal repentance and apology. Therefore, political groups that call for supporting the Greater East Asian War or defending the emperor system enjoy tacit support from the government and business. They openly operate within the establishment and obstruct the efforts by the Japanese people to address the question of war responsibility and to remember the crimes and atrocities of the Japanese military. Moreover, they are connected to the movements within the government that seek to justify Japan's war in the past and to create a national consciousness in support of war policy. This is considered necessary for Japan to revise the postwar constitution that renounced war, and to make Japan into a "normal country" that can wage war in the future.

In any case, the policy and posture of the Japanese government is completely opposite from that of the German government, which has made it an obligation for the German people to learn the history of the Nazi Holocaust. In spite of their irresponsible government, Japanese people are promoting the memory of the Nanking Massacre in several ways.

First, some Japanese are bearing witness through testimonies. Although there is still much pressure for them to keep silent, many former soldiers have testified about the crimes of the Nanking Massacre. Chinese victims and survivors have come to Japan to tell their experiences, and many Japanese groups have visited Nanking.

Second, some are fostering remembrance through pictures and films. Because of the Japanese control in Nanking and back at home, such materials were quite limited at the time. The photographs and films whose origins we know for sure are those by members of the Safety Zone, foreign journalists, and Japanese soldiers. Since such records are very important for the memory of the Nanking Massacre, deniers in Japan are now concentrating their attacks on them.

Third, some Japanese are instilling memory through history books and textbooks. Although textbook coverage of the Nanking Massacre has improved somewhat, because of the format and volume of Japanese textbooks its descriptions range from a few lines to half a page. As a result, it is entirely insufficient for the student to get a full historical picture of the event.

Finally, how can the Japanese remember the perpetration of the Nanking Massacre and develop such memory to build a history for the twenty-first century? I would like to end this chapter on two issues.

First, the question of war responsibility of aggression in China was left unresolved by the Japanese government and by the Japanese people of my parents' generation. Those of us born after the war shall take it over as a postwar responsibility and move the issue of Japanese war responsibility toward resolution. The legal action by citizen groups on behalf of Chinese war victims is one concrete measure. With Chinese victims as plaintiffs, such lawsuits demand the Japanese government or businesses pay compensation for wartime damages. Li Xiuying, who had been injured by Japanese soldiers in Nanking when they tried to rape her, has filed such a suit in the Tokyo District Court. Attorneys who have fought in the textbook case have organized a support group to back up her suit. As a founding member of this group I am preparing a legal affidavit to be submitted to the court. Such a suit demanding compensations for the damages to the Chinese victims is also an unprecedented step to enable the Japanese to remember their history of perpetration, to bring about repentance, apology, and compensation, and to settle war responsibility.

Second, in remembering the Nanking Massacre we need to analyze the causes from the particular aspects of Japanese war crimes as well as universal aspects of human behavior in war. By doing so, we can gain shared lessons to prevent such an inhumane and brutal genocide from ever happening again in the twenty-first century. This is what I learned at the "Nanking 1937 Conference" at Princeton in November 1997.

Notes

1. Kasahara Tokushi, "Nankin jiken," pp. 221–227.
2. Fujiwara Akira, 1997, pp. 33–34.
3. Fujioka Nobukatsu, 1996, pp. 26–30, 215–216.
4. Rengokoku saiko sireibu johokyoikukyoku, 1946, p. 251.
5. Tanaka Masaaki, "Nanking jiken no sokatsu," Tokyo: Kenkosya, 1987, p. 18.
6. Honda Katsuichi, "Chugoku no tabi" [A journey to China], Tokyo: Asahi shinbunsha, 1972.

References

Boeikenkyujo senshishitsu, Senshisosho, "Shinajihen rikugun sakusen (2)," Tokyo: Asakumo shinbunsha, 1976.
Eguchi Keiichi, "Jugonensenso shoshi," Tokyo: Aoki shoten, 1991.
Fujioka Nobukatsu, "Kingendaishi kyoiku no kaikaku," Tokyo: Meiji tosho, 1996.
Fujiwara Akira, "Nankin no Nihongun," Tokyo: Otsuki shoten, 1997.
Honda Katsuichi, "Chugoku no tabi" (A journey to China), Tokyo: Asahi shinbunsha, 1972.

————, "Honda Katsuichi syu 23 Nankin Daigyakusatsu," Tokyo: Asahi shinbunsha, 1997.

Hora Tomio, Fujiwara Akira and Honda Katsuichi, eds. "Nankin daigyakusatsu no kenkyu," Tokyo: Banseisha, 1992.

Ito Takashi and Ryu Ketsu, eds. "Ishi Itaro nikki," Tokyo: Chuo koronsha, 1993.

Kasahara Tokushi, "Ajia no nakno Nihongun," Tokyo: Otsuki shoten, 1994.

————, "Nankin jiken," Tokyo: Iwanami shoten,1997.

————, "Nankin nanminku no hyakunichi," Tokyo: Iwanami shoten, 1995.

————, "Nichu zenmensenso to kaigun: Panay go jiken no shinso," Tokyo: Aoki shoten, 1997.

————, "Nankin jiken to Sanko sakusen," Tokyo: Otsuki shoten, 1999.

Kasahara Tokushi, Matsumura Takao, and Yoshimi Yoshiaki, eds." Rekishi no jijitsu o do oshieruka," Tokyo: Kyouiku shiryo shuppankai, 1997.

Kyokasho kentei sosho o shien suru zenkoku renrakukai, ed. "Ienaga kyokasho saiban daisanji sosho kosai hen: vol. 2 Nankin daigyakusatsu, Chosen jinmin no teiko, 731 butai," Tokyo: Minshusha, 1997.

Tanaka Masaaki, "Nanking jiken no sokatsu," Tokyo: Kenkosya, 1987, p. 18.

Tawara Yoshibumi, "Kyokasho kogeki no shinso," Tokyo: Gakusyu no tomosha, 1997.

Rengokoku saiko sireibu johokyoikukyoku, ed. "Shinso bako—Taiheiyo senso no seiji, gaiko, rikukaikusen no shinjitsu," Tokyo: Kozumo shuppan, 1946.

Yoshida Yutaka, "Tenno no guntai to Nankin jiken," Tokyo: Aoki shoten, 1986.

————, "Nihonjin no sensokan," Tokyo: Iwanami shoten, 1995.

————, "Gendai rekishigaku to senso sekinin," Tokyo: Aoki shoten, 1997.

6

The Overall Picture of the "Nanking Massacre"

Higashinakano Shudo

There has been much discussion in recent years about the "Nanking debate" in Japan between revisionists who seek to minimize the Nanking Massacre while protecting Japanese citizens from "masochistic, anti-Japanese" history, and progressives who insist that Japan must face up to its World War II atrocities. While it is easy to disregard all revisionists as politicians and journalists with obvious political agendas, we feel it is important to represent their point of view by publishing a chapter that states their argument as well as it can be stated.

Higashinakano Shudo is a professor of intellectual history who has researched the Nanking Massacre quite thoroughly. Here he presents his argument that much of the evidence for the Massacre has arisen from "hearsay" evidence rather than being based on undeniable facts. —Eds.

The Fall of Nanking

Chinese towns had long been surrounded by walls, as was one of the capitals of the Shang dynasty in 1400 B.C. Nanking also was protected by a giant wall, 34 kilometers in length. The population in Nanking numbered a little more than a million people, decreasing to 200,000 just before the fall. This decrease occurred because people escaped from Nanking due to their fear of the scorched-earth operation of the Chinese forces.[1] The people who remained in Nanking were "the poorest of the poor" who could not afford to flee the town.

Europeans who remained in Nanking then established "a neutral zone where noncombatants could take refuge." On November 22, 1937, about twenty days before the fall of Nanking, the International Committee designated an area in the middle of Nanking as the Safety Zone.

The Safety Zone was such a primitive arrangement that even combatants could enter it simply by crossing the street. The Japanese forces announced that they would honor the Safety Zone and refrain from attack, but that they could not officially recognize the Safety Zone. Just before the fall the neutral zone was invaded by almost all Chinese soldiers inside the city wall. Unfortunately their fear of the Japanese forces later proved justified.

The *New York Times* on December 6 reported that Nanking had been placed under "martial law." Chiang Kai-Shek escaped from Nanking on December 7, 1937. The Nanking Defense Commander, Tang Cheng-Chih, made an important proclamation that "all noncombatants must concentrate in the internationally supervised Safety Zone" and should not move outside the Safety Zone with the exception of persons bearing a "special permit to be indicated by a symbol specially stamped on yellow armbands."[2] Many people thus gathered in the Safety Zone, and there was "crowding" inside the zone.[3] On December 9, Tang Cheng-Chih closed all the gates of Nanking tightly with sandbags. At eight o'clock in the evening of December 12, Commander Tang Cheng-Chih fled the city through Yi Chiang Gate (the northwest gate).

Nanking fell before dawn on December 13. The Chinese soldiers outside the city tried to escape by crossing the Yangtze River from Hsiakuan on the south shore of the river. In keeping with the universal and timeless battlefield principle of pursuing a fleeing enemy, the Japanese Army chased after and annihilated the Chinese Army. This fact was well known among Europeans in Nanking. It did not, however, result in charges of a violation of the prohibitions of Article XXIII of The Hague Regulations. This point must be kept in mind.

Almost all the citizens inside the city wall had taken refuge in the Safety Zone. The International Committee for the Nanking Safety Zone has stated that "on the 13th day, when your troops entered the city, we had nearly all civilian population gathered in the zone." Therefore, the area outside of the Safety Zone was "practically deserted" until the end of January of the following year.[4] This means that any persons found "outside" the Safety Zone would have been Chinese soldiers, and any dead bodies discovered there would have been those of Chinese soldiers.

The Chinese soldiers inside the city had taken off their uniforms and had hidden in the Safety Zone, disguised as civilians. In addition, they had concealed a large quantity of weapons. The Japanese forces decided to carry out "mop-up operations" for three days, beginning the day after the fall (December 14), for the purpose of self-defense or "self-preservation." Nobody knew when the Chinese soldiers dressed as civilians would make a counterattack. In fact, fierce fighting continued outside the city even after the fall. As described in John Rabe's diary, the Chinese forces bombed Nanking by air on January 2, 1938.

There was no street fighting. The task of mop-up operations of the Safety Zone was assigned to the Seventh Infantry Regiment. "About 6,500 were strictly dealt with" during these three days of the mop-up operations, according to the field diary (December 16) written by the commander of the Seventh Regiment. The phrase "dealt with" means that the regiment freed those people who were identified as civilians and executed only soldiers who were resistant and assumed a threatening attitude. The fact is that not all the disclosed Chinese soldiers were executed. However, a boy aged seventeen who claimed to be the only survivor told Robert Wilson, a surgeon with the International Committee for Nanking Safety Zone, on January 3, 1938, that 6,000 soldiers and 4,000 civilians were taken to the Yangtze River and shot to death. Thus, Europeans in Nanking began to criticize the Japanese for the reported executions during the mop-up operations. Looking back from the perspective of the present, this story marks the origin of the so-called Nanking Massacre.

Burial in Nanking

The detection of Chinese soldiers in the Safety Zone was incomplete. Once again the Japanese Army began the task of separating civilians from soldiers. This continued from December 24, 1937, until January 5 of the following year. After the completion of the first stage of this process, however, as noted in Document No. 46 (January 18, 1938) of the International Committee, the problem of food supplies had become more serious. Then the Japanese Army became completely occupied with that problem.

When the food problem had been resolved by the Japanese Army, at last they could take on the problem of burials. As shown by the January 22, 1938, entry in Rabe's diary,[5] "My protests and pleas to the Japanese embassy finally to get this corpse buried, or to give me permission to bury it, have thus far been fruitless." At this point burials had not yet begun.

If 300,000 people were massacred in Nanking, a corresponding number of dead bodies should have been buried there. In order to determine an accurate account of these burials, we must examine the supporting evidence, including: (1) time of burial, (2) testimony from persons performing the burials, (3) number of burials each day, and (4) total number of burials.

Maruyama Susumu, who was in charge of burials in Nanking, is still alive. He had been working in the Shanghai office of the South Manchuria Railway (Mantetsu), but was dispatched to the Nanking Special Service Agency in the latter part of December 1937. His mission in Nanking was to endeavor to improve the public welfare, and he told me that he directed the members of the Red Swastika Society to perform the burials, starting at the beginning of February 1938 and completing the process on March 15.[6] The records at the Red Swastika Society, however, indicate that burials took place from December 22, 1937, to October 30, 1938. Which dates are correct? Since Rabe's diary says that the burials started on February 1,[7] agreeing with Maruyama's account, it seems more likely that the burials started in February 1938.

When were the burials completed? In the *Report of the Nanking International Relief Committee*, Committee Chairman Miner Bates reported that the Red Swastika Society employed about 170 people to "complete" this task.[8] The fee was 40 cents per head, which means that $68 was paid out daily. Since the amount paid during "some 40 working days" was $2,540, the number of days of work can be calculated at 37.3. If we consider that on some days bad weather may have prevented burials from taking place, we can estimate that the operation took about 40 days. This figure agrees with the testimony of Maruyama that the burials were carried out from February 1 to March 15.

Who performed the burial operations? In the Tokyo Trials, representatives of the Republic of China insisted that Tsun-Shan-Tang and six other groups performed this task, in order to prove that 279,586 people were massacred. However, the Bates report "Relief Situations in Nanking" (February 1938), the *China Year Book 1939,* and the *Report of the Nanking International Relief Committee* all indicate that only the Red Swastika Society was involved in the burials.[9] Maruyama verified this fact in his testimony. We have to say, therefore, that only the Red Swastika Society carried out the burials.

How many corpses were buried each day? In his diary entry of February 14, Rabe wrote that 200 bodies had been buried daily up to that date. Maruyama verified that 200 bodies at most and ordinarily 180 were buried each day. If we assume that, in February, 200 bodies were buried each day and that the number of working days in this month was 25 days (excluding rainy days), then the data indicate the burial of at most 5,000 bodies in February. This figure agrees with the "Second Report of the Nanking Special Service Agency," which states that the Red Swastika Society buried 5,000 bodies by the end of February.[10] On the other hand, the burial notes of the Red Swastika Society reported burials of more than 30,000 in February.[11] I believe that this number has been inflated by 25,000.

How about the number of burials in March? Secretary Rosen stated in his report to the German Ministry of Foreign Affairs in Berlin that the number of burials was 500–600 each day.[12] If we use the larger number of 600 burials per day, the operation of 15 days means only 9,000 burials. The Rabe diary, however, states, "What shocked me most . . . is the observation that . . . there are still 30,000 to be dealt with, most of them in Hsiakwan." Rabe wrote these comments because the Red Swastika Society insisted on this number, but the society buried only about 2,000 bodies in total in Hsiakwan district in March, according to the record presented at the Tokyo Trials.[13] There were no 30,000 corpses in Hsiakwan.

Thus, the Red Swastika Society buried 5,000 in February and 9,000 in March, for a total of 14,000 bodies. However, the society claimed to have buried 43,000 bodies. Why was the number of burials inflated to such a degree? According to Maruyama, the Japanese forces paid the fee of 30 sen (0.3 yen) for each corpse,[14] at a time when the monthly salary of the police in the Republic of China was 3 to 5 yen. The International Committee also paid 40 cents per day. These amounts represented a large income for the burial group, so inflation of the burial numbers was natural in a sense. Moreover, Japanese officials were aware of the inflation. Maruyama recalled that it was said that the Japanese officials paid the money in order to improve the public welfare in Nanking in spite of their awareness of the inflation.

The *Report of the Nanking International Relief Committee* states, "For example, $2,540 was used to complete the necessary burial enterprises undertaken by the Red Swastika Society, which covered over 40,000 bodies otherwise uncared for."[15] This was because they believed the report of the Red Swastika Society.

Thus, with the exception of the Red Swastika Society, six of seven burial groups whose names were submitted by the Republic of China to the Tokyo Trials were found to be nonexistent. The 184,557 corpses that the six groups were said to have buried were also fictitious. Only the Red Swastika Society actually carried out the burials, completing the operation by burying 14,000 corpses.

I thus think that 14,000 corpses at most were picked up inside and outside the city wall. The buried corpses inside the city are estimated to be about 600 at most. This number includes rioters who were shot as a warning before the fall, Chinese soldiers who were left on a platform at the Nanking station as war dead, Chinese soldiers who died in battles at gates including the Chung Hua Gate, the Chinese soldiers shot by a supervising unit of their army at the North Gate, and the dead Chinese soldiers who fell from the city wall.[16]

International Law Relating to War Conduct

Did the execution of Chinese soldiers by Japanese forces outside the city after the takeover violate the International Law Relating to War Conduct (*jus in bello*)?

The Hague Regulations of 1907 prohibited "killing or wounding an enemy who, having laid down arms, or having no longer any means of defense, has surrendered." When a "belligerent," who has engaged in battle, becomes a prisoner of war (POW), the enemy must save his life. This was a great privilege for a belligerent. However, The Hague Regulations can be applied only to those belligerents who qualify under the regulations. What is meant by "belligerent"? The Hague Regulations define the following "qualifications of belligerents":

1. To be commanded by a person responsible for his subordinates;
2. To have a fixed distinctive emblem recognizable at a distance;
3. To carry arms openly;
4. To conduct operations in accordance with the laws and customs of war.

A belligerent can become a "lawful prisoner of war" only when he meets these four qualifications. If a belligerent does not qualify under these rules, he is not eligible for protection under the Hague Regulations, because he does not qualify as a prisoner of war. He is placed outside the protection of the International Law Relating to War Conduct. This important rule of qualification of belligerents was succeeded by a treaty concerning the treatment of POWs in 1949, which is still in effect today. These guidelines mentioned above were in effect at the time of the fall of Nanking. The Chinese soldiers had not yet surrendered officially after the fall. They hid themselves in the Safety Zone. Did these Chinese soldiers qualify as belligerents under the regulations?

Qualification of Belligerents No. 1

The Supreme Commander Tang Cheng-Chih fled to Wuhan by train just before the fall of Nanking. Officers and soldiers including the divisional commander also fled. Therefore, the Chinese forces became an uncontrolled group without "a person responsible for his subordinates."

Qualification of Belligerents No. 2

The Chinese soldiers, acting without a commander, took off their military uniforms and hid themselves in the Safety Zone. This act violated The Hague Regulations, which require belligerents to bear "a distinctive emblem recognizable at a distance."

Qualification of Belligerents No. 3

Not a few Chinese regular soldiers hid a number of weapons in the Safety Zone. This act violated the rule that they should "carry arms openly."

Qualification of Belligerents No. 4

The actions listed above, in other words, indicate that the Chinese soldiers violated The Hague Regulation No. 4, "to conduct operations in accordance with the laws and customs of war."

Thus, the Chinese regular soldiers violated the qualification-of-belligerents rule according to the International Law Relating to War Conduct, and became what were called "plainclothes soldiers" in China, that is, guerrillas. Long before the Americans had problems with Communist guerrillas in Vietnam, the Japanese Army had already encountered guerrillas in China. When they disregarded the qualification of belligerents rule, the Chinese soldiers lost their qualification to become lawful prisoners of war. However, the Japanese forces treated these unlawful POWs as they did other POWs, taking many of them to the POW camps and using them as laborers. When the registration of citizens was held from the end of 1937 through the beginning of 1938, even these "unlawful POWs" were registered as citizens. At the same time particularly resistant soldiers were executed. Did this treatment violate *jus in bello*?

An English report titled *Documents of the Nanking Safety Zone* was published in 1939 under the auspices of the Council of International Affairs, Chungking. These documents consist of protests that were prepared by the International Committee of the Nanking Safety Zone to the Japanese Embassy. The report also represents the official opinions of the Republic of China.

Document No. 1, dated December 14, 1937, begins with the sentence "We come to thank you for the fine way your artillery spared the Safety Zone." The last document was dated February 19, 1938, and announced the breakup of the International Committee for the Nanking Safety Zone. Among 69 protests made in 58 days (about 8 weeks), 52 described "cases of disorder," nearly all with the signature of Rabe.

However, it was in only one document that the International Committee referred to Chinese soldiers' qualifications as POWs. In Document No. 4, dated December 15, the International Committee insisted that "the Committee fully recognizes that identified soldiers are lawful prisoners of war."[17] No such statement appears in documents dated later than December 16. Therefore it means that the committee in effect withdrew this statement and regarded the Chinese soldiers as unlawful POWs.

How did European correspondents regard the qualification of the Chinese soldiers as POWs? One journalist left Nanking on December 16, but the others did on December 15, the second day of the mop-up operation of the Japanese forces. These correspondents watched the Japanese troops execute Chinese soldiers at the shore of Yangtze River.

For example, a journalist named Tillman Durdin of the *New York Times*, wrote on December 18 in an article titled "All Captives Slain," that he "watched the execution of 200 captives." He did not write "the execution of 200 POWs" because that statement would not have been true. The use of phrases such as "execution of men" rather than "execution of POWs," was not limited to Durdin. Journalists from Reuters and the *Chicago Daily News* wrote similar reports.[18] In other words, the journalists could not insist that the Japanese forces violated *jus in bello* because they executed the Chinese soldiers "without even a summary trial."

As another example, how did the diplomats in Nanking regard the qualifications of the Chinese soldiers as POWs? Dr. Georg Rosen was a secretary of the German Embassy at Nanking. His report runs as follows:

> When we were on board the British gunboat Bee in front of Nanking
> from December 12 to 20, Japanese Rear Admiral Kondo told British Rear
> Admiral Holt that there were 30,000 Chinese soldiers to be "mopped-up"
> on a large island in the Yangtze River downstream from Nanking. This
> mop-up operation, as it is called in the Japanese official announcement,
> means killing unarmed enemies and is against the general rules of con-
> duct of war.[19]

Rosen criticized the mop-up operation of the Japanese forces on an
island in the middle of the Yangtze River as a violation of The Hague
Regulations because he regarded the mop-up operations as the killing of
unarmed enemy soldiers. Significantly, this report was dated January
20, 1938. The Japanese forces had completed the mop-up operation inside the city wall in the middle of December, one month prior to Rosen's
report. Rosen knew about this other mop-up operation; nevertheless, he
could not criticize the December operation inside the city wall.

The next piece of evidence is the report of the British Consul E.W.
Jeffrey in Nanking: "The atrocities committed during the first two weeks
after the occupation of the city were of a nature and on a scale which
were almost incredible."[20]

This report, dated January 28, 1938, was redirected from the American Embassy at Nanking to the Department of State at Washington. The
target of his criticism was "atrocities." What did he mean by "atrocities"? In his report dated January 29 and filed on microfilm with the
Department of State, Jeffrey pointed out that "military lawlessness continues, due to a lack of centralized control. The majority of cases are of
ransacking."[21] This report was filed forty-seven days after the fall of
Nanking. Nevertheless, it does not include any mention of "massacre"
of civilians and captives by the Japanese troops.

Let me introduce one more example. Cabot Coville, an army attaché
at the American Embassy at Tokyo, visited Nanking to gather and exchange information for six days with six Europeans who remained in
Nanking. Secretary John Allison of the American Embassy told Coville
that "looting and rape by the Japanese troops continued for several
weeks,"[22] but he did not blame the Japanese for slaughters of civilians
or captives, that is, for violating *jus in bello*.

As I have proved so far, no written evidence exists of violation of the
Hague Regulations by the Japanese troops.

Problems of Verification as to Murder and Rape

Many descriptions with regard to the Nanking Incident are based on reports that were written after World War II. However, most of the reports have never been verified. For example, in the first chapter of the book *What War Means*, edited by Harold Timperley, author George Fitch says:

> They were first reported in the Zone at *eleven o'clock that morning, the 13th.* I drove down with two of our committee members to meet them, just a small detachment at the southern entrance to the Zone. They showed no hostility, though a few moments later they killed *twenty refugees who were frightened by their presence and ran from them.*[23] (Italics added.)

Fitch says that he watched the Japanese forces shoot the refugees at about noon on December 13 at the south entrance of the Safety Zone. However, the killings described above were mentioned by Fitch alone and are not found in any records written by Japanese, American, or German nationals. Moreover, the Japanese troops entered the Safety Zone for the mop-up operation the next day, that is, December 14. Therefore, at about noon on December 13, they were not yet at this location.

The same scene as that of the Fitch Report is found in *Documents of the Nanking Safety Zone*, which was edited about one year after the Fitch report.

> In the afternoon of December 13, we found a captain with a group of Japanese soldiers resting on Hang Chung Lu. We explained to him where the zone was and marked it on his map. We politely called his attention to the three Red Cross Hospitals and told him about the disarmed soldiers.[24]

Documents of the Nanking Safety Zone does not describe the murder of twenty refugees by the Japanese troops, because the event described by Fitch could not be confirmed.

Accusations of a "Nanking Massacre" of 10,000 victims began on the basis of an account offered by a seventeen-year-old boy who claimed he was the only survivor. According to his account, on December 14 when the Japanese forces began the mop-up operation in the Safety Zone, 10,000 people including this boy were taken from the zone to the shores of Yangtze River and all were killed. He said that they included 6,000 captured soldiers and 4,000 civilians. The boy barely escaped with his life. It was on January 3 that he told this story to Robert Wilson, a surgeon with the International Committee, twenty days after the supposed incident.[25]

Some questions arise. How did the boy recognize 6,000 people as soldiers and 4,000 as civilians when he barely escaped with his life? It was necessary to go through the gate of the giant wall in order to go from the shore of the Yangtze River to the hospital inside the city wall where Wilson worked as a surgeon. According to Rabe's diary entry of January 26, the Japanese forces "banned anyone from entering or leaving." Nobody could go through the gate without a good reason. Moreover, the movement of such a large group of 10,000 people would have been observed by many people, but there are no other eyewitness accounts at all. I cannot help concluding that it is because the supposed incident did not occur.

One additional story of mass slaughter relates to the segregation of soldiers from civilians that began on December 24. This story was also told by a Chinese who claimed to be the only survivor. The uncorroborated story was described by Bates in a memorandum that constitutes the third chapter of *What War Means:*

> Next morning, a man with five bayonet wounds came to the University Hospital. . . . That evening, he said, somewhere to the west, about 130 Japanese soldiers had killed most of *five hundred* similar captives with bayonet thrusts. When he regained consciousness, he found that the Japanese had gone and managed to crawl away during the night. He was not familiar with this part of Nanking, and was vague as to places.[26] (Italics added.)

Bates adds in his memorandum that the burial group saw the corpses, the number of which was increased from 500 to 3,000. It runs as follows: "Burial gangs report three thousand bodies at the point, left in rows or piles after mass executions."[27]

This Bates memorandum was included in the following publications (dates given are those of prefaces):

1. Harold Timperley, ed., *What War Means* (London. Victor Gollanz, March 20, 1938; New York: Books for Libraries Press, 1969), pp. 46–51.
2. *The War Conduct of Japanese*, edited by Hsu Shu-Hsi and prepared under the auspices of the Council of International Affairs,

Hankow, April 12, 1938 (Shanghai: Kelly & Walsh, 1939), pp. 139–146.

3. *A Digest of Japanese War Conduct,* edited by Hsu Shu-Hsi and prepared under the auspices of the Council of International Affairs, Chungking, January 28, 1939 (Shanghai: Kelly & Walsh, 1939), pp. 5–12.

4. "The War Conduct of the Japanese," in *The Chinese Year Book 1938–39,* edited by Hsu Shu-Hsi and prepared from official sources by the Council of International Affairs, Chungking, March 15, 1939, pp. 181–186.

5. *Documents of the Nanking Safety Zone,* edited by Hsu Shu-Hsi and prepared under the auspices of the Council of International Affairs, Chungking, May 9, 1939 (Shanghai: Kelly & Walsh, 1939), pp. 100–109.

The first book listed above referred to "3,000 corpses," but the other books, which were supervised by the Council of International Affairs at Hankow (later Chungking), deleted the number 3,000 since the facts could not be confirmed. In other words, Bates's records were not true.

I will next examine the *Documents of the Nanking Safety Zone.* This official document consists of protests handed to the Japanese Embassy by the International Committee for the Nanking Safety Zone and was compiled by the Council of International Affairs of the Republic of China. Document No. 10, dated December 18, stated that, for several days after the fall of Nanking, "cases are pouring in faster than we can type them out." This means that the International Committee was unable to take the time to confirm the truth of these reports.

Nevertheless, a total of twenty-five "murder cases" were presented to the Japanese Embassy by the International Committee, twenty-three of which were based on hearsay evidence. Out of these twenty-three cases, seven were unsigned and one contained only a family name with no first name. Courts do not accept hearsay or rumors as evidence, because such statements are not considered reliable.

Witnesses came forth in only two of the twenty-five cases. What were these two cases? One was the incident of the killings witnessed by Christian Kroeger and Rupert Hatz. However, this was clearly described as "legitimate executions" in a note to the Documents. The other case was witnessed and testified at the Tokyo Trials by John Magee. His testimony says that a "Chinese ran away when a Japanese soldier shouted *'Mate,* (wait) and was shot on December 17, four days after the Japanese occupation." What would happen if a man ran away in fear after a soldier shouted "Wait" as an emergency warning? Anyone would understand the behavior of the Japanese soldier. The determining evidence, however, is that on December 19, 1937, Magee writes in his diary, "The actual killing we did not see as it took place." This statement shows that he did not see the event himself. This is contrary to his testimony at the Tokyo Trials.[28]

No cases actually witnessed by the president of the International Committee, John Rabe, appear in his diary. If Rabe witnessed a case, he should have made an official protest to the Japanese Embassy, and we should have found that case in the *Documents*. There are no cases of unlawful murder witnessed by Rabe among the protests to the Japanese Embassy that he authorized himself. Rabe signed only three protest documents that referred to the existence of corpses, but he did not witness them.

Tsukamoto Koji worked in Nanking from December 1937 through August 1938 as a chief of the judicial section that dealt with trials of the Japanese forces. He testified at the Tokyo Trials that there had been two or three cases of murder.[29] This testimony is nearly in accord with the *Documents*. Therefore, I think that there were two or three cases of murder in Nanking. Even these cases were not due to the systematic conduct of the Japanese forces but were the results of misdeeds by individual Japanese soldiers. After World War II, during the period from November 6, 1945, to the end of December 1945, there was an incident in which American soldiers who were part of the force occupying the famous military port town of Kure, east of Hiroshima, committed 20 cases of fire or arson and murdered 14 people. A total of 1,874 cases of crimes were committed by the American soldiers or their allies in Kure from 1946 to 1951.[30] Just as this cannot be called a massacre by the U.S. or Allied forces, so the incidents of murder in Nanking cannot be called a massacre.

Incidents of Rape

Another accusation, along with the murder, is that of rape. A total of 251 cases of rape was mentioned in the *Documents*. I would like to consider the first three cases[31] in a time sequence.

1. The first example of rape in the *Documents* is Case No. 10. Four girls were said to have been raped at noon on December 14, the day the mop-up operation by the Japanese troops began.

2. Case No. 12 states that four women were raped on the evening of the same day.

3. Case No. 15 states that one woman was raped and three were taken away on December 15.

Who witnessed these cases and who recorded them? No names were found on the record. This means that these were instances of hearsay. In an article in the *New York Times* on December 18, Tillman Durdin wrote that "many Chinese men reported to foreigners the abduction and raping of wives and daughters." Durdin's statement was based on these kinds of rumors, because he left Nanking in the afternoon of December 15. Thus, these unreliable reports of "rape" were propagandized around the world.

One story of rape took place on December 17 after the ceremonial entry of the Japanese forces into Nanking. Rabe's diary entry of December 17 says: "Last night up to 1,000 women and girls are said to have been raped, about 100 girls at Ginling Girls College alone." Rabe's account is evidently based on hearsay rather than the testimony of witnesses. This kind of one-sided, exaggerated "propaganda" by the Chinese people appears in the second chapter of *What War Means*. The chapter was written by George Fitch.

> Friday, Dec. 17. Robbery, murder, rape continue unabated. . . . One poor woman was raped thirty-seven times. Another had a five month old infant deliberately smothered by the brute to stop its crying while he raped her.[32]

Bates made a similar report in the fourth chapter of *What War Means*, as follows:

> You can scarcely imagine the anguish and terror. Girls as low as *eleven* and women as old as *fifty-three* have been raped on University property alone. In other groups of refugees are women of *seventy-two* and *seventy-six* years of age who were raped mercilessly.[33] (Italics added.)

Both cases, if true, were quite shocking events. However, descriptions of these incidents were not included in *Documents*. The descriptions were not included because these cases could not be confirmed. Similarly, the description by Iris Chang that "children and babies were suffocated by clothes stuffed in their mouths or bayoneted to death because they wept as their mothers were being raped" does not have any concrete basis.[34]

Bates reported that "Able German colleagues put the cases of rape at twenty thousand. I should say not less than eight thousand."[35] But this is based on the Chinese "one-sided" exaggerated propaganda. In accordance with these reports, an editorial on January 21, 1938, in the traditional *North China Daily News* commented that rapes by the Japanese forces in Nanking amounted to "8,000 to 20,000" cases. However, the North China Daily News and Herald did not give this number of 20,000 rapes in the *China Year Book 1938*, edited by the paper's editors. There is no evidence that the company received vigorous protests about this. The edition of 1939 also did not give any account of 20,000 rapes. Because this number could not be confirmed as true, Chang insists that 20,000 to 80,000 women were raped in Nanking, but on what grounds is she making this statement?

Why were such a large number of rapes reported in Nanking? We can find the answer to this enigma in the *New York Times*:

> American professors remaining at Ginling College in Nanking as foreign members of the Refugee Welfare Committee were seriously embarrassed to discover that they had been harboring a deserted Chinese Army colonel and six of his subordinate officers. The professors had, in fact, made the colonel second in authority at the refugee camp. The officers, who had doffed their uniforms during the Chinese retreat from Nanking, were discovered living in one of the college buildings. They admitted their identity after Japanese Army searchers found they had hidden six rifles, five revolvers, a dismounted machine gun and ammunition in the building. The ex-Chinese officers in the presence of American and other foreigners confessed looting in Nanking and also that one night they dragged girls from the refugee camp into the darkness and the next day blamed Japanese soldiers for the attacks. The ex-soldiers were arrested and will be punished under martial law and probably executed.[36]

The Nanking Safety Zone was a neutral zone. Nevertheless, Rabe hid two Chinese colonels. American professors also hid Chinese officers. These acts were serious violations of neutrality. Concerning the stories of "rape" in Nanking, as Secretary General Paul Scharffenberg of the German Embassy in Nanking summed it up, "And as for all these excesses, one hears only one side of it, after all."[37]

To conclude regarding these claims of rape, sixty-one cases (24 percent) out of two hundred fifty one described in the *Documents* included the name of the witness. If these cases were true, they should have been reported to the Japanese forces, but in fact they were reported only to Europeans. The cases that were reported to the Japanese forces and in which a suspect was brought in by the Japanese forces numbered only seven (3 percent) out of sixty-one. Seven cases of rape was the entire scope of the Nanking Incident, as far as we can find in the *Documents,* which Timperley says "completes the story of the first two months of the Japanese Army's occupation of Nanking."[38]

A Follow-Up to Bates's View that 40,000 Were Massacred

Facts cannot be deleted from the record, but untruths will eventually be removed. For example, when record A is reported, a complete follow-up survey is necessary in order to clarify how record A will be handled. I want to follow up on "the view that 40,000 people were massacred," put forth by Bates, an advocate of the Nanking Massacre. A professor of Nanking University, Miner Bates insisted in his memorandum that "this incident is only one of a series of similar acts that had been going on for two weeks."[39] What he called "this incident" was the murder of captives, and he based his claim on one-sided accusations by Chinese people. He accused "the Japanese who neglected international law" of the mass massacre of soldiers over a period of two weeks: "Evidence from burials indicate that close to forty thousand unarmed persons were killed within and near the walls of Nanking, of whom some 30 percent had never been soldiers."[40]

Bates's view that 12,000 civilians were killed was based on the added note to *War Damage in the Nanking Area,* edited by Lewis Smythe. The note says that "A careful estimate from the burials in the city and in areas adjacent to the wall indicates that 12,000 civilians were killed by violence."[41] The person who wrote the preface to *War Damage in the Nanking Area* was Bates himself. However, the table of burials of the Red Swastika Society does not differentiate soldiers from civilians. There is no basis for identifying 70 percent of 40,000 as soldiers and 30 percent as civilians. This memorandum, written by Bates on January 25, 1938, constitutes the third chapter (pp. 46–51; see p. 51) of *What War Means,* edited by Harold Timperley. This book was published in July 1938, and the preface was dated March 23, 1938. This date is significant. As was mentioned earlier, Bates's memorandum was cited in five English books as well, four of which were edited by Hsu Shu-Hsi, an adviser to the Ministry of Foreign Affairs, and so were reported as the representation of official views. One section, "Killing Prisoners of War," in Book 4, cited entire sentences from Bates's "Memorandum" but deleted the critical portion, that is, the view that 40,000 were massacred. Books 2, 3, and 5 also deleted Bates's statement that "Evidence from burials indicates that close to 40,000 unarmed persons were killed within and near the walls of Nanking, of whom some 30 percent had never been soldiers."

If 40,000 were the true number killed, the Republic of China might have kept blaming Japan because that would have been the best material for propaganda. The fact that the advisor to the Ministry of Foreign Affairs expressly deleted the number means that there were no mass killing of POWs and civilians by the Japanese forces.

A Follow-Up of the View that the Nanking Massacre Occurred

I want to follow up on the use of the term "Nanking Massacre" in official records of the Republic of China. The *China Journal*, published in Shanghai and edited by Dr. Bruno Kroker, was "the leading monthly magazine" in English on China. "Events and Comments" in the issue of January 1938 accused the Japanese of "slaughter in the city [Nanking]." "Events and Comments" in the next (February) issue commented that "the fall of Nanking and Hanchow was followed . . . with Japanese looting, raping and wanton destruction." The word "slaughter" was deleted and the term "Nanking Massacre" was not used at all.[42]

The English magazine *China at War* was edited on the basis of "daily bulletins." It consisted of short, official announcements offered by the China Information Committee at Hangkow (Hanchow) for the purpose of arousing war sentiment. The inaugural issue, published in April 1938, described only looting and raping as the Nanking problem. The Republic of China did not confirm the massacre by the Japanese forces at Nanking.[43]

On May 27, 1938, five months after the fall of Nanking, the Council of the League of Nations issued a resolution condemning Japan.[44] This resolution also did not refer to the Nanking Massacre.

What did the Chinese Communist Party say? During a period of nine days beginning May 26, Mao Tse-Tung mentioned the fall of Nanking many times in his speech "On the War of Endurance," but he did not mention the massacre in Nanking. On the contrary, Mao said that "there were many sieges but they wiped out few," due to the "poor leadership" of the Japanese in both the battles in Shanghai and Nanking.[45] In other words Mao meant that since the Japanese troops did not wipe out the Chinese soldiers in Nanking, the Chinese soldiers could regain their strength and counterattack the Japanese forces. Therefore, the success of the counterattack was said to be due to the bad strategy of the Japanese forces.

On July 7, 1938, the first anniversary of the Sino-Japanese War, Chiang Kai-Shek emphasized "the atrocity by Japanese" in his "Statement to Friendly Nations" and "Message to Japanese People." He picked Canton as an example and did not say anything about the Nanking Massacre.[46]

China Forum was a weekly magazine published under the auspices of the Chinese League of Nations Union, Hankow. This English magazine propagated the official view of the government of the Republic of China. The issue of March 19 included an article by an unnamed author who wrote of the massacre of 80,000 people, twice the number given by Bates. Therefore, I paid special attention to the July 9 issue, which printed "One Year of the Sino-Japanese War: Review Questions for Study Groups." Review Question No. 10 was "What was the attitude of China after the fall of Nanking?" The model answer was that Chiang Kai-Shek encouraged the Chinese, saying, "We must not surrender but march onward" after the fall of Nanking.[47] This answer implies a voluntary withdrawal of the term "Nanking Massacre."

China Critic behaved in a similar fashion. One of the special features of *China Critic* was, according to the advertisement of the publishers, to include "official documents published for historical records in the future." The managing editor was Kwei Chungshu, who had been graduated from Wisconsin University and was the managing editor of the American paper *China Press* in Shanghai. The July 7 issue of *China Press* included an editorial titled "A Year of Undeclared War," which commented on "the fall of Nanking and the beginning of the Great Retreat."[48] It did not mention "the fall of Nanking and the beginning of a massacre." This was the official view of *China Critic*.

Revived Bates's View

The term "Nanking Massacre" was used for the period of four months after the fall of Nanking, but Bates's view that 40,000 were killed had been denied since April 1938. It was Edgar Snow who revived Bates's view in Europe and America, where little information on the subject prevailed. Snow published *The Battle for Asia* in 1941, a half-year before the beginning of the war between Japan and America. In his book, he insisted that "according to an estimate given to me by members of the Nanking International Relief Committee, the Japanese murdered no less than 42,000 people in Nanking alone, a large percentage of them women and children."[49]

Among the members of the Nanking International Relief Committee, only Bates insisted that 40,000 were killed. Snow simply used Bates's view. He overlooked the fact that Bates's view had already been rejected. Moreover, Snow reversed the ratio of soldiers to civilians and insisted on what even Bates did not mention, that is, that a large part of the victims were women and children. Snow did not have any new evidence to introduce Bates's view.

Agnes Smedley published *Battle Hymn of China* in 1943. She wrote that the Japanese "put to the sword some two hundred thousand civilians and unarmed soldiers."[50] This statement was an exaggeration of propaganda, including a number five times the one Bates had given.

What Did "Nanking Incident" Mean Before the War?

It is worthwhile looking back at the preface to *The China Year Book 1939.* "It has been the constant aim of the Editor, ever since the publication of the first issue of *The China Year Book*, to make its contents impartially factual, and to avoid including material that could in any way be considered partial, on controversial issues. For that reason, except for a brief commentary on the actual process of hostilities, the Sino-Japanese conflict has been dealt with entirely on the basis of official documents or speeches. . . . It is hoped that no documents, speech or statement essential to an understanding of the issues raised by the present hostilities has been omitted."[51]

The China Year Book was an English publication with an independent editorial policy from the time of its inaugural issue in 1912. Its editions of 1938 and 1939 present at the beginning a calendar giving important dates. For example, January 22 says "Death of Lenin 1924"; January 30 says "President Franklin Roosevelt's birthday 1882"; December 13 says "Nanking occupied by Japanese 1937"; and December 17 says "Japanese Triumphal Entry into Nanking 1937." There is no mention of the Nanking Massacre by the Japanese, while the column of March 24 says clearly "Nanking Outrages 1927." This event was "the Nanking Incident" carried out by the Chinese Nationalist forces.

According to *The China Year Book 1928*, Chiang Kai-Shek's Nationalist forces intruded into the Japanese Embassy, European embassies, and missionary institutions in Nanking on March 24, 1927, the day after the occupation of Nanking. They systematically killed Dr. L.S. Smith (British), Mr. Huber (British), Dr. J.E. Williams (the vice president of the University of Nanking, American), a French and an Italian missionary. British Consul General Bertram Giles, Major Nemoto Hiroshi (Japanese), and three others were wounded. The wife of the Japanese consul and others were systematically raped.[52] It was this big incident in Nanking that was described in *The China Year Book 1938* as a disgusting event before 1938. There was no trace of severe protest to the report in *The China Year Book*, because the 1939 edition described only the same "Nanking Outrages 1927." This term means that everybody recognized the justice of the record. Even in *The China Year Book*, which described world events in detail, one could find no mention of a "Nanking Massacre by the Japanese Forces."

Records of history can survive when everyone recognizes the truth. Therefore, facts are never deleted from the historical record. Untruths are destined to be deleted from the historical record. No records exist to confirm evidence of a "Nanking Massacre." Anyone who insists that a "Nanking Massacre" occurred must present proof of violations of the Hague Regulations by the Japanese forces, that is, proof that confirmed the accusations of massacre of POWs and civilians by the Japanese forces.

Notes

1. In a speech on July 28, 1937, Wang Chao-Ming stated, "We decided to burn out any Chinese and any pieces of land in order not to give them to the enemy. . . . We have to burn out all cities large or small." In a speech three days later, Chiang Kai-Shek supported Wang's decision. For Wang's speech, see Mastumoto Shigeharu, *Shanghai Jidai* (My days in Shanghai) (Chukoshinsho, Tokyo: Chuokosonsha, 1975), pp. 170–174.

2. Tillman Durdin, "Chinese Make a Stand," *New York Times*, December 8, 1937.

3. Hsu Shu-Hsi, ed., *Documents of the Nanking Safety Zone* (Shanghai: Kelly & Walsh, 1939), p. 114.

4. Ibid., pp.14ff. Harold Timperley, ed., *What War Means* (1938; New York: Books for Libraries Press, 1969), p. 143. Iris Chang asserts, "The zone eventually

accommodated some 200,000–300,000 refugees—almost half of the Chinese population left in the city," but there is no record from anyone who witnessed the other "half of the Chinese population left in the city," which she claims was there. The area outside the Safety Zone was "practically deserted." As the foreign community of Nanking referred to the "2,000 civilians in Nanking" on December 21, 1937, there lived "200,000 Chinese civilians." Less than a month from that time, on January 14 of the following year, Document No. 41 of the International Committee estimated the population at "probably 250,000 to 300,000 civilians." Document No. 46, dated January 18, and Document No. 48, dated January 22, referred to the estimated "250,000 Chinese civilians." The fact that the population of the Safety Zone (that is, Nanking) increased from 200,000 to 250,000 speaks to the fact that Nanking was safe. Cf. Iris Chang, *The Rape of Nanking* (New York: Basic Books, 1997), p. 139; A letter of the foreign community of Nanking to the Japanese Embassy of Nanking, dated December 21, 1937, in Miner Searle Bates's, papers, Record Group No. 10, Box 102. Folder 864. Yale Divinity School Library. New Haven, Connecticut; Hsu, ed., *Documents*, pp. 17ff, 84, 95.

5. Erwin Wickert, ed., *The Good Man of Nanking: The Diaries of John Rabe* (New York: Alfred A. Knopf), p. 147. Concerning my views on Rabe's diaries, refer to: Higashinakano Shudo, "Aratamete 'Rabe no Nikki' wo Tettei Kensho Suru" (Thoroughly examining the diaries of Rabe all over again), *Seiron*, April 1998; Higashinakano Shudo, "Yahari 'Rabe Nikki' wa Santo Shiryo: Itakura Yoshiaki-shi no Hihan ni Kotaeru" (The "diaries of Rabe" is after all a third-class historical material: My answer to criticism, by Mr. Itakura Yoshiaki), *Seiron*, July 1998.

6. Higashinakano Shudo, "Recollection of Maruyama Susumu: A Member of Nanking Special Service Agency (Staff of Mantetsu)," *Ajiadaigaku Nihonbunka Kenkyuusho Kiyo* (Journal of the Institute for Japanese Studies, Asia University), *No: 2* (1995): pp. 81–82. Concerning a photograph of the hanging scroll that was sent to Maruyama by Wang Changtien, also known as "Jimmy," on the occasion of Maruyama's return to Japan, refer to Higashinakano Shudo, *Nankin Gyakusatsu no Tettei Kensho* (Overall examinations of the "Nanking Massacre"), 3d ed. (Tokyo: Tendensha, 1998, 1999), p. 309.

7. John Rabe's Report to Hitler, in Erwin Wickert, ed., *Rabe no Nikki* (The diaries of Rabe) (Tokyo: Kodansha, 1997), p. 317.

8. Miner Bates, *Report of the Nanking International Relief Committee*, *November 1937 to April 1939*, 1939, p. 19, in Miner Searle Bates's papers, Record Group No. 10, Box 102, Folder 867.

9. Miner Bates, "Nankin no Kyusai Jokyo" (Relief situations in Nanking), in Nankinjiken Chosakenkyukai Hen (Study Group for Nanking Incident Research, ed.,) *Nankinjiken Siryoshu* (Collected materials on the Nanking Incident), vol. 1 (Tokyo: Aoki shoten, 1992), p. 174; Phyllis Ayrton, "The Refugee Problem in China," *China Year Book 1939* (Shanghai: North-China Daily News & Herald, 1939), p. 562; *Report of the Nanking International Relief Committee*, p. 19.

10. Inoue Hisashi, ed., *Kachu Senbu Kosaku Shiryo* (Materials on activities for stabilizing occupied mid-China) (Tokyo: Fuji Shuppan, 1989), p. 153.

11. "Records of the Red Swastika Society's Burial," in Hora Tomio, ed., *Nicchu Senso Nankin Daizangyaku Jiken Shiryoshu* [Collected materials on atrocious incidents in Nanking in the Sino-Japanese War) (Tokyo: Aoki shoten, 1985), pp. 378–380.

12. Georg Rosen, "Die Lage in Nanking" (The situation in Nanking), in *Deutsche Gesandschaft/Botschaft in China: Japanisch-Chinesischer Konflikt* (microfilm), Deutsches Bundesarchiv, p. 108.

13. "Records of the Red Swastika Society's Burial," pp. 378–380.

14. Higashinakano, "Recollection of Maruyama Susumu," p. 83.

15. *Report of the Nanking International Committee*, p. 19.

16. Higashinakano, *Nankin Gyakusatsu no Tettei Kensho* (Overall examinations of the "Nanking Massacre"), pp. 318–320.

17. Hsu, ed., *Documents*, p. 5.

18. Archibald Steele reported that he watched the execution of "300 Chinese," *Chicago Daily News*, December 15, 1937; see also "Auszug aus dem Vortrag von Mr. Smith (Reuter) ueber die Kriegerischen Ereignisse in Nanking in der Zeit vom 9. bis 15. Dezember 1937" (Excerpt of speech by Mr. Smith [Reuter] on military occurrences in Nanking from December 9 to December 15, 1937), in *Deutsche Gesandschaft/Botschaft in China*, pp. 182ff.

19. Georg Rosen, "Nanking's Uebergang" (Nanking's transition), in *Deutsche Gesandschaft/Botschaft in China*, p. 204.

20. Gray telegram, February 3, 1938, in *Records of the Department of State Relating to Political Relations Between China and Japan, 1930–1944* (microfilm), roll 49.

21. Ibid.

22. Nankinjiken Chosa Kenkyukai Hen (Study Group for Nanking Incident Research), *Nankin Siryoshu*, pp. 110–121.

23. Timperley, ed., *What War Means*, pp. 26ff.

24. Hsu, ed., *Documents*, p. 12.

25. Robert Wilson, in a letter to his family, January 3, 1938, manuscript DS796 N2W75, Hoover Institution Archives, Stanford University, Stanford, CA.

26. Timperley, ed., *What War Means*, pp. 47ff.

27. Ibid., p. 50.

28. Hsu, ed., *Documents*, p. 78.

29. Hora, ed., *Nicchu Senso Nankin Daizangyaku Jiken Shiryoshu*, vol. 1, p. 192.

30. Kure City Fire Department, *Kure Shobo-shi: Boro wa Kataru* (History of firefighting in Kure: Tales from the watchtower), (Kure City Fire Association, 1978), p. 401; Kure City Historical Committee, ed., *Kureshi-shi* (History of Kure City), vol. 8 (Kure City Hall, 1995), pp. 742, 746; *Mainichi Shinbun* (Mainichi Newspaper), September 23, 1953.

31. Hsu, ed., *Documents*, p. 11.

32. Timperley, ed., *What War Means*, p. 33.

33. Ibid., p. 53.

34. Chang, *The Rape of Nanking*, p. 94. Concerning Iris Chang's fearsome interpretation of historical materials, refer to: Higashinakano Shudo, "Airisu Chan no 'Reipu obu Nankin' no Kenkyu (2)–(4)" (A Study of Iris Chang's *The Rape of Nanking* (2)–(4)), *Seiron*, June-August 1999; or *A Study of "The Rape of Nanking,"* (Tokyo: Shodensha, 1999).

35. Timperley, ed., *What War Means*, p. 52ff.

36. "Ex-Chinese Officers Among U.S. Refugees, Colonel and his Aides Admit Blaming the Japanese for Crimes in Nanking," *New York Times*, January 4, 1938.

37. Erwin Wickert, ed., *The Good Man of Nanking: The Diaries of John Rabe* (New York: Alfred A. Knopf, 1998), p. 190.

38. Higashinakano, *Nankin Gyakusatsu no Tettei Kensho,* pp. 258–262.

39. "Memorandum of M.S. Bates, January 25, 1938," in Timperley, ed., *What War Means*, p. 51.

40. Ibid.

41. Lewis S. Smythe, *War Damage in the Nanking Area: December 1937 to March 1938, On the Behalf of the Nanking International Relief Committee*, (n.p., 1938), p. 8.

42. *China Journal,* January 1938, p. 4; February 1938, p. 59.

43. *China at War,* April 1938, p. 70.

44. "Resolution of the Council of the League of Nations, May 27, 1938." in *The China Year Book 1939*, p. 436.

45. Mao Tse-Tung, "Jikyusen ni tsuite" (On the war of endurance), May 26–June 3, 1938, in *Mo Takuto Senshu* (Collected works of Mao Tse-Tung) (Beijing: Gaiko Shuppansha, 1968), p. 237.

46. "Generalissimo's Statement to Friendly Nations" and "Message to Japanese People," July 7, 1938, in *China Year Book 1939*, pp. 416–420.

47. *China Forum,* July 9, 1938, pp. 51, 58.

48. *China Critic,* July 7, 1938, p. 6.

49. Edgar Snow, *The Battle for Asia* (New York: World Publishing Company, 1941), p. 57.

50. Agnes Smedley, *Battle Hymn of China* (New York: Knopf, 1943), p. 213.

51. H.G. Woodhead, in Preface to *The China Year Book 1939*, p. vii.

52. "The Nanking Outrages," chapter 16 of *The China Year Book 1928* (Tientsin: Tientsin Press, 1928), pp. 723–736.

Part Three
Remembering Nanking

7

Reporting the "Fall of *Nankin*" and the Suppression of a Japanese Literary "Memory" of the Nature of a War

Haruko Taya Cook

When a large-scale historical event such as the Nanking Massacre occurs, the parties involved are easily categorized by nationality or race, such as "Japanese" or "Chinese." While such categories do tell us something, these broad representations are far too simple. In Japan, for example, many people have struggled with the legacy of the war in many different ways.

Haruko Taya Cook discusses the censored Japanese press during the war, particularly in an inspiring piece of fiction entitled Living Soldiers, *which was published in Japan shortly after the Nanking Massacre. Cook's powerful pen examines not only the issue of censorship by government, but also a subtler censorship fearful writers and editors imposed upon themselves. Through this examination, Cook provides us with a deeper view of wartime Japanese society as well as the Japanese people's own struggle to learn the truth in spite of censorship.—Eds.*

Starting with the inception of the full-scale war with China following the Marco Polo Bridge Incident near Beijing on July 7, 1937, Japanese news organizations were hard-pressed to meet keen public demand for coverage of the "China Incident" (as it was soon named in Japan). The actions and condition of the hundreds of thousands of Japanese troops— mostly reservists called up to units sent abroad one after the other throughout the summer and fall—were the focus of intense competition among newspapers, magazines, movie news services, and semiofficial and official government agencies, all seeking both to report on the progress of the war and to sustain and develop popular support for what soon became a huge national effort in Japan, as it was in China as well. How those who could publish about it covered the story and one example of how it might have been available to the Japanese public had official censorship not intervened is the topic of this chapter.

The Press and the Battle

When the Japanese imperial forces began their advance to capture Nanking in November, more than 100 reporters and photographers from national and local news organizations followed the advance of Japan's troops. The largest single group operating in China was the thirty-three-member entourage sent by Dōmei Tsūshin, Japan's semiofficial news service.[1] As the fall of China's capital city and the symbol of the Nationalist Party's place in modern Chinese history approached, famous Japanese novelists, poets, essayists, and publicists—with newsreel cameramen and photo journalists along as well—flocked to the theater of operations as special correspondents, many dispatched by newspapers, magazines, and the military services themselves.[2] Soon reports under banner headlines and often individual bylines adorned newspapers and magazines back in the Japanese homeland, purporting to describe the army's advance.

The articles the newsmen wrote, and the pieces the people at home read, described the fall of Nanking during December 1937 and January 1938 through the lens of official sanction. They were narrowly limited versions of what was going on in China. Their focus was directed at the question of when the city of Nanking would fall into the hands of imperial Japanese forces. Public memory of events in Central China would largely be molded by the way issues were framed then. The *Tokyo Asahi Shimbun* headlines on December 7, 1937, read: "TO OUR DESTINATION, NANJING, ONLY A FEW LI," "NANJING IS A FLAME IN A BLOWING WIND," "OUR IMPERIAL FORCES MIGHT MAKE ENTRY TO THE CITADEL TODAY" and "THE FIERCE ADVANCE TO THE WALLS OF THE CITADEL." The *Asahi* newspaper set up a headquarters at the foot of Jijin Mountain, just outside the city wall, and dispatched reports illustrated by an accompanying map of the city of Nanking, about the "fierce" charges of December 11, providing the names of the units at the walls as if they were broadcasting live by radio:

All the artillery pieces in front of the XX Gate fired and roared at once, their echoes shaking the earth. This is the great cannonade that adorns the fall of the Citadel of Nanjing. [The men of] Wakisaka Unit continued their blood-spurting, severe combat over several tens-of-hours with several thousand enemy soldiers defending the walls in the vicinity of Guanghua Gate. In order to get behind these enemy forces, Isa Unit fought bloody battles by charging between Zhongshan Gate and Guanghua Gate. . . . The unprecedented bombardment of guns and cannons in the total offensive on Nanjing clouded the sun so that the Citadel of Nanjing grew dark. The reports and echoes of the great cannons deafened the ears. The outskirts of Nanjing were now a magnificent battlefield.[3]

Despite the rhetoric, the newsmen were only covering the story exactly along the lines provided by army headquarters. Their perspective is completely that of Japanese military authorities and not that of either troops or independent observers.

The occupation of the southern areas and the first entry of the Japanese troops into the city around noon on December 12 were expressed in large headlines like "THE JAPANESE FLAGS FLUTTERED ON ALL THE SOUTHERN WALLS OF NANJING," "RUSHED INTO THE CITADEL LIKE A TIDE," and "LARGE SCALE HEROIC STREET-TO-STREET FIGHTING IN DARKNESS." In a special telegram, the statement made at 8 P.M. by the Shanghai army was reported as follows:

Our Army broke through and occupied the Guanghua Gate and its eastern wall salient, and the Zhongshan Gate and its eastern wall salient, occupied all the southern walls of Nanjing Citadel around noon on the 12th, and hoisted Sun Flags [above them]. While eliminating dogged enemy resistance and repelling stubborn counterattacks by the enemy, the forces advancing into the city exchanged ferocious street-to-street fighting and pressed the enemy northward gradually.[4]

The *Asahi* newspaper's front-line headquarters dispatched passages full of heightened emotions and dramatic metaphors, justifying and glorifying the official announcements of the day's events in flowery phrases:

The Imperial Forces entered the Citadel of Nanjing. The conquering arrows of the imperial nation sharply pierced through the heart of Shina [Japan's slightly pejorative name for China] that was mad with murky anti-Japan sentiments. The time was 12:30, the 12th day of the 12th month. It was an historic moment that will eternally decorate world history. Looking up, the sun-disk flags flutter soul-stirringly. The kindling fires of justice that symbolize permanent peace in the East were raised by the hands of the officers and soldiers high into sky [above] the capital Nanjing.[5]

On the page, as a part of the news from the fronts section, there appeared a brief report of how four Chinese ships and large numbers of junks bearing about 1,000 fleeing Chinese soldiers away from the city were bombarded and "sent to the ocean [*sic*] bottom" in the Yangzi River. That small article, rather than expressing any concern over the fate of the defeated soldiers, provides one additional concrete, triumphalist piece of evidence marshaled by the journalists to demonstrate to their wartime readers the accomplishments of the imperial forces.

The overwhelming tones of victory and glory in which the reports from the fronts in China were couched seem to us today so malevolently distant from the realities of the time—not only about the enemy side but also about the Japanese side—that they virtually leap from the page. It seems impossible for knowledgeable readers today to miss the implications of the *Tokyo Asahi* report of December 16 that an estimated 60,000 enemy soldiers were reported "captured or annihilated" as a consequence of the mopping-up operation against "stragglers," described as "hiding and popping up again" throughout Nanking.[6] This description appears in the same sentence as "the acquisition of numerous war trophies," making the capture or killing of the defeated soldiers part of a successful and proud achievement.

The Reaction "Back Home" in Japan

In Japan, these developments in the conflict in China were greeted with excitement and exhilaration, at least if we are to judge from the pages of the country's newspapers. Even before the fall of Nanking, elementary school boys and girls waved flags, and students of the Tokyo Foreign Language School shouted *"Tenno heika banzai"* (Long live the emperor!) in front of the Imperial Palace. A wide range of victory celebrations was already in full swing on December 12, even though Japanese forces had not yet officially taken the whole city. "Victory sales" began along the market streets of Ginza, Kyobashi, and Nihonbashi. One noodle shop owner put "Fall of Nanjing Noodles" on sale for the occasion; the dish featured a piece of tempura as a bomb beside a sun-flag–shaped fish cake. An image of the crying face of Chinese President Chiang Kaishek on a large lantern was prepared for a celebratory parade, among other large numbers of lanterns for festive parades to come. A fishmonger delivered a celebration tai-fish to the residence of the army minister.

At 6 P.M. on December 12, it was reported that about 1,500 members of the National Defense Women's Association planned to march together with the geisha members of the Patriotic Women's Association.[7] Considering that the official announcement of the fall of Nanking only reached Tokyo the night of December 13, it is undeniable that the newspapers were doing quite a job of whipping up the feelings of the people for this conflict.

Intellectuals were vociferous as well, joining the almost-premature celebration of December 12. Sasaki Nobutsuna composed several poems for the occasion, choosing the five-seven-five-seven-seven syllable *waka* form. One poem read, "Our Imperial forces enter the Citadel of Nanjing, this day should be written in gold letters in our history." The novelist Yoshikawa Eiji wrote an essay analyzing the fall of Nanking as "a turning point in Eastern history" after voicing criticism of Chinese dependency on Britain since the Opium War of 1840–1842.[8] Photographs of the honored war dead also adorned the papers, captioned "Sublime! The protective flowers of the nation." They were displayed next to the photographs of the parades to celebrate the victory over China. Sugawara Harumi, thirty-three-year-old widow of Lieutenant Sugawara Umekichi, forty-one years old, of the Fujii Unit, who "fell like a flower" at Shikinsan (Jijin Mountain) in the battle of encirclement at Nanking, was quoted as follows: "All of us were anxious to receive a letter celebrating entry into Nanjing. I think my husband attained his desire in finding a place to die. I intend to bring up [our] two boys to be excellent military men as he wished."[9] This is how death was narrated in the tone and vocabulary of promoting war at this time.

Front-Line Reporters and their "Diaries"

Tokyo Asahi Special Correspondent Imai, who followed the Japanese troops from Shanghai to Nanking, told the audience at home that "the grand battles in the world of military history were staged magnificently and grandly at the site of a 'fortress impregnable since ancient times' . . . [not a terribly accurate description of Nanking, which had fallen to conquerors several times in its history, most spectacularly in the wake of the Taiping Rebellion in the nineteenth century], after one victory after another throughout four months from autumn to winter." His "diary entries" for the critical two days marking the fall of Nanking were published in *Asahi* on December 16, as follows:

December 12. Again, today all day long the sounds of shelling and gunfire echoed. At night, our unit reached the walls. Tonight or tomorrow
morning, the Japanese flags will be hoisted. We will enter the Citadel,
carrying the remains of Mr. Hamano. After the long hardship of accompanying the troops, I have a sense of something missing, thinking this
soon will be over. Lying on the straw-strewn floor I was sleepless waiting
for a dawn to arrive and imagining what delight will come. Half-way
through the night, the gunfire suddenly halted. The night of victory arrived on the battlefield.

December 13. A sublime day, four months since the incident in Shanghai. At the Zhongshan Gate the three sun-disk flags shine. In rapid suc-
cession, officers and soldiers entered the Citadel and shouted "*Banzai*" at
the top of the [city] wall. Even the remains of the war comrades hanging
from the chests [of the soldiers] wreathed their smiles across the white
cloths [that wrapped their boxes] and entered the city together with the
echoes of the military boots. Wave after wave of soldiers entered
[Nanjing].[10]

Why did Correspondent Imai, who followed the troops from Shanghai to the capital of China, become so blinded and so muted? This kind
of question might not have arisen in the minds of the family members
whose husbands and sons and brothers died on the fronts in 1937, but
more than sixty years later we need to ask whether the "ritualized" images of Shinto Nationalism and loyal soldiers really capture what happened in and about Nanking in those days.

Reports from the front had to be cleared through the Reporting Division of the Imperial Army in China, and then by the desk at their headquarters in Japan; obviously reporters were fettered by many rules
imposed by the military authorities and by their own newspapers. As I
will show later in this chapter, the Home Ministry had the power to
prohibit sales of any publication determined to violate its standards.
More importantly, many reporters, knowing these regulations, no doubt
censored themselves and refused to write what they really saw. (Perhaps
even more frightening is the possibility that they fully subscribed to the
values and actions of the army they were covering and saw nothing to
report at all.) In 1956, correspondent Imai lamented his inability to report the large-scale executions by machine guns at night near the *Asahi*
office in Nanking and Xianguan (Shakan), which he personally witnessed.
Describing the feelings he had nineteen years earlier, he reports that he
and another reporter said, " 'I really would like to write [about it].' 'Some-

day in the future. For awhile we cannot write. But we saw it.' 'Let's go once more [and confirm] with our own eyes.' Both of us stood up. Before we noticed it the sounds of machine guns halted."[11] Even acknowledging the restrictions of war, it is regrettable that Imai's pieces sent from Nanking convey so little of what went on in front of his own eyes.

Special Correspondent Nakamura of the *Asahi* reported on conditions in the city on December 14, 1937. "The horns of automobiles echo in the streets without sound of shelling," he wrote and, surprisingly, noted that 100,000 refugees remained in the city. "Nanjing has come to life again," he wrote. Along the streets of Nanking, Nakamura encountered fellow journalists who emerged from an automobile flying a U.S. flag and introduced themselves as Tillman Durdin of the *New York Times* and Arthur Menkin, a photographer for Paramount. To Nakamura's inquiry, "What were the last days like in Nanjing?" they responded, "Very scary." The most fearful things were shelling from the cannons, they told Nakamura, and the two Americans then described the routed Chinese soldiers' efforts to escape as a "tragic retreat" to Xianguan. Both Americans saw the "tragedies of the world," according to Nakamura. Considering what Tillman Durdin actually reported to the world outside China, in stunning stories that appeared in his paper detailing the horrors caused by the Japanese imperial troops in Nanking, the conversations exchanged among the three correspondents sound quite cryptic.

Writing the "Truth of War" Through Fiction

More than 100 newspaper reporters at the front in China failed to report what they witnessed in Nanking, so that a majority of the civilian population at the home front in Japan remained quite ignorant of the events known as the "Rape of Nanking" or the "Massacre of Nanking" to the world outside Japan. However, among literary authors, efforts were made to write what went on at the front in China. One such writer was Ishikawa Tatsuzō. His work must capture our attention because it reveals a great deal about the nature of that war and those who promoted it, fought it, and suffered from it.

A novelist, Ishikawa Tatsuzō (1905–1985), thirty-two years old in 1937, was commissioned by *Chūō Kōron*, one of the country's leading monthly magazines, to write a war novel. In 1935 Ishikawa had won the first Akutagawa Prize (Japan's leading prize for fiction) for *Sōbō* (The Common People), a novel about Japanese immigrants to Brazil based on his own experiences for a brief time in 1930.[12] When *Chūō Kōron* wanted an on-the-scene writer, its editors turned to him, and Ishikawa soon found himself headed for China with an open brief to write a novel about the war there.

Ishikawa left Kobe by military freighter on December 29, 1937, and landed at Shanghai January 5, 1938. Together with five Imperial Army officers he had met aboard the ship—men heading to Nanking to take up positions of platoon and company commanders, replacing those who had been killed in action—he made his way through several cities to the capital, 100 miles up the Yangzi River. He stayed in Nanking from January 8 to January 15.[13] During his brief visit in China, Ishikawa collected materials for his potential work, speaking with the men in the Thirty-Third Infantry Regiment of the Sixteenth Division.[14] He then returned to Japan.

Back home again, Ishikawa Tatsuzō produced a 330-page manuscript in just eleven days. "I exerted all my strength," he declared later. "I did not leave my desk while I was awake," setting down, "an average of thirty manuscript pages each day."[15] He entitled the work *Ikiteiru heitai* (Living soldiers) and submitted it to his magazine. Scheduled for publication in March 1938, the novel was suppressed by the authorities, and the case escalated with the indictment and prosecution of its author and publisher.

What was the nature of the work that was at the center of controversy early in Japan's war with China? What characteristics of the fighting that Japanese newsmen refused to write about did novelist Ishikawa dare to capture in the form of fiction? To answer such questions, let us examine the novel.

Ishikawa's *Living Soldiers* is the story of a platoon in the Japanese Army in the month before the capture of Nanking on December 12, 1937, and for some twenty days thereafter. At the onset of the novel a brief passage summarizes the history of the platoon up to the point where the novel begins. The reader learns that the unit landed at Dagu (Taku) in North China immediately after the fall of Beijing to the Japanese on July 31. The men then advanced through dust and swarms of flies throughout the lingering heat of the summer. For two months, they chased the enemy south on both sides of the Shikagawa. Around the time the fall frosts began, the platoon learned that Sekkasō had fallen to their forces. In these operations they lost two company commanders and one-tenth of the men, killed in action. Their division then took a ten-day rest, while awaiting its next orders. Memorial services were held for the war dead, but the men have heard nothing about when they may expect the arrival of a reserve unit to augment or replace them. In sum, then, the men Ishikawa introduces to us are experienced soldiers with more than two months of exposure to action on the North China front, just one part of the vast Chinese theater of war. Instead of being sent home, the men then find they are moving on to new battles. In fact, the military moves Ishikawa attributes to his platoon's division coincide with those of the Sixteenth Division from the Kyoto region, which became notorious at Nanking.[16]

After this short introductory passage, *Living Soldiers* opens with a scene in which Corporal Kasahara catches a Chinese youth near a burning house behind the regimental headquarters. Questioned by an interpreter named Nakahashi, the youth retorts that he has the right to set fire to his own house. Kasahara takes him to the creek nearby. At the sight of Kasahara pulling his sword from its scabbard, the youth falls to his knees in the mud and begs for mercy, screaming out something incomprehensible. Kasahara casually brings his sword down, then kicks the youth's lifeless body into the river. The scene is both graphic and explicit:

> Instantly the cries of the young man ceased and the field was restored to a quiet evening scene. The head did not fall off, but the cut was sufficiently deep. The blood gushed out over the shoulders before his body fell. The body leaned toward the right and dropped into the wild chrysanthemums on the bank, and rolled over once more.[17]

Ishikawa Tatsuzō does not describe the strategy and tactics of the great battles in which his men participate, although he uses the advance of the Japanese forces to Nanking as the chronological skeleton for the work. He focuses on the behavior and mental state of individual soldiers, noncoms, and officers who find themselves in a war, something he sees as "a matter for the state." The protagonists of the novel are a group of soldiers of Kurata Platoon, Nishizawa Regiment, Takashima Division. They are divided between two general types. The first is exemplified by Corporal Kasahara, a farmer who is able to keep a cool head in any combat situation and can kill without hesitation. Buddhist chaplain Katayama also belongs to this category. We come to know him as a man who can beat captured enemy soldiers to death with a shovel in one hand and a priest's Buddhist rosary in the other.

Shouting in his hoarse voice [Katayama] chased after enemy soldiers who ran away through one alley to another. Even the enemy soldiers were unfamiliar with the details of the town. Blind alleys and lanes are everywhere in Chinese cities and towns. When cornered in cul-de-sacs, the enemy abandoned their arms, jumped into the houses, threw away their uniforms and put on the residents' clothes. But, they did not have time to take care of the uniforms removed.

"You! . . ." soon after he shouted with his thick voice, the Buddhist chaplain beat horizontally with a shovel. Without a blade, the shovel thrust into the head half-way. With blood spouting [the man] collapsed.

"You! . . . You! . . ."

The Buddhist rosary on his wrist made dry sounds while he killed, beating one after another. He wiped away the sweat streaming from forehead to the beard with the sleeves of his military uniform, and slowly stepped out the alley using the bloody shovel as a cane.[18]

The second category of Ishikawa's soldiers are three men with enough literary education to qualify for status as members in the first rank of Japan's prewar "intellectuals." Second Lieutenant Kurata was once an elementary school teacher, Private First Class Kondō was formerly a medical student; and Private First Class Hirao had been a proofreader at a newspaper.[19] Kurata continues to keep a diary even after the most severe combats. He wonders whether or not he should write a letter bidding farewell to his pupils, since that might cause a shock to their young minds. He is one of those rare characters who are able to think from the enemy's perspective. Kondō, who arrived at the front with a medical student's respect for human life, comes to realize that life is not something to venerate and concludes that his intelligence is of no use in the war. A romantic, urban youth, Hirao suffers emotionally; his delicate mind is unable to maintain its balance, and he becomes totally confused.

The men of this group go through an agonizing process of losing their sensitivity, their reverence for life, and their "intellectual morality" in the face of their own deaths. After they are freed from delicacy and the ability to reason, they at last become comfortable at the front and can face combat. They cease to be men and seem to turn into animals. After one battle, Ishikawa describes them that way. Ishikawa's original draft, as presented to his editors, included the words struck out below but omitted from the work published in 1938[20]:

The friendly force headed for Changzhou chasing the stragglers, while the [Nishizawa Regiment] [replaced by Unit in the printed version] took rest in Wuxi for three days. It was in such a situation that the surviving men most desired women. They walked around with large strides inside the town and searched for women like dogs chasing a rabbit. This aberrant behavior was strictly controlled at the battle front in northern China. However, it was difficult to restrain their behavior here.

They came to feel proud and willful, as if every one of them was an emperor or a tyrant. When they failed to achieve their objectives in town, they went out to civilian houses far outside the wall. They could run into perils from stragglers who were hiding themselves and from armed natives in the area. But the soldiers had no sense of either hesitation or scruples. They felt as if none would be stronger than they themselves in the world. Needless to say, morality, law, introspection and humanity completely lost their power in the midst of such feelings.[21]

By the end of the novel, every character has taken on the characteristics of Kasahara, a man who does not flinch from slaughter. Ishikawa concentrates on the intellectuals, and we are shown how each is transformed from human being to a full-fledged soldier. The author seems to assert that war must draw out the worst in men. Ishikawa's all-mighty narrator states,

"A battlefield seems to have such mysterious and powerful effects that a battlefield makes every combatant the same in character even when one is unaware of it, and makes each think only of matters of the same level and demands the same [of everyone]."[22]

Living Soldiers reveals some of the characteristic ways in which the imperial Japanese forces conducted their war in China, bringing out the horror and atrocities committed against both enemy soldiers and Chinese residents in the areas through which they passed. First of all, the Japanese imperial forces advancing into south-central China abandoned the requisition policies that were exercised in the north for keeping the population passive. Despite many violations and exceptions, the policy in northern China was to purchase food and supplies in the areas in which they operated. ("Requisition" was the term used, and refusal was not possible, but a reasonably appropriate price was supposed to be paid.) Many of the provinces and subprovincial areas that were the theater of operations in the north were "homelands" of semiautonomous warlords who were potential "allies" of the invaders. The men on whom Ishikawa's novel is based found the rules changed when they moved to the Shanghai-

Nanking heartland of the Nationalist Party. The new mechanism adopted to feed their men by the advancing troops was "local acquisition," also described as "free forage." Such a policy, which was little less than a license to loot and confiscate anything, was justified by difficulties in transporting food for troops for which no supplies had been laid in and who were advancing at high speed ever deeper into the interior. Ishikawa's narrator states that it would have cost too much to do anything other than "free forage."[23] The list of items the troops foraged included rice, vegetables, sugar, pigs, horses, and oxen.

The soldiers Ishikawa portrays at the front are neither glorified nor beautified, although in combat they do fight bravely and are killed. Whenever fighting ceases, no matter how briefly it may be, he shows them foraging for food and "fresh meat"—the euphemism for women.

> The water buffalo has started walking along unconcernedly, [raising] a cloud of dust in the path. The men have begun to feel good. There are unlimited riches on this continent. And ~~[the men] seize~~ [them] as if the continent's riches were theirs. ~~The private possessions~~ of the residents now lie open to the desires of soldiers, as if [they] were wild fruit.[24]

An example of a battle can be seen in Ishikawa's description of the seizure of Wuxi. At first, the defenses of Wuxi are solid. After fierce offensive battles extending over two days, the gates in the walls are still not pushed through. The battle continues throughout the night. On the morning of November 26, Wuxi finally falls into the hands of the Japanese forces. The regimental flag bearer is killed when a bullet pieces the left side of his chest. Victorious, the Nishizawa Regiment takes a three-day rest while the remaining troops chase the stragglers to Changzhou (Jōshū). Against the background of these events, Ishikawa then describes behavior unbounded by morality, laws, or reflections.

> It was in this [type of] situation when the surviving men most ~~desired women~~. They wandered through the city, taking large strides, ~~and searched for women as if they were dogs chasing after rabbits. Such reckless behavior was strictly controlled~~ on the northern front, but it was impossible ~~to restrict their behavior~~ after arriving in this area [i.e., Central China].
>
> Each one of them came to feel proud and egocentric like an ~~emperor~~ and a tyrant. When they were unable to ~~attain their objectives in the city~~ they went out to the houses far outside the walls. . . . A soldier returned with a ~~silver ring on his medicinal finger~~ [his ring finger, in Japan used for scooping medicine].

When asked by his comrades, ~~"Where did you get it?"~~ he responded with a laugh, "This is ~~a keepsake from my dead wife."~~[25]

Ishikawa shows how Japanese soldiers slaughter the captured and set fire to the houses before they move on to their next fight. They brutally kill Chinese civilians, both men and women, on their advance to Nanking. The author seems to assert that those acts are carried out because of war. War seems to have its own logic, separate even from time and place.

Ishikawa does not rely on a binary of uncivilized versus civilized as a vehicle for writing *Living Soldiers*. Unlike other popular writers such as Hino Ashihei and Ueda Hiroshi, who presented Chinese people as inferior to Japanese, Ishikawa revealed an empathy for both Chinese and Japanese soldiers, referring to them as "patients who suffered from the same illness" imposed by their states."[26] His omnipotent narrator points out that Japanese soldiers find comfort in their casual conversations with Chinese, even while they "despise them."[27] Ishikawa shows the current military and political relations between the two nations while pointing out his criticism for the general contempt directed at China and the Chinese. In this limited sense, Ishikawa does not fall into the trap of Japan's "Orientalism," choosing to recognize it even when he does not name it."[28]

"On to *Nankin*!"

The soldiers of the novel continue their advance. They enter the city of Tanyō. All the soldiers begin to think about Nanking. They want to stay alive until the battle for Nanking. The fall of Nanking might mean a victorious return home, they hope. It gave them a great goal. Ishikawa depicts an incident, on the second day in Tanyō, in which Second Lieutenant Kaname of the Third Battalion is shot to death by a girl aged eleven or twelve while making his rounds, checking the security of his unit. The girl runs into a house, but then the soldiers shoot her to death, together with an old man. "All right! It's decided! If they have such ideas, we will kill all the Chinese. We make fools of ourselves if we restrain ourselves [from killing them]. Murder them!" Ishikawa's narrator describes the difficulty in distinguishing between combatants and noncombatants. It is the norm, he writes, for Chinese soldiers to remove their uniforms and mingle with the "good residents," while wearing the armband bearing the sun disk (which identifies them as sympathetic to

Japan). The closer the unit approaches to Nanking, the stronger and deeper the anti-Japan ideology permeates, he says. After the Second Lieutenant Kaname incident, the military authorities issue an order stating, "Because of the strong anti-Japanese ideology even among civilians in the western areas, one needs to look out for women and children. It is all right to kill, to shoot anyone who resists."[29] This order, described by the novelist, gives us insight into the Japanese military authorities' policy that in effect gave their men license to kill any civilians under suspicion.

When the enemy loses Changshu, Wuxi, and Changzhou,[30] many Chinese troops rush into the walled city of Nanking, which is further surrounded by hills and Mount Jijin. In this situation, *Living Soldiers* again indicates that military authorities approved the killing of any Chinese soldiers captured.

> In this kind of pursuit combat, the treatment of the captured was a problem for any unit. At a time when [we] were about to commence a desperate battle, [we] were unable to advance while guarding and taking along the captured. The easiest method of disposing of them is to kill. However, when [we] had once accompanied them, it was laborious even to kill [them]. "When one takes a captive, kill the captured at the site." It was not an order exactly. But these kinds of policies were dictated from above.
>
> In this kind of situation, Corporal Kasahara carried it out bravely. He continued to sever [the heads of] thirteen who were chained like a rosary, one by one.
>
> They were in official military uniforms, but were barefooted. [They] carried long, thin bags containing baked rice on their backs and wore blue cotton long-coats stuffed with cotton. Two of them appeared to be noncoms and were properly dressed and had shoes on.
>
> The thirteen were taken to a stream at the edge of an airport and made to line up. As soon as Kasahara unsheathed his dull sword with its nicked blade, he cut, lowering his sword deep into the tip of the shoulder of the first man. The remaining twelve instantly knelt down on the ground and prayed, screaming and slavering. Two in particular, the men who looked like noncoms, trembled miserably. Further, Kasahara cut the second and third soldiers without any time between.[31]

At great cost, the regiment presses on and succeeds in making Zijing Mountain, the ridge overlooking Nanking. During this attack, men sleep in a skirmish formation on the frosty mountainside, side by side with "fallen war comrades," protecting the corpses. A soldier takes his coat off and covers himself and his fallen buddy with it. At one point, the transcendent narrator of *Living Soldiers* describes the soldiers' feelings toward the dead and their remains:

> They did not have the eerie sensations and feelings of repugnance toward these remains that might be felt about ordinary dead or corpses; contrarily [they] felt particularly close [to the remains]. The bones themselves seemed to be still alive. They each might have felt already that his [own] life was only a temporary form and that within the day he might become just like the bones. They might be just living remains.[32]

Skillfully, Ishikawa presents the notion that, in battle, there is no clear distinction between life and death. Rather, a total confusion between the two takes place. He suggests that this confusion is reality for soldiers at war in China.

Ishikawa's portrayal of the enemy dead is extremely powerful, yet callous, using concrete language. Two examples of the matter-of-factness of enemy death make this clear.

> Still, the dead bodies were lying on the wide streets, too. They became black and withered as the days passed. Eaten away by cats and dogs overnight, the bodies grew leaner each succeeding day. One was literally a skeleton already, its legs mere bones. The corpses got so old that they looked like mere trash.[33]

And later,

> "Hey, Kondō, this guy has shoes on. [He] still intends to escape. Aha ha ha [laugh]!" A dead body covered by a straw mat lay in front of a tobacco shop [Kasahara] had chanced to pass. Five cats kept a sharp watch on it. The cats, on guard, glared into the street, the tips of their noses red and wet.[34]

Graphic and expressive descriptions of the horrors of the dead of one's own side are not to be found in the pages of *Living Soldiers*.[35] Instead, we see the bones of soldiers borne to the next battle by their comrades.

From the crest of Zijing Mountain, the soldiers see the city of Nanking in a "whirlpool of flames."[36] They enter the Chinese capital on December 13; go past Xianguan Station; and then make their way to the pier, where they see the Yangxi again. The narrator describes the scene: "The mopping-up operation in the walled city of Nanjing by the friendly forces were particularly ghastly this day." The enemy (Chinese) stragglers escape through the Jūkō Gate and attempt to cross the river, grabbing anything that floats, including logs, tables, and wooden doors. "The number was about 50,000 who [attempted to] cross the river, turning the water black. . . . The machine-guns open up, echoing. . . . The final coup de grace was administered to the floating stragglers by the attack of the [Japanese Navy] destroyers."[37] For the platoon, this battle is over.

Soon, Japanese merchants move up from Shanghai to establish commissaries in the city. "Comfort places"—brothels for the soldiers—are opened.

> They bought a ticket and waited in the long lines. One came out between the iron lattices and the next one was allowed to enter. The one who came out tightened his belt and grinned toward the lines and went back shaking his shoulders. This was an expression that he was "comforted."
>
> On the both sides of the alley, there were 5 or 6 tiny houses. In each house was a woman. The women were Chinese *kunyan*. The women had rouge on their cheeks with short hair. They had room to put cosmetics on at this time. They provided service to the military men of the enemy nation for thirty minutes, whose language and background were totally unknown. To provide safety to women, the military policeman stood with a bayonet at the entrance of the lattices.[38]

Things have settled down to "normal." But, after a brief stay in Nanking, the regiment moves on, bound for an unknown destination. The war continues. There is no final resolution for the men, and no end to the war even seems possible. Thus ends the novel Ishikawa Tatsuzō set down for his publisher.

The Publisher and the Story

Chūō Kōron (Central review) is perhaps best known as the monthly magazine that played a central role in Japanese democratization in the 1920s. Together with *Kaizō* (Reconstruction), *Chūō Kōron* reigned over the magazine world among the intellectuals, priding itself in upholding its liberal tradition even at the onset of war with China.

Something of a golden era for Japanese magazines came with the war. The stars who emerged through their fiction would become much-sought-after bearers of the story of Japan's war.[39] Each magazine was seeking both originality and sensation to capture the attention of the Japanese public and satisfy their demand for news.

When Ishikawa's manuscript was read by his publisher, the book struck all at *Chūō Kōron* as a powerful, dangerous piece. From the start, suppression of Ishikawa's new work was not completely unexpected by the editorial staff. Editor-in-chief Amemiya Yōzō later recalled:

> While reading this [the manuscript], I thought it would either be crushed or it would achieve a great hit. I made the decision to carry it with that [last] expectation. It was my ambition and gamble as editor-in-chief. . . . Reading it at the proof stage, I thought "this might be [it]." There was no other work to replace it. I touched up the work.[40]

When the March issue was published, *Living Soldiers* was placed in the back of the magazine, with separate pagination, beginning with a new page 1, as if in anticipation of censorship.

Ameniya's concerns were appropriate in the atmosphere of the late 1930s. Numerous publications were banned, and could not be sold or distributed.[41] Yet, as Hatanaka Shigeo—a member of the magazine's editorial staff at the time—describes it, there was a sense of resistance among the editorial staff: "[We] dared to publish, taking a calculated risk. Long-standing resentment toward those arrogant people who were conducting the war, and our dissatisfaction with the unreasonable war must have been factors in our psychology."[42]

At least this is what they say looking back on it decades later. Clearly, they ran a great risk in publishing *Living Soldiers*. They also had considerable experience at running such risks. *Chūō Kōron* and *Kaizō*, each with a monthly circulation of approximately 100,000 in the early 1930s (compared to about 1 million for a leading daily newspaper like the *Asahi Shimbun*), have even been called by one student of prewar mass media "an excellent test of permissiveness" for censorship based on political content.[43] Again and again, the journal *Chūō Kōron* was "tested." Its liberalism of earlier days had slipped considerably by the time the "China Incident" began in July 1937.[44] According to Hatanaka Shigeo, *Chūō Kōron* provided opportunities to publish to authors who were accused, arrested, and released under the Peace Preservation Law of 1925. At the same time, the magazine also carried writings from military men to stave off censorship. Hatanaka said that kind of article was referred to jokingly among the magazine's staff as "our magic shields."[45]

In fact, the editors who published Ishikawa's novel were not as bold in their defiance of government-imposed standards as they recalled later. Prior to the scheduled publication in the March 1938 issue, *Chūō Kōron* conducted its own extensive prepublication self-censorship. As a result, Ishikawa's 330-page manuscript was reduced by 80 manuscript pages. Numerous words, phrases, lines, and even pages, were deleted, as we shall see below. The traces of the cuts were clearly noticeable throughout. Lines of periods, ellipses, empty circles, and sometimes completely blank spaces pockmarked the pages of the magazine in place of the omitted words. Moreover, the last two chapters were completely deleted, indicated merely by two dotted lines.[46] It seems appropriate to ask, in light of the mentality of the editorial staff described above, why was the novel cut so severely? Indeed, it may even well be asked, why did they attempt to publish?[47]

The publishing date of the March issue was scheduled to be February 19, 1938. On February 17, a copy of the March issue of *Chūō Kōron* containing *Living Soldiers* was submitted for inspection to the Book Section of the Home Ministry—responsible for keeping control over literature—while the magazines went to the distributors. The editorial members at *Chūō Kōron* spent February 18 anxiously, dreading a possible phone call from the authorities, but it was not until that night— while Ishikawa and the editorial staff were celebrating the novel's publication—that they learned that the Home Ministry had issued an announcement prohibiting publication of *Living Soldiers*.[48] The editors, office clerks, errand boys, and the whole distribution net now had to race through the darkened streets of Tokyo to local police stations, where the issues were stacked in great bundles. The novel had to be cut from each magazine individually, meaning that 105 printed pages had to be sliced out of about 600 bound pages,[49] leaving a flappy-covered remnant with only the table of contents showing that *Living Soldiers* had been at the back of the issue.

Keeping the Lid on *Living Soldiers*

Ishikawa Tatsuzō knew that it would not be enough to present his work as a novel; he felt he had to emphasize that it was fiction. His brief postscript to the novel declares, "This manuscript is not a faithful record of actual battles. The author has attempted a free creation. Please understand that the names of units and officers and soldiers are all fictitious."[50]

In other words, the first censorship of this work was no doubt undertaken by Ishikawa himself. The Nishizawa Regiment in *Living Soldiers* entered the city of Nanking on December 13, 1937. The omnipotent narrator introduces the unit's entry into the city with the phrase, "The mopping-up of the friendly force within the walled city was most ghastly," as we saw above.[51] It then describes Japanese machine guns opening fire on Chinese stragglers in the river. Such mopping-up operations, inside and outside the city walls, continue in the novel on December 14, 15, 16, and 17. The reader is never told what the protagonists did on these days. Ishikawa says no more about Chinese civilians or captured soldiers in Nanking.

Interestingly, in light of the later notoriety and arguments over the fate of the city, many other contemporary Japanese observers were not so delicate. For example, a special telegram from the Shanghai office of the *Asahi* on December 15, 1937, reported:

> All imperial units that brought about the fall of the Nanjing citadel gathered within and outside the walls; some [units] participated in operations to mop-up the [enemy] stragglers who hid and then reappeared—and were engaged in putting the city in order. It has been estimated that those captured and annihilated by our forces amount to more than 60,000 men in the battle to capture Nanjing.[52]

A telegram from the *Shanghai Yomiuri,* flashed out at 6:00 P.M. on December 29, stated:

> Damage to the enemy resulting from the attack on the Nanjing defense line to the complete capture of Nanjing has been announced in part. According to precise studies, the number of abandoned enemy bodies alone amounted to the large figure of 84,000, while the total of "our" killed-in-action and injured were about 4800.[53]

Ishikawa's novel purports to be about the month prior to the fall of Nanking. We know, however, that he did not even arrive in the city until January 8. Historically, those days in December—just after the breaching of the Walled Citadel—are when what became known throughout the world as the "Rape of Nanking" began. Many who have unearthed the full horrors of the Japanese Army's actions have said that the massacre went on well into the next year.[54]

When *Living Soldiers* went to the publisher, the next stage in the process of censorship began. By comparing the author's submitted text version to the actual *Chūō Kōron* issue of March 1938 that survived the war, we can examine the publisher's own insight into the effort to avoid censorship by the Home Ministry at the time and under the conditions affecting freedom of expression.[55] The first major cuts were directed at military security issues, and we see the uniform substitution of the word "units" for all references to "divisions" and "regiments." The terms for commanders at each level and military ranks were replaced by "unit commander." Place names survived as they were, with the exception of Dalian (Dairen), in Manchuria, which was deleted and replaced by two ellipses instead of the characters. Nanking, however, is named repeatedly, and seems to glower at us from the pages of the book today.

The editors carefully removed words or phrases that indicate the sexual desires of men, including such things as "sensed brutal carnal desire," "want to torment women," "buy a woman," "bring prostitutes," "geisha,"[56] "forage for fresh meat," and *kūnya* (a Chinese term for a young girl).[57] Also removed were expressions of contempt for life, or particular attachments to it, such as: "[They] won't go back home any more"; [They] bit their lips in silence"; "Life is something like garbage on the battlefield"; and "It is great to be alive."[58]

Graphic depiction of cruel murders of Chinese women by soldiers, the soldiers' ruthless pillaging of food and "fresh meat," and the killing of captives or torching civilian houses were cut severely. One example may show how this was done during the offensive on Mushuku. In this scene, a woman's crying reaches the soldiers when the shooting stops. The group discovers a whimpering seventeen- or eighteen-year-old Chinese girl in a house with her dead mother, who has been killed by a bullet. Night falls. The girl's crying continues with an added tone of lamentation. The soldiers become irritated. The original and the published but suppressed versions of what Ishikawa next described are below. (The words struck out in the example were indicated by ellipses in the version *Chūō Kōron* attempted to publish, showing that some words had been deleted.)

"I'll ~~kill her~~."

So said Private First Class Hirao over his shoulder and dashing out holding his rifle, crouching low. Five or six men stamped out of the trench and ran along the trench chasing him.

They rushed into the pitch-dark house. ~~A figure of a sobbing woman~~ was crouching in the starlight that streamed in through a window broken by shells as it was in the evening. Hirao ~~grabbed the back of her neck and dragged her. The woman was holding the corpse of her mother~~ and didn't let go. One soldier ~~twisted her hands~~ and separated ~~the corpse of the mother. Dragging the lower half of her body across the floor~~, they brought ~~the woman~~ out the door.

Hirao ~~pierced~~ the area of ~~the women's chest with a bayonet~~, while screaming in a shrill voice, as if he had gone mad. All the other soldiers also kept ~~thrusting at her head, stomach, and all over with their bayonets~~. ~~The woman was hardly alive~~ in about ten seconds. ~~She lay~~ worn out ~~on the dark soil~~ like a flat piece of ~~futon. The fresh smell of blood~~, stiflingly and warm, wafted up to the flushed faces of the soldiers.

Second Lieutenant Kurata stretched himself out back in the trench and sensed it from the atmosphere, but he did not say a word. When the excited soldiers returned to the trench, repeatedly spitting saliva, Corporal Kasahara mumbled in a laughing voice, smoking a cigarette in his crouched position, "What a wasteful thing they did, really!"

It is impossible to exaggerate how much his saying that saved Second Lieutenant Kurata from his pain.[59]

While the reader today can see that specific physical acts were removed by the publisher, the implications of these acts survived in the remaining text. In another passage later in the book, explicit descriptions of the slaughter of captured soldiers were edited out. Nonetheless, the reader is still told that the captured Chinese were killed because the Japanese could not drag captives along in their desperate offensive, as in the passage quoted in full above in which Corporal Kasahara cut off ~~"[the heads of] thirteen who were chained like a rosary~~, one by one."[60]

The omission of the final two chapters was the largest deletion made by the magazine's own editors. Chapters 11 and 12 in Ishikawa's original manuscript tell how Privates First Class Hirao and Kondō and Corporal Kasahara go out to look for geisha in Nanking. While drinking sake, Kondō is tormented by his memory of a Chinese woman he once stabbed. Drunk, and mentally deranged, he shoots and wounds a Japanese geisha with a pistol. This leads the military police to an investigation of Kondō, but he is allowed to rejoin his unit, which departs for a new destination. Although it is possible only to speculate on why these two chapters were cut, since no explanations are offered, it seems a reasonable guess that what distinguished the soldiers' actions in this incident is not the act of violence, which did not even prove to be fatal, but the fact that the victim was a Japanese woman.

When the March issue of *Chūō Kōron* containing Ishikawa Tatsuzō's novel was suppressed at the end of February, the author was taken to the Metropolitan Police Office for investigation. His questioning lasted only one day, and he was then released. This is probably why it was such a surprise when, on August 4, nearly six months after the initial arrest, the prosecutor indicted Ishikawa (as author), Amemiya Yōzō (the magazine's editor-in-chief), and Makino Takeo (the department head most related), for violation of the Newspaper Regulations. The first trial began on August 31, 1938.[61]

Records of the pretrial investigation and the trial itself illuminate the state of the author's mind at that time. Ishikawa eloquently explained his motivation for going to the front. "The people view soldiers at the Front as gods," he said, "They think that a paradise will be built immediately on the soil occupied by our forces. [They think] that the Chinese masses are cooperating in this. . . . War," he continued, "is not such a carefree matter. However, I believed that to let the people know the truth of the war was essential in order to get the people to acknowledge the emergency and to adopt a determined attitude toward the situation."[62]

In testimony at his first public trial, Ishikawa described his method:

> I thought that I would be able to grasp the real situation of the war better by mingling with and speaking to soldiers than by having contact with officers. . . . I saw and heard the true feelings of human beings at the front.

What he learned from soldiers was "the progress of battles, from the landings in front of the enemy [outside Shanghai] to the fall of Nanjing" and "how [men] killed the enemy." He personally witnessed, too, "the disastrous scene after the battle in the parts of the city near Xiaguan, Zhongshan Gate, and Suixi Gate."[63] Students of the "rape of Nanking" know that Xiaguan was among the sites where the most horrific massacres were alleged to have occurred in Nanking. His testimony confirms Ishikawa's presence in Nanking either when atrocities were taking place or just after they had occurred, and also provides evidence that he spent time with soldiers who could have been directly involved.

The vast range of issues raised by the Japanese behavior at Nanking cannot be addressed here, but it is possible to get some sense of what Ishikawa actually observed. As mentioned earlier, the regiment with which Ishikawa spent time was the Noda Regiment, in the Thirtieth Brigade of the Sixteenth Division from Kyoto.[64] Thirtieth Brigade Commander Sasaki Tōichi was known as one of the Imperial Army's experts on China during the war.[65] He left a substantial body of writings. One of these, which he himself titled *Senjō kiroku: Chūshi sakusenhen* (Battle records: Operations in central China) was not published during the war years, although he had completed it and it was typeset and ready for publication prior to the end of the conflict.[66] It includes descriptions of the battles for Nanking from the perspective of the brigade commander. The entry in Sasaki's record for December 13 reads:

> Afterwards the captured came to give up in large numbers, reaching several thousands. The infuriated men massacred them, one after the other, defying their superior officers, looking back on the blood shed by many of their comrades, and [recalling] ten days of hardships, each would like to say, "Slaughter them all, whether they're soldiers or not."[67]

On December 14, Sasaki described mopping-up operations inside and outside the wall. Some stragglers hid themselves in villages and mountains and continued shooting. Therefore,

> [We] unsparingly and instantly slaughtered those who resisted or did not show submissiveness.[68]

Such descriptions, unusually frank but still circumspect, may help the reader glimpse the landscape Ishikawa's soldiers passed through, and we may sense what Ishikawa might have learned by looking through their eyes, if not his own.[69]

Isikawa did not set his protagonists in scenes of massacre within Nanking, although he presented them as engaging in brutal murders of Chinese civilians and captives. This could be interpreted as an instance of censorship by the author himself. Perhaps he was consciously avoiding any precise mention of the Nanking massacre in anticipation of the trouble that writing about it might cause him. Yet *Living Soldiers* seems a prelude to the army's entry into the enemy's capital city, and the cruel acts of the imperial forces in the following days are presaged by the author. Ishikawa is saying that killing did not begin after the capture of the capital but was an ongoing activity of the Japanese soldiers.

Ishikawa seems to assert that it is war that causes these acts. Judge Hatta asked Ishikawa at his trial whether or not this kind of writing would "result in injuring [the people's] trust in Japanese military men." Ishikawa's responded directly:

> I tried to damage that. On the whole, it is a mistake for the people to consider soldiers at the front as gods. I believed that the people should see the real appearance of human beings and build true trust based on that. Therefore, I thought I would destroy the mistaken views that people had.[70]

This statement sounds outrageous and unbelievable in the atmosphere of wartime, but his assertion of the intention to damage trust in military men may be taken at face value. This can be true, however, only if it is acknowledged that disclosing the cruel nature of soldiers at war is not necessarily an antiwar sentiment but rather an appeal to "reality" over "romanticism" in a grim life-and-death struggle.

During his pretrial investigation, Ishikawa maintained that, "when I wrote the cruel scenes, I believed they shouldn't end merely in cruelty. I wrote as if the [cruel] behavior took place for justified reasons."[71] For example, Ishikawa himself pointed out to his prosecutors that in the manuscript a Chinese cook is stabbed to death by Private First Class Takei for stealing a piece of sugar that had been saved for the regimental commander's dinner. Ishikawa asserted in 1938 that the killing was justified, but the novel does not leave it there. The incident causes Private First Class Kondō to realize that "a piece of sugar was exchanged for a life" and forces him again to agonize over what life is.[72] It seems that in Ishikawa's logic the fact that he is making a desperate attempt to convince the authorities that he did not deliberately try to injure the image of the Imperial Army may have actually led him in this case to undercut the perceptive argument about the effects of war and violence on men that he so skillfully set out in his novel.

On September 5, 1938, the second day of his trial, Ishikawa Tatsuzō was sentenced to four months of imprisonment with three years of probation for "depicting the slaughter and pillage of non-combatants by, and relaxed military discipline among, the soldiers of the Imperial Armed Forces, and for writing things which disturb peace and order." He was also judged guilty for having put his name on the work. The charge "disturbing peace and order"—an all-encompassing "thought crime"— was levied not only because the passages themselves were likely to cause unrest but because they were written "in the present public knowledge that the China Incident is in progress."[73] Thus the court held that not only was the depiction of the soldiers' behavior a crime, but also that this vague and subjective offense had been committed while his country was at war. Editor-in-chief Amemiya Yōzō received the same sentence. The head of the publishing department, Makino Takeo, was sentenced to a fine of 100 yen. The next day, the prosecution appealed the sentences the court handed down, showing that they considered the sentences far too lenient.[74]

Of course, the vast majority of the readers in Japan did not have an opportunity to see even the *Chūō Kōron* dotted-line version of *Living Soldiers* that the Home Ministry's suppression order kept from publication during the war. But police censorship procedures were not airtight and breaches occurred. According to the *1939 Publishing Yearbook,* a partial translation of *Living Soldiers* appeared in a major Chinese newspaper in Shanghai, under the title *Soldiers Who Have Not Yet Died.* It was used as a tool to attack Japan. The yearbook also reported the discovery that a major newspaper in San Francisco was about to publish a translation, and only last-minute intervention by the Japanese consulate and furious negotiations blocked it.[75]

The Writer and the War

The major Japanese offensive against the Wuhan ("Bukan" to the Japanese Army) cities had begun while Ishikawa's trial was being held. The Cabinet Information Division dispatched its own well-known authors to the front in August 1938 to cover Japan's ongoing battle in China. These so-called Pen Units included twenty-two established male authors, such as Niwa Fumio, Ozaki Shirō, Yoshikawa Eiji, and Kikuchi Kan, and one female author, Yoshiya Nobuko. Painters like Fujita Tsuguji and Nakamura Ken'ichi were dispatched to the front in 1938.[76]

Chūō Kōron suggested that Ishikawa again travel to the front as a special correspondent, but since he was a convicted criminal facing a prosecutor's appeal, permission from the army would be required for him to make the trip. To his surprise, the army's press office not only granted permission, but even provided him with a letter of introduction to the head of the reporting division in Shanghai. It would seem necessary to conclude from such attitudes that the stories Ishikawa wrote in *Living Soldiers* did not bother the army enough to make him persona non grata with officials eager to promote the cause in China.[77] There appears to have been some discordance in censorship between the army and the Home Ministry. While it can only be speculation, it is possible that events unfolded this way for Ishikawa because the military police—Kempeitai—and the special higher police—the Tokkō—were at this time sorting out their respective responsibilities over thought crimes at the onset of the war. In any event, on September 12, just one week after his conviction for "disturbing peace and order," Ishikawa found himself on a flight from Haneda airport, bound again for the war zone.

Ishikawa spent about two months with the army in China from the end of September 1938. Upon his return, he completed *Bukan Sakusen: Senshi no ichibu to shite* (The Wuhan operation: As part of war history), which appeared in the January 1939 issue of *Chūō Kōron*. This time, publisher censorship was hardly required. The author's self-censorship was vigorously at work. His approach is manifestly obvious in his brief postscript:

> The objective was to let the home front know the breadth, depth, and complexity of the war. In other words, as the author, I tried to construct a faithful history of the battles. . . . My attempts to study individuals resulted in a legal problem caused by something written. This time, I have sought to avoid individuals and to observe the movement as a whole.[78]

This attitude probably accounts for Ishikawa's use of a chronology of military operations as his vehicle in *The Wuhan Operation*. Rather than focusing on men in the vanguard of the army, he portrays behind-the-line activities such as automobile transport units, a field hospital, and ship engineering units. There are no central characters, like those in *Living Soldiers,* who reveal their anguished minds in the heat of battle. Graphic descriptions of brutal behavior are totally absent.

Nevertheless, the author does not completely avert his eyes from the soldiers. Ishikawa picks up the "strange fear of being alive" felt by a soldier facing a landing opposed by the enemy.[79] In the final chapter, the seriously wounded Private First Class Kawakami thinks, "When the oblivious Japanese people forget the severity of this war, all that remains is merely this disabled, injured body."[80] Undoubtedly, Ishikawa had to compromise himself in his work, but he did not utterly succumb to the authorities, infusing his works with compelling images of the exploitation of the wartime situation by greedy Japanese merchants and the "National Defense Women's Association," who follow the army and "comfort" the troops.[81] In *The Wuhan Operation* he never adopts the tone of beautification and glorification of the war that we can see in many other writings of the time. Such popular expressions as "sacred war," "imperial forces," and "imperial nation"—which permeate and virtually punctuate novels of this period—appear only once each in the entire novel.[82]

Ishikawa spent the remainder of the war in literary activities. He visited Saigon for the navy. He was an active member of the Bungaku Hō kokukai (Association to Serve the Nation Through Literature).[83] Nevertheless, he again ran afoul of the authorities when he dared to write that the Japanese fighting spirit could not be raised to its capacity due to the fact that the people were not free to express their thoughts.[84] Ishikawa's wartime works were often cut and sometimes they were suppressed, but he always had sponsors and he was frequently in print until the end of the war.[85] *Chūō Kōron*, the magazine that had started him on his war literature way, was not as fortunate. The magazine was shut down in July 1944 for repeated violations of an ever-stricter standard of military and police censorship. Some of its editorial staff, including Hatanaka Shigeo, were imprisoned and treated harshly until the final days of the war and even beyond.[86] What happened during the occupation is the subject for another paper.[87]

Final Thoughts

The question of why the Japanese forces behaved atrociously and aggressively remains unanswered. The primary logical explanation—that war brings out the worst in human beings—which Ishikawa provided for the readers of *Living Soldiers* may not satisfy our inquiry. However, the work certainly tells what happened on the fronts in China, however limited in scope it may appear in retrospect. Furthermore, it indicates the nature of the war in which Japanese troops fought—the killings of the captured, the murky distinction between combatant and noncombatant, the pillaging of all kinds in the advance to Nanking—and shows that those policies were clearly approved by the military authorities. *Living Soldiers* is thus a critical literary document and an important source for those of us seeking to bring out the many suppressed truths in the Japan-China War.

It is quite impressive that after a brief stay at the front—merely eight days—Ishikawa Tatsuzō, a young novelist without his own military experience, put down on paper portraits of men in the battle to capture Nanking that are believable even fifty years later. Despite the multilayered censorship of the time, he also conveyed, through his powerful images, the sweat, smells, and sounds of that war in China. The question of why so many newspaper reporters stopped reporting any of those and became the salesmen of the war also needs to be answered.

Notes

1. Hata Ikuhiko. *Nankin Jiken: Gyakusatu no kōzō* (The Nanjing Incident: The structure of a massacre) (Tokyo: Chūō Kōronsha, 1986), p. 15.

2. A broader discussion of the writers' war can be found in Haruko Taya Cook, "Voices from the Front: Japanese War Literature, 1937–45," unpublished M.A. thesis, University of California–Berkeley, 1994. See Ben-ami Shillony, "The Pen as a Bayonet," in his *Politics and Culture in Wartime Japan* (Oxford: Clarendon Press, 1981), pp. 110–120, esp. p. 117. Donald Keene has written of these times in "The Barren Years," *Monumenta Nipponica*, 33 (Spring 1978), pp. 67–112, and in "Japanese Writers in the Greater East Asian War," *Journal of Asian Studies*, 23 (February 1964), pp. 209–225, which can also be found in his *Landscapes and Portraits* (Tokyo: Kodansha International, 1971). See, too, Donald Keene's survey of modern Japanese war literature in his *Dawn to the West: Japanese Literature in the Modern Era, Fiction* (New York: Henry Holt, 1994), pp. 906–961. "Wartime Travel in China," in Joshua A. Fogel, *The Literature of Travel in the Japanese Rediscovery, 1862–1945* (Stanford, CA: Stanford University Press, 1996), pp. 276–296, is an excellent guide to that neglected subject.

3. *Tokyo Asahi Shimbun*, December 12, 1937. Japanese units were called by their commanders' names rather than numbers for reasons of security, so "Wakisaka Unit" and "Isa Unit" refer to specific Japanese divisions, the latter the Ninth Division from Kanazawa. "Shikinsan" to the Japanese meant Jijin Mountain; Japanese names for the city gates were "Chūzanmon" and "Kōkomon."

4. *Tokyo Asahi Shimbun*, December 13, 1917. "Chukamon" is the name of Zhongshan Gate. *Nisshōki* (translated here as Sun Flags) is a more formal term for *Hi-no-maru* (the Japanese flag).

5. Ibid.

6. *Tokyo Asahi Shimbun*, December 16, 1937.

7. Ibid.

8. *Tokyo Asahi Shimbun*, December 12, 1937.

9. Ibid.

10. *Tokyo Asahi Shimbun*, December 16, 1937.

11. See "I was There," *Special Edition, Bungei Shunjū*, 1956, quoted in Hata Ikuhiko, *Nankin Jiken: Gyakusatsu no kōzō* (The Nanjing Incident: The structure of a massacre) (Tokyo: Chūō Kōronsha, 1986).

12. Ishikawa was the third son of a schoolteacher in Akita prefecture who traced his descent to both warriors and Buddhist priests. If one examines his autobiographical short stories, they seem to evoke a complex and psychologically troubled childhood. His formal education was often interrupted by moves or the financial difficul-

ties of his family—they had to move in with relatives—though he did spend one year at the English Department of Waseda University. He then worked as an editor for industrial papers, writing his fiction in obscurity until his Akutagawa Prize thrust him into prominence. See Nihon kindai bungakukan, ed., *Nihon kindai bungaku daijiten* (Japanese modern literature dictionary), vol. 1 (Tokyo: Kodansha, 1977), pp. 100–104.

13. Pretrial Investigation Report, cited in Yosunaga Taketo, "Senjika no bungaku" (Wartime literature), Part 2, in *Dōhisha Kokubungaku*, no. 2 (Kyoto: Dōshisha Daigaku, 1966), p. 64. Also see Ishikawa Tatsuzō, "Keikenjeki shōseturon" (Experimental theory of the novel), in *Ishikawa Tatsuzō ūsakuhinshū*, vol. 25 (Tokyo: Shinchōsha, 1974), pp. 327–328.

14. Hata Ikuhiko, *Nankin Jiken*, p. 19. The Sixteenth Division was headquartered in Kyoto, while the city of Tsu was the home of the Thirty-Third Regiment of infantry, a part of that division.

15. Ishikawa, "Keikentcki shō scisuron," p. 329.

16. Eguchi Keiichi and Shibahara Takuji, eds., *Nichū sensō jūgun ni'ki; Ichi shichōhei no sensō taiken* (A diary of active service in the Japan-China War: A transport soldier's battlefield experiences), (Kyoto: Hōrotsu Bunkasha, 1989), pp. 21–81.

17. Ishikawa Tatsuzō, *Ikiteiru heitai* (Living soldiers), vol. II in *Sensō bungaku zenshū* (War literature collection), 8 vols. (Tokyo: Mainichi Shimbunsha, 1972), p. 8. Citations are taken from this edition where possible, and are cited under the title *Living Soldiers*.

18. Ibid., pp. 27–28.

19. In the 1930s, when educational opportunities were limited and available jobs scarce, these people were viewed as intellectuals. So, too, were the readers of the *Chūō Kōron*.

20. The struck-out words and phrases were present in the original draft Ishikawa presented to his editors. They cut them from the text when it was printed in the March 1938 *Chūō Kōron*, which was then suppressed nevertheless. That censorship is discussed later in this chapter, but the complete passages are included here to show their full strength.

21. Ishikawa, *Living Soldiers*, p. 41.

22. Ibid., p. 29.

23. Ibid., p. 41.

24. Ibid., p. 19.

25. Ibid., pp. 40–41.

26. Ibid., p. 26.

27. Ibid., p. 44.

28. The depiction of Japan's aggression, in the very best late-imperialist tradition of behavior, can be viewed as within the structure of Orientalism as presented by Edward W. Said in *Orientalism* (New York: Random House, 1978). But Ishikawa does not fall into the trap of Japan's "Orientalism."

29. Ishikawa, *Living Soldiers*, pp. 48–49.

30. Mushuku is Wuxi, Jōshū is Changzhou, and Jōjuku is Changshu.

31. Ishikawa, *Living Soldiers*, pp. 49–50.

32. Ibid., pp. 44–45.

33. Ibid., p. 66.

34. Ibid., p. 66.

35. Asai Tatsuzō, a photographer for *Dime News* at the front in China, said that he did not take pictures of the corpses of the Chinese dead or the Japanese dead because of his certain knowledge that such pictures would not be included in any final films presented at home. Moreover, he said, "You can't really direct your camera at the corpses of your kind." Haruko Taya Cook and Theodore F. Cook, *Japan at War: An Oral History* (New York: New Press, 1992), pp. 205–206.

36. Ishikawa, *Living Soldiers*, p. 60.

37. Ibid.

38. Ibid., p. 69. "Comfort women" and "comfort places" are euphemisms used by Japanese servicemen and civilians during the war. A comfort woman sexually served military men at or near the front. Some were "volunteers"—occasionally women already in the sex trade—while other women were dragooned into sexual service either directly or after being recruited for domestic work or other labor. Comfort women who served officers were primarily Japanese, and those who served soldiers were often Koreans, Chinese, and other women native to the occupied areas. The Japanese military officers organized this structure in cooperation with private business people. See Senda Kakō, *Jūfgun ianfu: seihen* (Military comfort women: Main part) (Tokyo: Sanihi Sheba, 1992), and his earlier *Zoku jfgun ianfu* (Sequel: Military comfort women) (Tokyo: Kōbunsha, 1985).

39. Magazine publishing did extremely well in 1938, despite the rationing of paper that included a tighter allocation of paper for publishing, annual sales growing by 3.7 percent in that year alone, from 72,733,000 in 1937 to 75,474,200 in 1938. The annual report of the publishing industry noted that both general magazines and mass magazines owed much of their growth to their decision to carry war literature. What began as magazine features were eventually to become war novels and war movies. The yearbook stated that even the prohibition on the publication of *Ikiteiru heitai* (Living soldiers) by *Chūō Kōron* became the fuse that led to Kaizō's October 1938 issue, which contained Hino Ashihei's best-selling *Mugi io heitai* (Wheat and soldiers). See Tōkyōdō Nenkan Henshūbu, ed., *Shuppan nenkan Shōwa 14 nenban* (Publishing yearbook for 1939) (Tokyo: Tōkyōdō, 1939), p. 12.

40. See *Shūkan gendai*, September 24, 1961, p. 52.

41. Between 1934 and 1939, the sale and distribution of 4,234 items was prohibited under the Publishing Regulations and Newspaper Regulations. Of these, 1,426 items were declared to be disturbances of peace and order and 2,808 were said to be destructive of public morals. See Hatanaka Shigeo, *Nihon fashizumu no genron dan'atsu: shōshi* (Suppression of free space in Japanese fascism: An abridged history) (Tokyo: Kōbunken, 1986), p. 19. Richard H. Mitchell, *Thought Control in Prewar Japan* (Ithaca: Cornell University Press, 1977), discusses the establishment and implementation of the Peace Preservation Law. His *Janus-Faced Justice: Political Criminals in Imperial Japan* (Honolulu: University of Hawaii Press, 1992) looks even more closely into the political dimension of "thought-crime."

42. Hatanaka Shigeo, "'Ikiteiru heitai' to 'Sasameyuki' o megutte" (On *Living Soldiers* and *Sasameyuki*) in *Bungaku* (Literature), vol. 29, no. 12 (December 1961), p. 93.

43. Gregory J. Kasza, *The State and the Mass Media in Japan, 1918–1945* (Berkeley: University of California Press, 1998), pp. 44–51, has discussed this for the early 1930s. Hatanaka Shigeo said each monthly issue of *Chūō Kōron* was selling

about 60,000 copies when Ishikawa signed his contact to write about the China War in 1937.

44. Kasza documents the process of expanding military control in the 1930s. Ibid., pp. 121–167. The role of the special higher police, the *Tokkō*, is discussed by Elise K. Tipton, *The Japanese Police State: The* Tokkō *in Interwar Japan* (Honolulu: University of Hawaii Press, 1990), esp. pp. 56–73.

45. Interview with Hatanaka Shigeo at his home in Tokyo on February 23, 1989. See also Haruko Taya Cook and Theodore F. Cook, *Japan at War: An Oral History* (New York: New Press, 1992), p. 64.

46. A copy of the 1938 March issue of *Chūō Kōron* is available on microfilm at the Diet Library in Tokyo. The cover of the magazine has a seal indicating a purchase date of February 18, 1938 (unclear), by the Imperial Library. In addition, "fiction column (all)" and "removal" are handwritten on the upper part of the cover.

47. For an extended discussion of the issues of censorship raised here, see Haruko Taya Cook, "The Many Lives of *Living Soldiers*: Isikawa Tatsuzō and Japan's War in China," in Thomas Rimer and Marlene Mayo, eds., *War Reconstruction and Creativity* (Honolulu: University of Hawaii Press, forthcoming).

48. From the point of view of the Book Section of the Home Ministry, Mitchell has speculated that "*Chūō Kōron*'s most serious sin was not the contents of the story, but the fact that specimen copies given the police read different from earlier copies." Mitchell, *Censorship in Imperial Japan*, pp. 287–291.

49. See Cook and Cook, *Japan at War*, p. 65.

50. Ishikawa, *Living Soldiers*, p. 83.

51. Ibid., p. 60.

52. Shimbun Taimususha, ed., *Shina jihen senshi: kōhen* (War history of the China Incident: Part 2) (Tokyo: Kōtoku hōsankai, 1938), pp. 203–215, esp. p. 203. This collection of newspaper reports touted Japan's war on the Continent.

53. Ibid., p. 215.

54. See the discussion in Cook and Cook, *Japan at War*, pp. 39–40. See also H.J. Timperley, *Japanese Terror in China: Documents Revealing the Meaning of Modern War* (New York: Modern Age Books, 1938), for the classic description of the horrors; the appendixes include violent incidents occurring well into February 1938, pp. 157–166. Recent treatments include Fujiwara Akira, *Nankin Daigyakusatsu* (The Nanjing great Massacre) (Tokyo: Iwanami, 1988); Hata Ikuhiko, *Nankin jiken*; *Gyakusatsu no kōzō* (The Nanjing Incident: The structure of a massacre) (Tokyo: Chūō Kōronsha, 1986), and Nankin Senshi Henshū Iinkai, ed., *Nankin Senshi* (History of the Nanjing battle), 2 vols. (Tokyo: Kaikō sha, 1989). See the recent compendium of sources on the incident in Daqing Yang, "A Sino-Japanese Controversy: The Nanjing Atrocity as History," *Sino-Japanese Studies*, vol. 3, no. 1 (November 1990), pp. 14–35. Two recent studies of value by Kasahara Tokushi are his *Nankin jiken* (The Nanjing Incident) (Tokyo: Iwanami, 1997) and *Nankin nanminku no hyakunichi: Gyakusani o mita gaikokujin* (The one hundred days of the Nanjing Safety Zone: Foreigners who saw the Massacre) (Tokyo: Iwanami, 1995). Of course, Iris Chang's *The Rape of Nanking: The Forgotten Holocaust of World War II* (New York: Basic Books, 1997) is a broad treatment of the issue.

55. Isikawa Tatsuzō, *Ikiteiru heitai* (Living soldiers) (Tokyo: Kawade Shobō, 1945). This copy, passed by the censors of the Supreme Commander Allied Powers (SCAP) responsible for screening Japanese publications in occupation-era Japan, is

held in McKeldin Library, University of Maryland-College Park, as part of the Gordon Prange Collection. The National Diet Library in Tokyo holds a copy of the original magazine issue.

56. Strictly speaking, *geisha* refers to Japanese women highly trained in the arts of music, dance, and service. It is extremely expensive to be served by geisha. But the term "geisha" is often used in a loose, broad meaning to refer to all serving women, almost euphemistically for a dancing girl or prostitute. Ishikawa's men use the word in the latter sense.

57. Ishikawa, *Living Soldiers*, passim.

58. Ibid., pp. 12, 39, 70.

59. Ibid., pp. 37–38.

60. Ibid., pp.49–50.

61. Hamano Kenzaburō, *Ishikawa Tatsuzō no sekai* (The world of Ishikawa Tatsuzō) (Tokyo: Shinchō, 1976), p. 121.

62 Yasunaga, "Wartime Literature 2," p. 53.

63. Ishikawa, *Living Soldiers*, p. 64. The Japanese pronunciations and references to Chinese place names were Shakan, Suiscimon, and Chūzanmon.

64. Ibid., p. 65.

65. Sasaki Tōichi died of illness in the Fushun prison in 1955 while he was in Chinese custody.

66. Shōwa sensō bungaku zenshū henshū iinkai, ed., *Shōwa sensō bungaku zenshū, Bekkan: Shirarezaru kiroku* (Shōwa war literature collection, an extra volume: The unknown records) (Tokyo: Shūeisha; 1965), p. 463.

67. Ishikawa, *Living Soldiers*, p. 254.

68. Ibid., p. 257.

69. Repeatedly, Hata Ikuhiko expresses his admiration for Ishikawa's work and notes in particular how remarkable it was that a writer with no military experience could capture so well how soldiers' violence could take place with the silent approval, or even the encouragement, of higher military authorities. Hata Ikuhiko, *Nankin Jiken: Gyokusai no kōzō* (The Nanjing Incident: The structure of a massacre) (Tokyo: Chūō Kōronsha 1986), pp. 19–21.

70. Hamano, *Ishikawa Tatsuzō no sekai*, p. 118.

71. Yasunaga, "Wartime Literature 2," p. 67.

72. Ishikawa, *Living Soldiers*, p. 42.

73. During the trial, Judge Hatta cited nine sections of the book, summarized in the trial record four groups, that he felt depicted illegal and cruel acts such as soldiers stealing an ox from an elderly Chinese woman. See Tsuzuki Hisayoshi, *Senji taiseika no bungakusha* (Literary men under the wartime system) (Tokyo: Kasama Shoin, 1976), pp. 15–16.

74. Yasunaga, "Wartime Literature 2," p. 51. Ishikawa's second trial was held in April 1939. The same sentence was handed down. Ishikuwa's prison term was reduced to three months due to the general amnesty announced on the occasion of the celebration of the 2,600th anniversary of Japan, celebrated in November 1940, according to Hamano, *Ishikawa Tatsuzō no sekai*, pp. 121–122.

75. Tōkyōdō Nenkan Henshubu, ed., *Shuppan nenkan Shōwa 14 nenban*, p. 61. The authorities concluded that some complementary copies of the magazines had been sent out and crossed to China, America and the Soviet Union via sailors. Due to this incident, the Newspaper Regulations were revised so that the publishers had

to submit magazines for review three days prior to the publishing dates rather than two days.

76. See Tsukasa, *Senji taiseika*, pp. 52–61.

77. Hamano, *Ishikawa Tatzuzō no sekai*, p. 126.

78. Yasunaga, "Wartime Literature 2," p. 70.

79. Ishikawa Tatsuzō, *Buken sakusen* (The Wuhan operation) (Tokyo, Bungeishunjū, 1976) p. 57.

80. Ibid., p. 199.

81. Ibid., pp. 114–115, 181. In this novel, Ishikawa never uses the term "comfort women" or *ianfu*, but instead uses *Kokubō fujinkai* (National Defense Women's Association) to mean women serving the troops sexually. This is a colossal euphemism. That organization, officially sanctioned and supported throughout the country, was composed largely of the sisters, mothers, aunts, and female neighbors of Japanese soldiers. It served to mobilize the communities, and helped to send the men off to war with parades and cheers. It steeled the national will to the demands of war. The National Defense Women's Association also contributed to the dispatch of entertainers, including famous actors and personalities to pay visits to the theater of war. Yet there is no doubt what the groups Ishikawa refers to actually do near the front. His is no USO show!

82. Donald Keene. *Dawn to the West: Japanese Literature in the Modern Era: Fiction* (New York: Henry Holt, 1984), pp. 915–916.

83. See Sakuramoto Tomio, *Nihon Bungaku Hōkokukai, Dai Tōa Sensō ka no bungakusha tachi* (The Japanese Association to Serve the Nation Through Literature. The writers of the greater East Asia war) (Tokyo: Aoki shoten, 1995), passim.

84. See *Mainichi Shimbun*, July 14, 1944.

85. While his trial was in progress, Ishikawa wrote a 300-page manuscript; Shinchōsha published *Kekkon no seitai* (The ecology of marriage) in November 1938. This time, Ishikawa adopted the I-novel style, writing from a first-person perspective and basing the book on his own marriage. From 1940 to the end of the war, his literary work drastically decreased, although his essays and discussions on contemporary topics appeared in newspapers and magazines. Mainichi newspapers began to serialize his novel *Naruse Nanpei no gyōiyō* (The behavior of Naruse Nanpei) in July 1945, but they were prevented by the government from continuing the publication after fifteen installments had come out. The reduction of literary publications during this stage of the war was not limited to Ishikawa alone, of course. See Tsuzuki Hisayoshi, *Senji taiseika no bungakusha*, passim, and *Nihon kindai bungaku daijiten*, pp. 100–103.

86. See Cook and Cook, *Japan at War*, pp. 222–227. Mitchell also tells Hatanaka's story in *Censorship in Imperial Japan*, pp. 326–328.

87. See Cook, "The Many Lives of *Living Soldiers*," for an extended discussion of the censorship of *Living Soldiers* under the Allied occupation of Japan.

8

Refighting the Nanking Massacre: The Continuing Struggle over Memory*

Takashi Yoshida

History can be defined as the chronological record of events. The attempt to write what really happened though is much more complex. Because of such factors as the historian's background and the circumstances under which the research is conducted, the creation of historiography is constantly challenged by various sides to controversies. The Nanking Massacre is no exception. In the years following, debates about the Nanking Massacre have been frequently influenced by many factors, including the political agendas of the governments and individuals involved, the international geopolitical atmosphere, and economics.

Takashi Yoshida regards this historiography problem itself as an important and inspiring topic. Examining diverse arguments from China, Japan, and the United States, Yoshida confronts a wide range of controversial topics head-on, from immediate postwar debates to Iris Chang's recent best-selling book The Rape of Nanking. *—Eds.*

Although 1997 marked the sixtieth anniversary of the Nanking Massacre, the persistent debate it has provoked demonstrates that the event has yet to recede either in world history or in public memory. Instead, the Nanking Massacre has become increasingly controversial ever since it was first perpetrated. The proliferation of accounts of the history of

---

*This essay, completed in June 1998, reflects the state of scholarship and available information on the Nanjing Massacre, as well as my personal knowledge of the field, as they existed at that time. For a more current and detailed analysis of the history and memory of the Nanjing atrocities, see my dissertation, titled "The Nanjing Massacre in History and Memory: Japan, China, and the United States, 1937–1999," Columbia University, 2001.

the Nanking Massacre, changes in international politics in Asia, and emotional issues of ethnic and national identity all have contributed to the battle over how the Nanking Massacre is to be recounted and remembered.

Before beginning the discussion, I would like to clarify a point of terminology. In Japanese historiography, progressive historians have wielded the dominant influence, and conservatives and nationalists have been attempting to revise postwar historiography regarding Japan's imperial past ever since the end of the war. Therefore, I will use the term "revisionist" in my paper to indicate the Japanese conservatives who have been challenging postwar wartime history written by progressives. This practice is the opposite of what we find in the U.S. historiography, in which "revisionist" usually refers to progressive, liberal historians revising conservative orthodoxy.

I. Historiography of the Nanking Massacre in Japan, China, and the United States

A. The Asia-Pacific War (1931–1945)

During the Asia-Pacific War each of the nations fighting the war perceived the Nanking Massacre in the context of its own war effort. In Japan, the urge to capture Nanking and to punish "the delinquent Chinese brotherhood" was widely supported. When Nanking fell on December 13, 1937, lantern parades celebrated the victory throughout Japan.[1] Literature, too, celebrated the Japanese victory in Nanking. Both *Shina jihen chūyūdan, kangekidan* (Brave and moving stories of the China Incident) (1938) and *Pen no jūgun* (Pen that follows the army) (1939) emphasized the virtuous morals, bravery, and self-sacrifice of Japanese soldiers in Nanking, as well as their friendship and generosity toward "good"—that is to say, cooperative—Chinese people. Not until after the end of war did most people in Japan associate the fall of Nanking with mass killing.

In China, on the other hand, both the Guomindang and the Communist forces were fully aware of the atrocities that occurred in Nanking, but they regarded the event as just one of many inhumane Japanese assaults on the people of China. Chinese-language newspapers, regardless of their political stance, reported Japanese atrocities in Nanking. For instance, *Dagongbao*, a newspaper considered to be nonpartisan, first reported looting, burning, and murder by the Japanese military on December 17, 1937, and from December 25 on, articles on the atrocities in Nanking frequently appeared in the newspaper.[2] In addition to the accounts in Chinese newspapers, publications such as the Japanese translation of H.J. Timperley's *Japanese Terror in China* (1938) and Shuhsi Hsu's *Documents of the Nanking Safety Zone* (1939), written in English, fully revealed the suffering of the Chinese people in Nanking, in the hope that the world could stop Japanese atrocities in China.

In the United States, too, the brutalities of the Japanese soldiers in Nanking were fully covered in newspapers, magazines, and books. For instance, the *New York Times* and the *Chicago Daily News*, both of which detailed Japanese war efforts in China, reported Japanese atrocities in Nanking during the event.[3] Books such as Timperley's *Japanese Terror in China,* as well as shorter written accounts, also fully described the atrocious treatment of the Chinese civilians in 1937–1938 by the Japanese Army. With the demonization of the Japanese following the American declaration of war against Japan, the Nanking Massacre, as well as other Japanese atrocities such as the Bataan Death March, became increasingly potent symbols of the supposed barbarism of the Japanese race.[4]

B. The Domination of Cold War Politics (1945–1971)

With the end of the war, the Nanking Massacre was for the first time subjected to scrutiny in the international political arena. The Tokyo War Crimes Trials (1946–1948) served as a stage for openly documenting Japanese wartime atrocities, including the Nanking Massacre, to the Japanese public. Beginning in 1947, approximately 200,000 wartime political, economic, and social leaders, as well as teachers and administrative staff members who supported wartime militarism, were purged from schools, the press, private companies, national and local offices, and boards of education. Eager for social change, a majority of the Japanese public (70 percent of interviewees, according to a survey by the U.S. Strategic Bombing Survey) supported Allied occupational policies, including the trials.[5] All the Japanese national newspapers supported the trials and circulated the trials' details throughout the country. For instance, on July 27, 1946, the testimony of Robert Wilson, a doctor who witnessed Japanese brutalities in Nanking, prompted *Asahi Shimbun* to write, "The horrible acts of the Japanese Army have now been revealed to the people for the first time."[6] *Yomiuri shimbun*, on the other hand, condemned the irresponsibility of the Japanese journalists who witnessed the Nanking Massacre, but stopped short of reprimanding the military.[7] The Nanking Massacre, however, failed to become a reminder of the atrocious Japanese military conduct against the Chinese people. Rather, it became a reminder of the atrocious Japanese military that dragged Japan into a reckless war with the United States and that led Japanese to tremendous suffering.

In China, as well, the image of the Massacre was shaped by concerns of national interest, though these interests were quite different. As the Cold War began and the United States became China's enemy, the Chinese government used the Nanking Massacre in its propaganda to accuse American missionaries of facilitating Japanese brutality in Nanking and to condemn the Guomindang for its inability to protect the Chinese people. Following the outbreak of the Korean War, for instance, the national monthly journal *Xinhua Yuebao* in 1951 charged the American missionaries with being "imperialists and fascists" who stayed in Nanking during the Nanking Massacre for the purpose of aiding the Japanese invaders.[8]

On the other hand, in the United States, although public documents regarding the trial were published by the government in the late 1940s, no in-depth study of the Nanking Massacre was published in either the 1950s or the 1960s. Because of the Cold War and Japan's strategic importance in Asia, the Nanking Massacre all but disappeared from the public eye in the United States.

C. The Proliferation of the Histories of the Nanking Massacre (1972–1989)

The reopening of diplomatic relations between China and the American camp in 1972 began a new era in the history and memory of the Nanking Massacre. The Nanking Massacre reemerged on the surface of the public memory in Japan, China, and the United States, and narratives and analyses of the Nanking Massacre proliferated in this third period. In Japan, for instance, an intense battle over how the Nanking Massacre should be recounted and remembered started among diverse groups of different political persuasions (which can be divided roughly into the progressives who confronted and the conservatives who cherished the memory of the "Greater East Asian War") and through diverse media (school textbooks, mass media, and the memories of individuals who had experienced the war). In 1972, both progressive historian Hora Tomio and the *Asahi Shimbun* journalist Honda Katsuichi, who had been outraged at American atrocities in Vietnam, published books that discussed Japanese atrocities in China, including the Nanking Massacre. Their works detailed events in Nanking that had long rested undisturbed in Japanese public memory.[9] Offended by these efforts to remind the nation of the Nanking Massacre, an incident they did not want to confront as a matter of national history, conservative revisionists such as Yamamoto Shichihei (a public commentator) and Suzuki Akira (a writer) attacked the credibility of Honda's account of the alleged killing competitions among Japanese officers, which Honda based on reports from Chinese survivors.[10] However, this debate petered out before the issue became the subject of international attention.

The fight over the history of the Nanking Massacre was revived at a new level of intensity by the 1982 Japanese textbook controversy, which contributed to a significant increase in the number of publications about the Nanking Massacre in Japan, China, and the United States. In Japan, the Study Group on the Nanjing Incident was set up in 1984. Since the founding of the group, its members, such as Fujiwara Akira (a professor emeritus of Japanese history at Hitotsubashi University), Honda Katsuichi (a journalist), Yoshida Yutaka (a professor of Japanese history at Hitotsubashi University), and Kasahara Tokushi (a professor of Chinese history at Utsunomiya University), have published more than fourteen books and numerous articles focusing on the Nanking Massacre. In contrast, revisionists such as Tanaka Masaaki (a World War II veteran) and Itakura Yoshiaki (an independent researcher) have published works that deemphasize the Nanking Massacre or have even asserted that it was fabricated entirely by the Chinese and American governments. Both camps have their allies, and they have fiercely competed for the memory and history of the Nanking Massacre for more than a decade.

Japanese wartime history is no longer merely national; it has become international. In China and in the United States, the historiographical conflict over the Nanking Massacre in Japan has agitated "historians" of the Nanking Massacre. In China, local governments, scholars, novelists, filmmakers, and bearers of personal memories all began to take initiatives in writing the history of the Nanking Massacre, especially after the 1982 textbook controversy. In 1985, the Memorial in Commemoration of the Victims of the Nanjing Massacre was opened to the public in Nanking. In the memorial, human skeletons, photographs, and written accounts of the Japanese atrocities were displayed. The official Chinese estimate of those killed by the Japanese invaders was set at 300,000. In the United States, Chinese immigrants became increasingly involved in writing a history of the Nanking Massacre in the late 1980s, and Chinese-American organizations began to play a key role in telling the story of the Nanking Massacre to the American public. For instance, in the late 1980s, these organizations published open letters in newspapers such as the *New York Times*, in which they refuted denials of Japanese conservative politicians.[11]

D. The Internationalization of the Nanking Massacre (1989–Present)

The end of the Cold War and the death of Emperor Hirohito in Japan, both in 1989, facilitated the process of the internationalization of the history and memory of the Nanking Massacre. Newly discovered government documents, letters, newspapers, diaries, and other historical materials in Japan, China, and the United States have made it possible to conduct a fuller analysis of what happened in Nanking. John Rabe's diary, which illuminates inhumane assaults by Japanese soldiers, was located by Iris Chang during her research on the Nanking Massacre. In 1997 the Yale Divinity School Library published oral history documents by the American missionaries who actively helped Chinese refugees. Kasahara Tokushi's *Nankin nanminku no hyakunichi* (One hundred days in the Nanking Safety Zone) (1995) analyzed the Nanking Massacre from the viewpoint of the people who experienced the Nanking Massacre (Chinese, Japanese, and bystanders) by using a massive array of oral history documents that he and other members of the Study Group collected in China, Japan, and the United States.

In addition, international conferences on the Nanking Massacre held in these three countries, such as Nanking 1937 at Princeton University in November 1997 and the International Symposium on the Nanjing Massacre in Tokyo on December 13–14, 1997, have contributed to educating the public on the issues relating to the Nanking Massacre.[12] In Japanese courtrooms, more than twenty-seven lawsuits have been brought against the Japanese government since 1990 for its misconduct during the war, including the Nanking Massacre.[13] Chinese survivors of the Nanking Massacre have demanded compensation from the Japanese government for suffering that they endured, and their claims have been more eagerly supported by historians, lawyers, and grassroots activists in Japan than by the reluctant Chinese government. Since 1998 more than 200 lawyers have been working on legal cases brought on behalf of Chinese victims of Japan's wartime atrocities.[14] Moreover, the Nanking Massacre has become a symbol of suffering that in one sense unifies "Chinese," regardless of political, racial, and national differences.[15] For instance, the Global Alliance for Preserving the History of WWII in Asia & Pacific, founded in 1994, has thirty-eight member organizations all over the world, each of which is supported by individual members. In the United States, there are twenty-four member organizations. Sponsoring lectures, publications, and photo exhibitions, these groups have been playing a central role in educating the American public in the 1990s.[16]

Japanese conservative revisionists, therefore, have had to respond to critics both inside and outside Japan in the 1990s—critics whom the revisionists regard as enemies. Fujioka Nobukatsu, a professor of education at the University of Tokyo, is probably the most visible spokesman of revisionism in the 1990s. He and his allies now blame the Japanese government, which was formerly considered an exemplar of conservativism, for disseminating "masochistic" versions of Japanese wartime history in school textbooks. Revisionists claim that these textbooks are filled with "dark" and "evil" Japanese atrocities and that the books overlook similar atrocities by other countries that have taken place in world history.[17] They have argued that Japan should have a national history that its nationals can be proud of, but that current history textbooks, especially those used in junior high school, have been eroding national pride among the Japanese youth. For instance, revisionists cannot tolerate the fact that current junior high school textbooks, in use since April 1997, all discuss the Nanking Massacre as a historical event. Even more intolerable to them is the number of the deaths of Chinese people reported by these textbooks. Six out of the seven junior high school textbooks' death tolls estimate that more than 200,000 were killed in Nanking during the Nanking Massacre, the figure that emerged from the Tokyo War Crimes Trials (1946–1948); four out of these six also mentioned 300,000, the figure insisted upon by the Chinese government.[18] Since Fujioka and his supporters condemn these figures as "fabrications" by the Chinese and American governments and claim that only forty-seven civilians were killed in Nanking, the figures mentioned in the textbooks are the objects of their rage.[19] To these revisionists, the death tolls insisted upon by the Chinese government (300,000) and by the Tokyo War Crimes Trials (200,000) were nothing but propaganda aimed at making Japan and the Japanese look "reckless and inhumane."[20]

These revisionists—trapped by their devotion to a nation-oriented history that privileges national "subjects" and often ignores the horrible experiences of others—are not unique to Japan. In the United States, China, and many other nations, one encounters people similar to the Japanese revisionists who assign different values to the lives of different peoples; who justify state-supported mass violence in the name of defending a nation; and who are outraged by past wrongs committed by other states, but cannot recognize those committed by their own.

This international struggle over the Nanking Massacre illuminates the complex battle between those still mired in nation-oriented history and those who are striving to move beyond it. In a world in which atrocities similar to the Nanking Massacre continue to be perpetrated, we can certainly learn an important lesson from the Massacre. We can use it to prevent both the terrible immediate damage of such a tragedy and the mental anguish that becomes a legacy passed on from one generation to another.

II. From "Victim Consciousness" to "Victimizer Consciousness"

In Japan, as in other nations, many different voices have spoken over the years. Even during the Asia-Pacific War, when the nation was making its effort to win the war, one could find antiwar Japanese activists in every aspect of the society, even though they failed to achieve their goal. One such activist organization that existed at the Chinese front was Nihonjin Hansen Dōmei (The Japanese alliance against the war). It had more than 200 members, all of whom were former Japanese soldiers who had been taken captive by Chinese communists. Chinese communists treated Japanese rank-and-file soldiers as allies and educated these Japanese soldiers that the real enemy was not the Chinese people but bourgeois capitalists. The former Japanese soldiers, who were moved by the communists' humane treatment and agreed to fight against the common capitalist enemy, actively engaged in antiwar operations at the front line. They printed and scattered leaflets in order to provoke antiwar sentiments among the Japanese soldiers. They often sent Japanese soldiers "comfort bags," which contained not only soap and towels but also notes bearing the *un*comfortable message that the Japanese soldiers were fighting on the wrong side. In addition, they often cut into phone conversations and explained why they were now fighting with Chinese communists—their former enemy. They appeared on the battlefront with megaphones and loud speakers, encouraging their former allies to surrender and to join Chinese communists in the fight against Japanese militarism.[21]

Immediately after Japan's defeat in 1945, according to the U.S. Strategic Bombing Survey, only 5 percent of the Japanese people expressed the wish that Japan should return to the prewar system.[22] Allied occupational policies were widely supported by the public, and the people regarded wartime leaders as responsible for postwar miseries such as starvation. Although few were able to view the Asia-Pacific War from the viewpoint of victimizer rather than that of victim, the left and liberals overwhelmed the society, including the universities and mass media. Marxist historiography, which substituted scientific history for previously accepted Japanese myth, became an orthodoxy in the Japanese academy.[23] A description of the Massacre, though not in detail, even appeared in the history textbook edited by the Ministry of Education in 1946.[24]

Although accounts that stressed Japan's role as a victimizer that had devastated Asia were published in the 1950s and 1960s, it was not until the 1970s that such accounts became more popular among the public.[25] The Vietnam War gave them an opportunity to think over Japan's wartime past, and liberals not only published writings from the viewpoint of the victims of aggression but also began to take this viewpoint into the classrooms. In the 1970s, the journalist Honda Katsuichi published books that included the personal testimonies of Chinese survivors, accompanied by photographs of many dead, often decapitated bodies.[26] The historian Hora Tomio published historical accounts analyzing the Nanking Massacre.[27] In Nagano in 1970, the annual meeting of Rekishi kyōikusha kyōgikai (Council for history teachers), mainly composed of elementary and secondary school teachers, underscored the importance of a historical pedagogy that focused on the victimizer's aspect of the Japanese wartime past.[28] From the defeat until the 1960s, the war and its visible aftermath were still close enough to provide children with a personal awareness of the terrible past and a conviction that the war was wrong. By the 1970s, however, schoolteachers found that many children had little knowledge of the war and needed to be taught about it.[29]

It was, however, after the textbook controversy in 1982 when teaching that underscored Japan's role as a victimizer became widespread.[30] Adachi Yoshihiko, a high school teacher in Hyōgo prefecture, for instance, wondered why "we [teachers] kept silent about 'Nanking,' while openly discussing 'Auschwitz'" and stressed that teachers should teach the Asia-Pacific War from the viewpoint of both victim and victimizer.[31] A junior high school teacher in Hokkaido, Komatsu Yutaka, also argued that the focus of the teaching of the war should be the role of Japan as a victimizer. Komatsu examined history textbooks then in use and argued that the textbooks were one-sided since they lacked discussions of the devastation in Asia during the war caused by Japanese aggression.[32] Therefore, both Adachi and Komatsu used additional materials as supplements to the textbooks in order to teach their students about the victimizer's aspect of Japanese wartime history. Adachi used Honda Katsuichi's Chūgoku no tabi (Travels in China), while Komatsu used photocopies of a book about Korean forced labor in wartime Hokkaido.[33]

After the death of Emperor Hirohito in 1989, the teaching of Japan's role as a victimizer gained still more momentum. Furthermore, a series of lawsuits have been instituted against the Japanese government in Japanese courts. Among those demanding compensation have been survivors of forced-labor gangs and former "comfort women." Their stories began to lead liberals to consider the issue of compensation.[34] These topics received much attention from school teachers.[35] Yamamoto Masatoshi, a high school teacher in Hokkaido, for instance, reported to his class on the "comfort women" and recorded his students' responses in January 1993.[36] Such movements were reflected in textbooks. History, civics, and geography textbooks that have been used in junior high schools since 1997 include discussions of "comfort women" and the issue of compensation, as well as the Nanking Massacre.[37] In junior high school history textbooks published in 1997, the descriptions of the Nanking Massacre included the high casualty figures mentioned earlier.[38]

Textbooks and history teaching were not the only evidence that "victimizer consciousness" was on the rise. War memorials in Japan also began to allude to the wartime devastation in Asia caused by Japanese aggression. In 1988 the Ōkunoshima Poison Gas Museum was opened on Ōkunoshima Island, Hiroshima. The museum exhibits documents and photographs proving Japan's usage of chemical weapons on the Chinese front. In 1991, when the Maruki Art Museum in Saitama completed its expansion, the new building housed an exhibit titled "The

Nanking Massacre." In the same year, the three-story Peace Osaka was founded and began to show exhibits that included Japanese atrocities in China, Korea, and other parts of Asia. In 1992, Ritsumeikan University's International Peace Museum was opened in Kyoto, teaching visitors about ways of life and war crimes in the Japanese-occupied areas in an exhibit called "The Fact of the Fifteen-Year War (1931–45)." In 1994, an east wing was added to the Hiroshima Peace Memorial Museum to house artifacts from the Meiji period to the Showa period, including evidence of Japanese aggression in China. In 1996, the Nagasaki Atom Bomb Museum was opened to the public, who were able to see an exhibit entitled "The War Between China and Japan, and the Pacific War," which included artifacts and photographs from the Nanking Massacre.[39] As John Dower has pointed out, Japan's wartime role as a victimizer has become a subject of extended discussion among the public in recent years.[40]

Active Japanese civic groups certainly deserve credit for promoting such discussion among the public. Approximately 27,000 activists supported the prosecution of the Ienaga Textbook Trial. This trial, a series of legal actions that continued off and on for thirty-two years, contributed to a more detailed description of Japanese war crimes and atrocities in textbooks.[41] In 1989, the Ministry of Health and Welfare was unwilling to investigate massive human bone deposits that had just been discovered in Tokyo. Frustrated by the official inaction, a civic group began a nationwide tour in July 1993. Featuring a panel discussion and photo exhibitions, the tour traveled to fourteen locations and received approximately 40,000 visitors.[42] Nihon no sensō sekinin shiryō sentā (Center for research and documentation on Japan's war responsibility) was opened in 1993 and has published its quarterly journal since then. Issues regarding Japan's war crimes have been discussed by many leading and prominent scholars in Japan such as Arai Shin'ichi, Kasahara Tokushi, Yoshida Yutaka, and Yoshimi Yoshiaki. In 1995, demanding that the Japanese government apologize to and compensate Chinese people who had suffered from Japanese atrocities, a group of activists founded the Chūgokujin sensō higaisha no yōkyū o sasaerukai (Society to Support the Demands of Chinese War Victims). The society has organized panels, lectures, and trips to war memorials in China.[43] Another organization, the Ajia josei kikin (Asian Women's Fund), has often been criticized as a superficial gesture designed by the government to divert attention from its deeper responsibilities. Nevertheless, the fund collected 482,200,000 yen from the public between August 1995 and March 1998.[44]

It is under such circumstances that revisionist movements have become intensified in the 1990s. The backlash has assumed various forms: repeated remarks denying Japanese wartime atrocities and aggression by conservative politicians in the 1990s; the vicious attack on school textbooks by Fujioka Nobukatsu and his supporters; and a controversial film, *Puraido* (Pride) (1998), which romanticized Tōjō Hideki, a class A war criminal who received the death penalty at the Tokyo Trials. However, these phenomena do not in any way prove that revisionism has triumphed. Rather, they should be analyzed as a response to the recent emphasis on Japan's role as a victimizer and as a barometer of conservatives' frustration and their growing sense of crisis.

Justice Minister Nagano Shigeto's denial of the Massacre, like Environmental Agency Chief Sakurai Shin's negation of Japanese wartime aggression in 1994, was a response to Prime Minister Hosokawa Morihiro's repeated public statements in 1993 that the Asia-Pacific War was an aggressive and reprehensible war.[45] Fujioka and his allies were responding to current junior high school textbooks that openly discussed Japanese wartime atrocities and crimes. The film *Puraido* (Pride) was a reaction to the "masochistic" wartime and prewar Japanese history that has dominated the society in recent years.[46]

It is quite unfortunate that mass media, particularly those outside Japan, have disregarded, if not ignored, Japanese progressives and liberals and have paid much attention to Japanese revisionists. This bias is partly due to the sensational appeal of the revisionists' claims and partly due to ignorance within the media about the Japanese society. For instance, denials of Japanese aggression by Japanese conservative politicians have always been reported both nationally and internationally, but politicians attempting to make the government legally responsible for researching wartime damages have received little, if any, attention.[47] Fujioka's best-selling book became notorious both nationally and internationally, but the availability of more than thirty books and dozens of articles that dispute Fujioka's claim has been ignored.[48] Although the film *Puraido* (Pride) attracted attention from foreign critics, the film *Nanking 1937: Don't Cry Nanking*, directed by Wu Ziniu, which was screened in Tokyo from May 2 through June 5, 1998, did not receive any praise except from liberal journals such as *Shūkan kinyōbi*.[49] In addition, protests against *Pride* and denunciations of the film by Japanese progressives received scant coverage, particularly among non-Japanese media.[50]

III. *The Rape of Nanking*: Illumination or Simplification?

In 1997, Iris Chang published *The Rape of Nanking: The Forgotten Holocaust of World War II*, which became a best-seller in the United States. Without any doubt, Chang's book contributed to the spread of knowledge of the Massacre among the general American audience and gave voices to people who were still suffering greatly from memories of the Massacre. Nevertheless, the book has certain limitations and, ironically, is guilty of errors similar to those committed by Japanese revisionists.

Chang's book is an angry one.[51] Chang is infuriated by "the Japanese" who "as a nation are still trying to bury the victims of Nanking not under the soil, as in 1937, but into historical oblivion."[52] She falsely assumes that Japanese society is completely dominated by the deniers of the Massacre. In the postwar period, Japanese progressives have dominated the society, Japanese lawyers and citizens' groups have been fighting for non-Japanese plaintiffs in order to win cases, and liberal teachers in schools, particularly since the 1980s, have emphasized Japan's role as a victimizer. However, all these forces are completely missing from Chang's picture. Chang monolithically labels a nation of broadly varied opinions and positions simply as "the Japanese." What she means by "the Japanese" is actually "Japanese revisionists," a small but vocal minority who have been furious about the current Japan, which they see as dominated by "masochistic" history.

Japanese revisionists such as Fujioka Nobukatsu are also furious about "the Japanese." What Fujioka means by "the Japanese," however, is the Japanese who, in the opinion of the revisionists, were "brainwashed" by the Japanese progressives and the Tokyo Trials.[53] Fujioka and his allies have dismissed Japanese school textbooks that openly discuss wartime Japanese atrocities and the issue of compensation as "masochistic." They are offended by the recent trend that, in their view, erodes Japan's national pride and the honor of the Japanese soldiers who fought for the nation. Although Chang claims that "to express true opinions about the Sino-Japanese War (i.e., to affirm the Japanese aggression and wartime atrocities) could be—and continues to be—career threatening, and even life threatening,"[54] the same assertion applies at least equally to revisionists. Many examples can be given of revisionists who have will-their professional careers, cabinet seats, or even their lives in the name of their beliefs. Like their progressive counterparts, revisionists such as Fujioka have received death threats from political extremists but have continued their work undeterred.[55] The degree of the conservatives' frustration can be seen in the number of cabinet members who were forced to give up their posts because of their denials of Japanese aggression, including the Massacre. Tanaka Masaaki, who wrote *"Nankin gyakusatsu" no kyokō* (The fabrication of the Nanjing Massacre) was born in 1911, but he has still been active in giving public lectures even in the 1990s.[56] There are few angers strong enough to compel men to expend such energy on behalf of a cause, even into their late eighties.

Another similarity between Chang's book and the work of Japanese revisionists is that both views are very simple and black-and-white. In Chang's estimation, the Japanese are demons, and the Chinese are innocents. She leaves no room for Japanese soldiers who maintained humanity; for Chinese people who collaborated with the Japanese military; for Chinese soldiers who burned buildings and killed Chinese civilians to steal their clothes.[57] No political struggles among nationalists, communists, and war lords find their way into her book. The book presents the Nanking Massacre with storybook simplicity: the Chinese were like sitting ducks in Nanking and the Japanese exterminated them all in a demonic manner. Chang seems to suggest that the Chinese people, who, with their military, outnumbered the Japanese troops by far more than two to one,[58] waited around to get killed without offering any resistance. Such an assumption cannot fail to test the credulity of thoughtful readers.

Japanese revisionist accounts are equally one-dimensional. In *Daitō-A sensō e no michi* (The road to the Greater East Asian War), written by Nakamura Akira, another prominent revisionist ally of Fujioka, there are no "delinquent Japanese" who committed atrocities in Nanking as well as other parts of Asia; no "un-Japanese" who disagreed with government policies and resisted; no "ugly Japanese" who ordered their followers to die without dying themselves; or no "good" Chinese and Koreans who fought and died for Japan. In denying the Nanking Massacre, Nakamura bases his argument on his own racial preconceptions. According to him, the Massacre could not possibly have occurred because the Japanese are not atrocious by nature; it is rather Chinese who are congenitally atrocious, and atrocities are "habitual" in China.[59] Like many other revisionists, Nakamura makes a simple and clear argument: Japan fought a "defensive war"; Japan was not a victimizer.[60]

Moreover, both camps very much disregard history. For Chang, the ultimate goal of her book is to teach to the Japanese the lesson that the Nanking Massacre was one of the worst, if not the worst, horror in human history. Written with a view to forcing diehard deniers of the Massacre to admit their distortions, the book is built on Chang's outrage toward the Japanese invaders of Nanking. Without meaning to do so, she accuses the Japanese as a race of ignoring Japan's wartime atrocities and war crimes. Chang stresses grotesque stories and photos instead of trying to understand why ordinary Japanese men committed a massacre in Nanking. Furthermore, the book contains a number of both large and small errors.[61]

Likewise, the ultimate goal of the revisionists is not to examine and understand history so as to construct a better future, but simply to "restore Japanese pride." The deniers of the Massacre have been playing the numbers game since the early 1980s and claiming that the so-called Nanking Massacre never occurred because neither 200,000 nor 300,000 noncombatants were killed during the event.[62] In revisionist accounts, readers will find a series of stories and photographs stressing Japanese humanity and friendliness to Nanking residents, but will not find stories of the Chinese massacred by Japanese soldiers.[63] Revisionists often disregard and ignore the empirical practice of history in order to support their claims. They formulate their arguments based on other revisionist sources, and their work often misquotes, exaggerates, and even manipulates the documentary evidence.[64]

Furthermore, Chang as well as Japanese deniers of the Massacre tend to balance cruelties against each other in an attempt to find out who suffered most. This balancing is often skewed, because it values some lives more than others on the basis of race and nationality. The problem with this type of analysis is that it can easily degenerate into a fruitless "cruelty game" in which each side accuses the other of more outrageous behavior instead of trying to weigh objectively the circumstances that produced the tragedies. Chang compares the inhumanity of the Massacre with other atrocities, such as the Holocaust and Hiroshima and Nagasaki, and the tone of the book suggests that the Massacre is the worst mass extermination in human history in terms of the number of deaths per day.[65] In contrast, Japanese deniers of the Massacre compare the Massacre with the inhumanity of Allied war crimes and Chinese atrocities against Japanese civilians, and insist that the Massacre does not deserve special attention.[66]

IV. A Monument to Hatred or a Path to Peace

History is a powerful tool. It can promote patriotism and nationalism as well as hatred toward a specific group. During the Asia-Pacific War, Japan's wartime Pan-Asianism helped to justify aggression as well as to foster the rise of discrimination against other Asian races and culture, whereas American emphasis on Japanese atrocities such as the Bataan Death March contributed to the demonization of the Japanese as a race.[67]

Both Iris Chang and Fujioka Nobukatsu have written best-sellers. What would happen if their books were used as school textbooks? Intentionally or not, Chang's book, which depicts the Japanese as perpetrators first of an orgy of atrocities in Nanking and later of a massive historical cover-up, would tend to inspire students toward hatred of "the Japanese." On the other hand, Fujioka's book, which defines war as a "game" and justifies killings in the name of self-defense—including the wartime usage of atomic bombs by the United States—would instill students with feelings of parochial nationalism and racism.

History should contribute to the future. Chang should realize that many different voices exist in Japan, and that she can better achieve her goal—that is, eliciting an apology and compensation from the Japanese government for the victims of the Massacre—by cooperating with academics, lawyers, journalists, and peace activists in Japan who have been working on the same issue as she for the same goal, rather than categorizing all Japanese as deniers of the Massacre. No matter how she stresses horrors of the Massacre, deniers of the Massacre in Japan will never be persuaded, any more than American veterans who justify the killing of Japanese, Koreans, Chinese, and POWs in Hiroshima and Nagasaki can be expected to change their beliefs. So, too, racist organizations like the Ku Klux Klan (KKK) will never accept racial equality, and deniers of the Holocaust will not withdraw their nonsense.

Similarly, Fujioka and his fellow revisionists should realize that they can feel "national pride" and contribute to the future of the world without attempting to revive a nation-centered history that justifies Japan's past war crimes. Instead of trying to persuade the Japanese public that the established wartime Japanese history is "masochistic," they should consider the future of a more peaceful world in which people do not legitimize killing in the name of a defensive war. Indeed, if pride is as important as the revisionists believe, they may take enormous pride in a

Japan whose historical judgments are guided, not by nationalism or ethnocentrism, but by human decency.

Then, which books should be used as a textbook in order to teach the Massacre? Unfortunately, books in English that focus on why ordinary Japanese men committed atrocities in Nanking are hard to find, though it is easy to find books and articles discussing what happened in Nanking, such as H.J. Timperley's *Japanese Terror in China* and Tillman Durdin's articles in the *New York Times*.[68] Assuming the absence of language barriers, the best combination of the readings would be Kasahara Tokushi's *Nankin jiken* (The Nanking incident) (1997) for general analysis of the Massacre; Nanjing datusha shiliao bianji weiyuanhui (Committee for the compliation of sources on the Nanjing massacre), *Qin-Hua Rijun Nanjing datusha shiliao* (Historical materials on the great Nanjing massacre by the Japanese troops that invaded China) (1985) for Chinese eyewitness accounts; Ono Kenji's *Nankin daigyakusatsu o kiroku shita kōgun heishi tachi* (The soldiers who recorded the Nanjing massacre) (1996) for Japanese soldiers' diaries; and John Rabe's diary or Martha Smalley's *American Missionary Eyewitnesses to the Nanking Massacre, 1937–38* (1997). These readings will help students to understand the horrors that took place during the Massacre, while also prompting them to consider why the Japanese soldiers committed such mass atrocities in Nanking.

Haggling over the actual death toll in Nanking and attempting to compare one cruelty with another are not constructive at all. The death toll could differ depending on considerations of space and time. Predictably, scholars will differ on how long the Massacre lasted and how to distinguish Nanking from surrounding areas. According to the figures posted at the war memorial in Beijing prior to 1995, for instance, 9,325,000 Chinese were killed between 1937 and 1945; in addition, 9,470,000 were wounded and 2,890,000 were counted as missing (excluding Taiwan, Jilin, Heilongjiang, and Rehe). In 1995, revised to include all of China, the figure was raised to 35,000,000 casualities during the Japanese aggression from 1931 through 1945.[69] Similarly, different numbers of the victims of the atomic bombs are offered by various sources at different times, partly because of the elusiveness of a clear definition. Obviously a person killed instantly on August 6, 1945, should be counted as a victim of the Hiroshima bomb. But what of the person whose life was taken by atomic poisoning months or even years later? And what is the definition of "atomic poisoning"? Immediately after the war, the figures were thought to be 75,000 in Hiroshima and 40,000 in Nagasaki. By 1972, estimates had risen to 140,000 in Hiroshima and 70,000 in Nagasaki. As of August 1994, the numbers had grown to 186,940 in Hiroshima and 192,275 in Nagasaki.[70] Both Japanese and Chinese figures will certainly increase, say ten years from now; even so many decades after the fact, neither Japanese aggression nor the atomic bombs have entirely finished their work.

The numbers game does not shed any light on the actual sufferings of the victims, and the cruelty game does not help the world to avoid the same kind of mistake. Atrocities are still commonly happening in the world today. People hate and kill each other based on race, religion, and nationality. The Massacre should be studied in order to help achieve a future in which the lives of human beings are all deemed equally sacred and we are no longer motivated by hatred of a specific race. If the criterion of history is an improved, balanced understanding of human behavior, both Japanese revisionist accounts and Chang's *The Rape of Nanking* fall short of the mark.

V. Conclusion

The study of the Nanking Massacre can be used either for promoting hatred of "the Japanese" or for preserving lives in the future. The issue of how to study the Massacre in order to prevent mankind from committing similar atrocities has become an increasingly challenging one, as reactions to the Massacre have become further internationalized. It has been a common tactic for a state to resurrect and stress bygone atrocities by the "Other" in order to unite the nation and agitate hatred toward the Other. It is hardly difficult to think of examples of how the Other was demonized during the Asia-Pacific war in Japan, China, and the United States. Even today, one can easily find such examples in conflicting nations. For instance, before Yugoslavia was dismembered, histories of massacres were suppressed for fear that their dissemination would undermine national unity. However, since the split-up of Yugoslavia, these stories have been manipulated by nationalist leaders of republics, especially Slovenia and Serbia. Old animosities have been deliberately revived in order to promote ethnic nationalism.[71]

Remembering Japanese wartime atrocities, such as the Nanking Massacre, can unite those who identify themselves as "the Chinese," regardless of their political, economic, ethnic, generational, and national differences. Both mainlanders and Taiwanese, both old and young, both the rich and the nonrich, both the "purely" Chinese and the multiracial, both communists and capitalists, both the Chinese-born and the foreign-born, all would be able to agree that Japanese wartime atrocities were quite dreadful and must be remembered. I completely agree that such atrocities were inhumane and must be remembered. However, they should be remembered in order to avert similar evils in the future, not to promote hatred toward a specific group of people and not to promote ethnic nationalism. Few would dispute the fact that race does not define one's personal character. Therefore, it is no surprise that Japanese liberals have spoken out and acted as mentioned in an earlier section of this chapter. It is also no surprise to discover that not all Japanese were inhuman villains even during the wartime. Yet it seems that racism with regard to other countries is still widely acceptable in the United States as well as in Japan and elsewhere, even though domestic racism is regarded as uncivilized and unhealthful.

One should remember that many Japanese soldiers who committed atrocities in Nanking were ordinary people who had never before killed people, never committed looting, or never committed rape. Yet many of these ordinary people, most of whom had not been highly educated, transformed themselves into murderers and rapists on the way from Shanghai to Nanking. Race can be used to predict neither decency nor barbarism. A person of any background might have become a perpetrator if subjected to conditions similar to those that the Japanese troops went through. War is not a natural disaster but a human disaster, and its remedy exists in our hands. The study of the Nanking Massacre can make us think of such fundamental issues as how one can maintain humanness under inhuman conditions.

Notes

1. For instance, approximately 400,000 people in Tokyo participated in lantern parades on December 14, 1937. See Kasahara Tokushi, *Nankin jiken*, p. 163.

2. Nankin jiken chōsa kenkyūkai, *Nankin jiken shiryō shū*, 1992, vol. 2, pp. 6–9.

3. Nankin jiken chōsa kenkyūkai, *Nankin jiken shiryō shū*, 1992, vol. 1, pp. 380–480.

4. John Dower, *War Without Mercy* (New York: Pantheon Books, 1986), pp. 43–48.

5. U.S. Strategic Bombing Survey, Morale Division, *The Effects of Strategic Bombing on Japanese Morale* (Washington, DC: June 1947), p. 154.

6. "Children, Too, Were Massacred: Revealed Massacre at Nanjing," *Asahi shimbun*, July 26, 1946, p. 2.

7. "Our Gratitude to the Chinese People," *Yomiuri Shimbun*, July 31, 1946. See General Headquarters, Supreme Commander for the Allied Powers Allied Translator and Interpreter Section, *Press Translations and Summaries Japan*, Reel 17.

8. Daqing Yang, "Contested History: Remembering the Nanjing Massacre in Japan and China," p. 18.

9. Hora Tomio, *Nankin jiken* (1972); Honda Katsuichi, *Chūgoku no tabi* (1972).

10. See, for instance, Yamamoto Shichihei, *Watashi no naka no Nihongun* (1975); Suzuki Akira, *Nankin daigyakusatsu no maboroshi* (1973).

11. See, for instance, "The Nanking Massacre: A Message of Future to Japan," *New York Times*, December 26, 1990, p. D16.

12. Over 770 people participated in the two-day conference in Tokyo.

13. Aitani Kunio, "Sengo hoshō saiban no genjō to kadai," p. 2.

14. Onodera Toshitaka, "Sengo hoshō saiban tōsō no kadai to tenbōn (Problems and prospectives of the legal struggle over postwar compensation), *Hō to Minshu shugi* (Law and democracy), p. 13.

15. I am grateful to Mark Eykholt for sharing his paper titled "Aggression, Victimization, and Chinese Historiography of the Nanjing Massacre," which was presented at the 49th Annual Meeting of the Association for Asian Studies in Chicago on March 13, 1997.

16. The Global Alliance for Preserving the History of WWII in Asia, *GA Newsletter*, March 1998, vol. 5, no. 5, pp. 132–134.

17. Fujioka Nobukatsu and Nishio Kanji, *Kokumin no yudan*, pp. 241–244.

18. Tawara Yoshifumi, *Kyōkasho kōgeki no shinsō*, pp. 170–172.

19. Fujioka and Nishio, *Kokumin no yudan*, p. 213.

20. Watanabe Shōichi, "Nankin daigyakusatsu wa nakatta," pp. 184–185.

21. Hansen dōmei kiroku henshūiinkai, *Hansen heishi monogatari* (Tokyo: Nihon Kyōsantō, 1963), pp. 1–9. Also see Kaji Wataru, *Nihon heishi no hansen undō*, 2 vols. (Tokyo: Dōseisha, 1962); and Fujiwara Akira, *Shiryō Nihon gendai shi 1: Guntai nai no hansen undō* (Tokyo: ōtsuki shoten, 1980).

22. U.S. Strategic Bombing Survey, Morale Division, *The Effects of Strategic Bombing on Japanese Morale*, p. 152.

23. Carol Gluck, "The Past in the Present," p. 70.

24. For instance, *Nihon no rekishi ge*, a history textbook for junior high and high schools, writes, "atrocities committed by our [Japanese] army at the time of the capture of Nanking resulted in the fullest Chinese anti-Japanese struggle." See Tawara Yoshifumi, *Kyōkasho kōgeki no shinsō* (Tokyo: Gakushū no tomo sha, 1997), p. 169.

25. See, for instance, Chūgoku kikansha renrakukai, *Sankō* (Tokyo: Kōbunsha, 1957), and *Shinryaku* (Tokyo: Shin dokusho sha, 1958). In these accounts, veterans confessed their war crimes in China during the war. Also see Hora Tomio, *Kindai senshi no nazo* (Tokyo: Jinbutsu ōraisha, 1967).

26. Honda Katsuichi, *Chūgoku no tabi* (Tokyo: Asahi shinbunsha, 1972), and *Chūgoku no Nihongun* (Tokyo: Sōjusha, 1972).

27. Hora Tomio, *Nankin jiken* (Tokyo: Shin jinbutsu ōraisha, 1972), and *Nankin daigyakusatsu* (Tokyo: Gendaishi shuppankai, 1975).

28. Rekishi kyōikusha kyōgikai, *Rekishi kyōiku 50 nen no ayumi to kadai* (Tokyo: Miraisha, 1997), p. 353.

29. Ibid., p. 351. The song "Sensō o shiranai kodomotachi" (Children who do not

know the war) became a hit song in 1970. Regarding books that discuss the teaching of history from the point of view of the aggressed, see, for instance, Tokutake Toshio, *Sensō to kyōiku* (Tokyo: Hato no mori shobō, 1972).

30. The 1982 annual meeting of Rekishi kyōikusha kyōgikai discussed the role of history education as well as the textbook authorization system; 1,199 people attended this meeting. See Rekishi kyōikusha kyōgikai, *Rekishi kyōiku 50 nen no ayumi to kadai*, p. 555.

31. Adachi Yoshihiko, "Sensō ni katan saserareta minshū," *Rekishi chiri kyōiku*, August 1982, no. 339, pp. 8–9.

32. Komatsu Yutaka, "Kagai no men o chūshin ni sueta 15 nen sensō no gakushū," *Rekishi chiri kyōiku*, August 1982, no. 339, pp. 14, 17.

33. Adachi, "Sensō ni katan saserareta minshū," p. 8; Komatsu, "Kagai no men o chūshin ni sueta 15 nen sensō no gakushū," p. 17.

34. More than twenty-seven lawsuits have been brought in the Japanese courts between 1990 and 1995. See Aitani Kunio, "Sengo hoshō saiban no genjō to kadai," *Kikan sensō sekinin kenkyū*, Winter 1995, no. 10, p. 3.

35. Rekishi, *Rekishi kyōiku 50 nen no ayumi to kadai*, p. 258.

36. Yamamoto Masatoshi, "Jūgun ianfu no jugyō o tsukuru pointo," *Rekishi chiri kyōiku*, January 1993, no. 497, pp. 92–93.

37. For more detailed analysis, see Tawara Yoshifumi, *Dokyumento "Ianfu" mondai to kyōkasho kōgeki* (Tōkyō: Kōbunken, 1997).

38. Tawara Yoshifumi has examined all the postwar history textbooks in both junior high and high schools and traced how descriptions of the Massacre have changed through time. See his *Kyōkasho kōgeki no shinsō* (Tokyo: Gakushū no tomo sha, 1997), pp. 158–169.

39. Rekishi kyōikusha kyōgikai, *Heiwa hakubutsukan, sensō shiryōkan gaido bukku* (Tokyo: Aoki shoten, 1995); Hiroshima Peace Memorial Museum, *The Outline of Atomic Bomb Damage in Hiroshima* (1994); Murakami Hatsuichi, *Dokugasutō no rekishi* (1992).

40. John Dower, "Three Narratives of Our Humanity," in *History Wars*, eds. Edward Linenthal et al. (New York: Metropolitan Books, 1996), p. 70.

41. Tawara Yoshifumi, "Kodomo to kyōkasho zenkoku netto 21 kessei e," *Akahata*, May 25, 1998, p. 4.

42. Watanabe Noboru, "Sensō, sengo sekinin o tou, 731 butaiten o kaisai shite," *Kikan sensō sekinin kenkyū*, winter 1993, no. 2, p. 57.

43. The society's newsletters are available on the Web at http://www.threeweb.ad.jp/~suopei.

44. *Ajia josei kikin nyūsu*, March 18, 1998, no. 10, p. 3. For instance, the Violence Against Women in War–Network Japan (VAWW-NET Japan) argues that the government is trying to deflect criticism and evade responsibility for the war by performing token gestures, like soliciting donations from the public. The VAWW-NET Japan, which organized the international conference on violence against women in October 1997, is planning to stage a "Women's War Crimes Trial" in December 2000.

45. "Saki no sensō 'shinryaku sensō' to meigen," *Asahi Shimbun*, August 11, 1993, p. 1. Also see Kisaka Jun'ichirō, "Ajia taiheiyō sensō no rekishiteki seikaku o megutte," *Nenpō Nihon gendai shi* (Tokyo: Gendai shiryō shuppan, 1995), p. 3.

46. Tanaka Masaaki, one of the deniers of the Massacre, was involved in making

the film. His view of the Tokyo Tribunal was very much reflected in the film: The tribunal was victors' justice; the Allies ignored their war crimes; witnesses of the Massacre had rarely seen the actual events to which they attested; and Judge Radhabinod Pal's separate opinion, which found no basis for convicting the alleged Class A war criminals, was not read before the court. See Tanaka Masaaki, *"Nankin gyakusatsu," no kyokō*, pp. 282–352.

47. Tanaka Kō and Motooka Akitsugu, both of whom are now members of the Minshutō (Democratic Party), have been working for the bill since mid-1997. For the most updated information, see *Let's* (June 1996), no. 15, the newsletter published by the Center for Research and Documentation on Japan's War Responsibility. On May 14, 1997, approximately 170 politicians and supporters of the bill gathered at the No. 2 Members' Office Building.

48. Tawara Yoshifumi listed thirty such books in his "'Dai sanji kyōkasho kōgeki' no aratana dōkō," *Kyōkasho repōto '98* (Tokyo: Shuppan rōren, 1998), p. 23. Regarding articles that dispute Fujioka and his supporters, see journals such as *Sekai, Shūkan kinyōbi, Rekishi chiri kyōiku*, and *Kikan sensō sekinin kenkyū*.

49. On May 9, 1998, a Chinese spokesman of the foreign ministry said that he was stunned by the fact that the film attempts to romanticize Tōjō, a key person of Japanese wartime aggression. For a review of *Nanking 1937*, see Kasahara Tokushi's article in *Shūkan kinyōbi*, April 24, 1998, no. 216, p. 42. Although the *Christian Science Monitor* reported that a member of a local right-wing group disrupted the screening of *Nanking 1937* in Yokohama, the article did not mention that the film was screened without disturbance in Tokyo for about a month (June 22, 1998).

50. For protests against the film, see, for instance, Honda Katsuichi, "Baikokudo tachi ga tsukutta eiga," *Shūkan kinyōbi*, May 29, 1998, no. 220, p. 57. Honda insisted that those who had made the film were "traitors" who intended to isolate Japan from the world and would provoke international contempt toward the nation. On April 20, 1998, a group called Critics of the Film *Pride* was established by scholars and critics such as Fujiwara Akira and Senda Kakō. Within a month approximately 550 individuals and organizations expressed their support for the group.

51. I am grateful to Joshua Fogel, who has kindly shared with me his forthcoming critical review of Iris Chang's book, which is to appear in the *Journal of Asian Studies*. Professor Fogel and I are in substantial accord in our view of Ms. Chang's work, and readers will observe that this section and Professor Fogel's review address some similar points.

52. Iris Chang, *The Rape of Nanking: The Forgotten Holocaust of World War II* (New York: Basic Books, 1997), p. 220.

53. Fujioka Nobukatsu and Nishio Kanji, *Kokumin no yudan* (Tokyo: PHP kenkyūjo, 1996), pp. 2–3. Fujioka Nobukatsu, "'Sensō no jugyō' no paradaimu tenkan o dō hakaruka," *"Kingendaishi" no jugyō kaikaku 1* (September 1995), pp. 14–15.

54. Chang, *The Rape of Nanking*, p. 12.

55. Kobayashi Yoshinori, *Shin gōmanizumu sengen 4* (Tokyo: Shōgakkan, 1998), p. 13.

56. Tanaka told this author that his mission was to educate the public that the Nanking Massacre was a fabrication. He argued that Japanese media was dominated by "anti-Japanese." (Interview with Tanaka Masaaki on June 19, 1996.)

57. See, for instance, John Rabe, *The Diary of John Rabe: Nankin no shinjitsu*, transl. Hirano Kyōko (Tokyo: Kōdansha, 1997), pp. 91, 95, 98.

58. For instance, Robert Wilson, who testified at the Tokyo Trials, estimated that the population declined from one million to one-half million (Pritchard, p. 2551). Although Chang supports the figure of one-half million in her book (*The Rape of Nanking*, p. 81), she seems subsequently to have increased this number. In a phone interview with an Associated Press (AP) journalist on June 12, 1998, she cited the estimate of Sun Zhaiwei, which lies between 600,000 and 700,000 (AP, June 12, 1998).

59. Nakamura Akira, *Daitō-A sensō e no michi* (Tokyo: Tendensha, 1990), pp. 444–456. In order to support his claim, he discusses the alleged ancient Chinese custom of cannibalism and Chinese methods of torture, among other atrocious practices.

60. Ibid., p. 19.

61. The most crucial misunderstanding is Chang's ignorance of postwar Japanese historiography and of progressive influences within the academy. Less serious weaknesses include inaccurate Japanese names, dates, and titles. See, for example, David Kennedy's review in the *Atlantic Monthly* (April 1998), pp. 110–116. Hata Ikuhiko, " 'Nankin gyakusatsu' shōko shashin o kantei suru," *Shokun!* (April 1998), vol. 30, no. 4, pp. 82–93.

62. See, for instance, Fujioka Nobukatsu and Nishio Kanji, *Kokumin no yudan*, pp. 211–214. Itakura Yoshiaki, " 'Nankin daigyakusatsu 20 man' setsu e no Itsusu no hanshō," *"Kingendaishi" no jugyō kaikaku 1*, pp. 71–79.

63. See, for example, Tanaka Masaaki, *"Nankin gyakusatsu no kyokō"* (Tokyo: Nihon kyōbunsha, 1984).

64. Tanaka Masaaki is known to have misquoted and fabricated more than 900 passages from General Matsui Iwane's diary. When Fujioka Nobukatsu claimed that only forty-seven civilians were killed in the International Safety Zone, he based this assertion on Itakura Yoshiaki's work (*Kokumin no yudan*, p. 213).

65. Chang, *The Rape of Nanking*, pp. 5–7.

66. See, for instance, Watanabe Shōichi, *Kakute shōwashi wa yomigaeru* (Tokyo: Kuresutosha, 1995), pp. 313–315.

67. John Dower, *War Without Mercy* (New York: Pantheon Books, 1986), pp. 8, 51–53.

68. H.J. Timperley, *Japanese Terror in China* (New York: Modern Age Books, 1938); Tillman Durdin, "US Naval Display Reported Likely Unless Japan Guarantees Our Rights; Butchery Marked Capture of Nanking," *New York Times*, December 18, 1937, pp. 1, 10. Also see Tillman Durdin, "Japanese Atrocities Marked Fall of Nanking After Chinese Command Fled," *New York Times*, January 9, 1938, p. 38. Timperley estimated "at least 300,000 Chinese military casualties for the Central China campaign alone and a like number of civilian casualties" (p. 15). He estimated that only 200,000 people out of one million remained in Nanking (p. 23). Durdin estimated the total Chinese dead as 33,000 in Shanghai on December 22 ("Japanese Atrocities Marked Fall of Nanking," p. 38).

69. Ishii Akira, "Sengo Nit-Chū kankei no kiseki," *Gaikō fōramu*, September 1997, no. 110, pp. 95–96.

70. John Dower, "Three Narratives of Our Humanity," n. 28, p. 263.

71. Robert Hayden, "Recounting the Dead: The Rediscovery and Redefinition of Wartime Massacres in Late- and Post-Communist Yugoslavia," pp. 168–169.

Bibliography

Adachi Yoshihiko. "Sensō ni katan saserareta minshū" (The people who were mobilized for the war). *Rekishi chiri kyōiku*, August 1982, no. 339, pp. 8–12.

Aitani Kunio. "Sengo hoshō saiban no genjō to kadai" (The present status and task of postwar trials concerning government reparations). *Kikan sensō sekinin kenkyū*, Winter 1995, no. 10, pp. 2–9.

Ajia josei kikin (Asian women's fund). *Ajia josei kikin nyūsu* (Asian women's fund news), March 18, 1998, no. 10.

Chang, Iris. *The Rape of Nanking: The Forgotten Holocaust of World War II*. New York: Basic Books, 1997.

"Children, Too, Were Massacred: Revealed Massacre at Nanjing." *Asahi shinbun*, July 26, 1946, p. 2.

Chinese Alliance for Memorial and Justice. "The Nanking Massacre: A Message of Future to Japan." *New York Times*, December 26, 1990, p. D16.

Chūgoku kikansha renrakukai (The group of returnees from China). *Sankō* (Three "all" operations). Tokyo: Kōbunsha, 1957.

———. *Shinryaku* (Invasion). Tokyo: Shindokushosha, 1958.

Dower, John. "Three Narratives of Our Humanity." In *History Wars*. Eds. Edward Linenthal et al. New York: Metropolitan Books, 1996.

———. *War Without Mercy: Race & Power in the Pacific War*. New York: Pantheon Books, 1986.

Durdin, F. Tillman. "US Naval Display Reported Likely Unless Japan Guarantees Our Rights; Butchery Marked Capture of Nanking." *New York Times*, December 18, 1937, pp. 1, 10.

———. "Japanese Atrocities Marked Fall of Nanking After Chinese Command Fled." *New York Times*, January 9, 1938, p. 38.

Fujioka Nobukatsu. *Kyōkasho ga oshienai rekishi* (History that textbooks do not teach). Tokyo: Sankei shuppan, 1996.

———. "'Nankin daigyakusatsu 30 man' no uso" (The fabrication of 300,000 in the Nanjing Massacre). In *Kokumin no yudan: rekishi kyōkasho ga abunai* (Negligence of the nation: The danger of history textbooks). Eds. Fujioka Nobukatsu and Nishio Kanji, pp. 209–215. Tokyo: PHP kenkyūjo, 1996.

———. *Ojoku no kingendai shi: ima kokufuku no toki* (Modern Japanese history: The time has come to get over the disgrace). Tokyo: Tokuma shoten, 1996.

———. "Sensō no jugyō no paradaimu tenkan o dō hakaruka" (How to change the paradigm of classes on the war). *"Kingendaishi" no jugyō" kaikaku 1*, September 1995, pp. 12–17.

Fujioka Nobukatsu and Nishio Kanji. *Kokumin no yudan: rekishi kyōkasho ga abunai* (Negligence of the nation: The danger of history textbooks). Tokyo: PHP kenkyūjo, 1996.

Fujiwara Akira. *Shiryō Nihon gendai shi 1* (Historical materials of modern Japanese history 1: Antiwar movements in the military). Tokyo: Ōtsuki shoten, 1980.

Gaouette, Nicole. "Frustrated Japanese Revise Past." *Christian Science Monitor*, June 22, 1998.

General Headquarters, Supreme Commander for the Allied Powers, Allied Translator and Interpreter Section. *Press Translations and Summaries—Japan*. Reel #17.

Gluck, Carol. "The Past in the Present." In *Postwar Japan as History.* Ed. Andrew Gordon, pp. 64–95. Berkeley: University of California Press, 1993.

Hansen dōmei kiroku henshū iinkai (Committee against the war). *Hansen heishi monogatari* (The story of antiwar soldiers). Tokyo: Nihon kyōsantō, 1962.

Hata Ikuhiko. " 'Nankin gyakusatsu' shōko shashin o kantei suru" (Examining photographs that prove the "Nanjing Massacre." *Shokun!,* April 1998, vol. 30, no. 4: pp. 82–93.

———. *Nankin jiken* (The Nanjing Incident). Tokyo: Chūō kōronsha, 1986.

Hiroshima Peace Memorial Museum. *The Outline of Atomic Bomb Damage in Hiroshima.* Hiroshima: Hiroshima Peace Memorial Museum, 1994.

Honda Katsuichi. "Baikokudo tachi ga tsukutta eiga" (The film made by traitors). *Shūkan kinyōbi,* April 24, 1998, no. 220, p. 57.

———. *Chūgoku no Nihongun* (The Japanese army in China). Tokyo: Sōjusha, 1972.

———. *Chūgoku no tabi* (Travels in China). Tokyo: Asahi shinbunsha, 1972.

Hora Tomio. *Kindai senshi no nazo* (Riddles of Modern War History). Tokyo: Jinbutsu ōraisha, 1967.

———. *Nankin daigyakusatsu: "maboroshi" ka kōsaku hihan* (The Nanjing Massacre: Criticism of the making of an illusion). Tokyo: Gendaishi shuppankai, 1975.

Hsu Shuhsi. *Documents of the Nanking Safety Zone.* Shanghai: Kelly & Walsh, 1939.

International Society for Educational Information (ISEI). *Japan in Modern History: High School.* 2 vols. Tokyo: ISEI, 1995.

———. *Japan in Modern History: Junior High School.* Tokyo: ISEI, 1994.

———. *Japan in Modern History: Primary School.* Tokyo: ISEI, 1993.

Ishii Akira. "Sengo Nit-Chū kankei no kiseki" (The trajectory of postwar Japan-China relations). *Gaikō fōramu,* no. 110, special issue, September 1997, pp. 94–107.

Itakura, Yoshiaki. " 'Nankin daigyakusatsu 20 man' setsu e no hanshō" (Refuting the 200,000 deaths of the Nanjing Massacre). *"Kingendai shi" no jugyō kaikaku 1,* September 1995, pp. 71–79.

Kaji Wataru. *Nihon heishi no hansen undō* (Antiwar movements among Japanese soldiers). 2 vols. Tokyo: Dōseisha, 1962).

Kasahara Tokushi. "Nanking 1937: Don't Cry Nanking." *Shūkan kinyōbi,* April 24, 1998, p. 42.

———. *Nankin jiken* (The Nanjing Incident). Tokyo: Iwanami shoten, 1997.

———. *Nankin nanminku no hyakunichi: gyakusatsu o mita gaikokujin* (100 days in the Nanking Safety Zone: Foreigners who witnessed the Massacre). Tokyo: Iwanami shoten, 1995.

Kennedy, David. "The Horror." *Atlantic Monthly,* April 1998, pp. 110–116.

Kisaka Jun'ichirō. "Ajia, taiheiyō sensō no rekishiteki seikaku o megutte" (Historical characteristics of the Asia-Pacific War). *Nenpō Nihon gendai shi* (1995), pp. 1–43.

Kobayashi Yoshinori. *Shin gōmaniszumu sengen 4* (A declaration of arrogance, new version), vol. 4. Cartoon. Tokyo: Shōgakkan, 1998.

Komatsu Yutaka. "Kagai no men o chūshin ni sueta 15 nen sensō no gakushū" (The 15-Year War: Focus on Japan's role as a victimizer). *Rekishi chiri kyōiku,* August 1982, no. 339, pp. 14–23.

Murakami Hatsuichi. *Dokugasutō no rekishi* (History of the Poison Gas Island). Hiroshima: Murakami Hatsuichi, 1992.

Nakamura Akira. *Daitō-A sensō e no michi* (The road to the Greater East Asian War). Tokyo: Tendensha, 1990.

Nanjing datusha shi liao bianji weiyuanhui (Committee for the compilation of sources on the Nanjing Massacre). *Shinhua ri jun Nanjing datusha shi liao* (Historical materials on the great Nanjing Massacre by the Japanese troops that invaded China). Nanjing: Jiangsu guji chubanshe, 1985.

Nankin jiken chōsa kenkyūkai (The study group on the Nanjing Incident). *Nankin jiken shiryōshū* (A collection of historical materials on the Nanjing Incident), vol. 1. America *kankei shiryō hen* (Historical Materials in Regard to the United States). Tokyo: Aoki shoten, 1992.

———. *Nankin jiken shiryōshū* (A collection of historical materials on the Nanjing Incident), vol. 2, *Chūgoku kankei shiryō hen* (Historical materials in regard to China). Tokyo: Aoki shoten, 1992.

Nezu Kikujirō. *Pen no jūgun* (The pen that follows the army) Tokyo: Daiichi shobō, 1939.

Nihon no sensō sekinin shiryō sentā (Center for research and documentation on Japan's war responsibility). *Let's*, no. 15 (June 1996).

Ono Kenji, et al., eds. *Nankin daigyakusatsu o kiroku shita kōgun heishi tachi* (The soldiers who recorded the Nanjing Massacre). Tokyo: Ōtsuki shoten, 1996.

Pritchard, John R. *The Tokyo War Crimes Trial*, 22 vols. New York: Garland, 1981.

Rabe, John. *The Diary of John Rabe: Nankin no shinjitsu* (The truth about Nanjing). Transl. Hirano Kyōko. Tokyo: Kōdansha, 1997.

Rekishi kyōikusha kyōgikai (The Council for history teachers). *Heiwa hakubutsukan, sensō shiryōkan gaido bukku* (The handbook of war museums and memorials). Tokyo: Aoki shoten, 1995.

———. *Rekshi kyōiku 50 nen no ayumi to kadai* (The history and objectives of fifty years of history education). Tokyo: Miraisha, 1997.

"Saki no sensō 'shinryaku sensō' to meigen" (Characterization of the previous war as an "aggressive war"). *Asahi shinbun*, August 11, 1993, p. 1.

Sakurai Joji. "Revisionist Academics Contest Best Seller 'Rape of Nanking.'" Associated Press, June 12, 1998.

Shina jihen chūyūdan, kangekidan (Brave and moving stories of the China Incident). Tokyo: Kōdansha, 1938.

Smalley, Martha. *American Missionary Eyewitnesses to the Nanking Massacre, 1937–38*. New Haven: Yale Divinity School Library, 1997.

Suzuki Akira. *"Nankin daigyakusatsu" no maboroshi* (The illusion of the "Nanjing Massacre"). Tokyo: Bungei shunjū, 1973.

Tanaka Masaaki. *"Nankin gyakusatsu" no kyokō* (The fabrication of the "Nanjing Massacre"). With a foreword by Watanabe Shōichi. Tokyo: Nihon Kyōbunsha, 1984.

Tawara Yoshifumi. " 'Dai sanji kyōkasho kōgeki' no aratana dōkō" (The background of the third textbook challenge). *Kyōkasho repōto '98*. Tokyo: Shuppan rōren, 1998, pp. 20–26.

———. *Dokyumento "Ianfu" mondai to kyōkasho kōgeki* (Document: The issue of "comfort women" and attacks on school textbooks). Tokyo: Kōbunken, 1997.

———. "Kodomo to kyōkasho zenkoku netto 21 kessei e" (Organizing the national net 21 for children and textbooks). *Akahata*, May 25, 1998, p. 4.

―――. *Kyōkasho kōgeki no shinsō* (Behind the attacks on school textbooks). Tokyo: Gakushū no tomo sha, 1997.

Timperley, H.J. *Japanese Terror in China*. New York: Modern Age Books, 1938.

Tokutake Toshio. *Sensō to kyōiku* (War and education). Tokyo: Hato no mori shobō, 1972.

U.S. Strategic Bombing Survey, Morale Division. *The Effects of Strategic Bombing on Japanese Morale*. Washington, DC: June 1947.

Watanabe Noboru. "Sensō, sengo sekinin o tou 731 butaiten o kaisai shite" (In the wake of Unit 731 exhibition: Questions about war and postwar responsibility). *Kikan sensō sekinin kenkyū 2*, Winter 1993, pp. 57–62.

Watanabe Shōichi. *Kakute shōwashi wa yomigaeru* (Finally the history of Showa will revive). Tokyo: Kuresutosha, 1995.

―――. "Nankin daigyakusatsu wa nakatta" (There was no Nanjing Massacre). In *Soredemo "No" to ieru Nihon* (A Japan that can still say "no"), eds. Ishihara Shintarō, Watanabe Shōichi, and Ogawa Kazuhisa, pp. 177–185. Tokyo: Kōbunsha, 1990.

Yamamoto Masatoshi. "Jūgun ianfu no jugyō o tsukuru pointo" (Approaches to organizing classes on comfort women). *Rekishi chiri kyōiku*, January 1993, no. 497, pp. 92–93.

Yamamoto Shichihei. *Watashi no naka no Nihongun* (The Japanese military through my eyes), 2 vols. Tokyo: Bungei shunjū, 1975.

Yang, Daqing. "Contested History: Remembering the Nanjing Massacre in Japan and China." *Sino-Japanese Studies 3.1*, November 1990, pp. 14–35.

Part Four
Healing the Wounds

9

The "Black Milk" of Historical Consciousness: Thinking About the Nanking Massacre in Light of Jewish Memory

Vera Schwarcz

To delve deeply into an atrocity such as the Nanking Massacre can involve analysis that is often quite difficult to bear. Moreover, while doing such delving, it is easy to overlook the fact that all atrocities in human history have common features and that the sufferings of all people who have undergone such traumatic events are similar.

Part of the healing process is the inevitable battle with memory. Vera Schwarcz reminds us with elegant, poetic prose that the memory of trauma transcends nationality and ethnicity. A scholar of Chinese history as well as a descendent of Holocaust survivors, Schwarcz compares the response to atrocity among Jews and Chinese, with special attention to the problems of memory and healing. —Eds.

> Black milk of daybreak we drink it at evening
> we drink it at midday and morning we drink it at night
> we drink and we drink
> we shovel a grave in the air there you won't lie too cramped
> A man lives in the house he plays with his vipers he writes
> he writes when it grows dark to Deutschland. . . .

> Paul Celan, "Deathsfuge"[1]

We are mistaken if we imagine history to be a gently nursing mother. True, historical consciousness provides essential nutrients for survival.[2] It enables us to compress the past and shape it into a narrative that makes the present and the future somewhat less bewildering; but telling the story of the past is far from reassuring. In fact, the more fully we tell the tale, the less certain are the "lessons" to be drawn from events such as the Holocaust or the Nanking Massacre. The wish for a didactic histori-ography may be likened to the hope for white milk with which an infant approaches the mother's body. We know that some children get sick from mother's milk. It is even more common for writers who wrestle with historical trauma to take refuge in dark metaphors that have little to do with inspirational messages from the past.

The German-Jewish poet Paul Celan understood the limitations of historical consciousness. A survivor of the Holocaust, he continued to write in the *mutterschprache* (Mother tongue) that killed his mother and father. The same words that Nazis used to dehumanize and exterminate Jews had to be revived after the war to make "sense" out of nightmares and ashes. Celan's poem "Deathsfugue" sought to bring together con-crete details about the death camps as they emerged in 1944–1945, when the world was just discovering the crematoria, when newspapers began to carry reports of Jews having to play music as their fellow inmates were marched to extinction, when photographers began to release their dreadfully tantalizing images of naked women who had been shot at close range or subjected to inhuman experimentation by Dr. Mengele. With all these "facts" released upon an unprepared world, Celan opted for the elusive language of poetry. "Black milk" was not a metaphor for those who survived Auschwitz. It was an accurate summary of what they took out of the death camps: a dark vision of history's failure to console, to inspire or even to explain man-created evil.

Is "black milk" the legacy of the Nanking Massacre as well? It de-pends how much we are willing to probe into the crevices of both memory and amnesia that surround the events of 1937–1938. The Princeton Uni-versity Nanking 1937 Conference commemorating the sixtieth anniver-sary of the atrocities that began in 1937 testified to the willingness of a new generation of Chinese students to wrestle with historical trauma. The undergraduates who organized this substantive discussion were born after the terrors experienced by their grandparents' generation in China. Some of them had grown up on the mainland, others in Taiwan and Singapore. Nonetheless, this exceptional group was drawn together by a determination to reappropriate a history that had become obscure through pain, amnesia and outright denial by some Japanese authorities. During a few days of long and heated discussions, the students listened to their elders describe a past that had been too difficult to share before.

The "black milk" poured forth not only from the podium presentations that focused on historical research about the numbers killed and raped in Nanking. More importantly, the hallways were full of talk, and students could hear the bitter passion of elders now engaged in such organizations as the Alliance in the Memory of the Victims of the Nanjing Massacre and the Alliance for Preserving the History of World War II in Asia. By 1997, memory and history were deemed to be fragile entities that required protection and preservation, whereas they had not been much treasured before. Older Chinese intellectuals had often buried the painful memories. Young students now created a forum for the exploration of a history that bound together disparate generations.

These youths had chosen to take time out of their academic studies in biology, physics, electrical engineering, and mathematics in order to remember the painful past. They were, perhaps somewhat unconsciously, reenacting the tradition of May Fourth—the student movement of 1919 that burst into public life out of a similar conviction that educated youth have a distinctive moral responsibility in Chinese public life.[3] The Princeton undergraduates, like their predecessors in Tiananmen Square in 1919 (and then again in 1989!) took upon themselves the Confucian burden of critical consciousness. With less fanfare and sloganeering than earlier student movements, they chose to take a close look at dark corners of the national past. By taking so much time away from their "proper studies," they reminded all of us how important history can be for the creation and maintenance of social identity. By looking at the facts and implications of the Nanking Massacre with open eyes, these students enlarged their sense of self and community. Remaining in the classrooms and laboratories of their specializations, they could have nurtured the *xiaowo*—the limited self that is grounded in practical goals. By organizing this conference, they laid the foundation for the *dawo*—the larger persona that is both the subject and object of the painful history in Nanking.

This journey from the small to a more encompassing sense of "I" is, according to Elie Wiesel, the main reason to study the Jewish Holocaust. Far from claiming exclusive ownership of the term that has come to sum up Jewish suffering during World War II, Wiesel's Nobel Prize acceptance speech argues for a concrete expansion of social empathy. The more we understand the details of the terror that befell our own people, the more compelled we will become to take to heart the grievances of others.[4] In this context, Iris Chang's recent book *The Rape of*

Nanking is not far off the mark when it describes the events of 1937 as "the forgotten Holocaust."[5] Chang's point of departure, like that of the Princeton undergraduates, is outrage at silenced memory of China's pain. To excavate the wound, however, takes more than archival discoveries such as the newly published diaries of John Rabe, the German Nazi who ended up saving so many lives in war-torn Nanking. New sources by themselves, as Iris Chang well knows, do not cast new light on history. They have to be accompanied by a new responsiveness to the shadows that had been hidden before.

When Chinese writers appeal to the Holocaust as an interpretive framework, they call to mind Jewish "expertise" in the art of commemoration. To be sure, Holocaust memorials are now omnipresent on the American landscape, and the Holocaust occupies more space in public education than does the Nanking Massacre. Nonetheless, those who are working to close the gap must look beyond the well-lit rooms where didactic messages prevail. In looking beyond museums, we are finally in a position to ask more subtle, more difficult questions: At what point in a nation's history is the remembrance of victimization conceivable? When and how does a narrative of victimization become necessary for nation building? What are the cultural resources that suppress such narratives, and what are the traditions that nourish the individual and collective urge to memorialize the nameless dead?

Having just returned from a year in Israel, I am mindful that these questions linger on in Jewish consciousness today. Even after all the museum building of the past two decades and the codification of the Holocaust in the public rituals of the Jewish state, the "black milk" of history continues to trouble Jews and non-Jews alike. The unique trauma that decimated European Jewry has been echoed in the history of other peoples brutalized by war: Cambodians under the rule of Pol Pot as well as Chinese trapped in Nanking. For many Jews (Israelis and others too), the *Shoah* (as the Holocaust is called in Hebrew) provides the most concrete ground for empathy with the suffering of others. The more Jews grapple with the ungraspable factitiousness of Auschwitz, the more they must hear—and respond to—the voices of pain that cut through other histories as well. Such responsiveness to history may be the most important outcome of memorializing the Nanking Massacre.

Yet before empathy, we must seek to understand the prolonged silence that once surrounded the events of 1937–1938. First, we have to construct the chronologies of remembrance and forgetting in both the

Chinese and the Jewish responses to historical trauma. Only later can we understand more fully what is meant by the "forgotten Holocaust." It is at the point where analogies break down that we may discover what Chinese and Jewish memory have to teach us and the world. Finally, as we press beyond the rhetorical utility of generalizations such as "the" Holocaust, it may be possible to start hearing the discrete voices of survivors themselves. Slowly, one by one by one, they bring us back to the "black milk" of Paul Celan: to a grief unassuaged either by reparation payments from Germany or formal apologies by the Japanese state.

Chronologies of Remembrance and Forgetting

It is, I believe, no accident that the Princeton University conference took place sixty years after the events of 1937–1938. Geographical and temporal distance from the site of historical trauma augmented the processes of memorialization. Chinese students who may not have thought about or been allowed to reflect much about the horrors of the Japanese occupation on the mainland found the murderous past more accessible from abroad. This return to historical memory is analogous to commemorations of the Tiananmen Square Massacre that began after 1989 among overseas students and intellectuals.[6] In fact, the intensity of interest in the Nanking Massacre today may in part be due to the enforced amnesia about 1989 that lingers in China today. The less one can speak about recent pain, the greater the commitment to document the once-forgotten atrocities in Nanking.

This tension between remembrance and forgetting, however, is not exclusively China's predicament. It marks the historical consciousness of Jews as well—though they may be seen by others as more vigilant guardians of memory. In fact, as Andreas Huyssen points out in his preface to *The Act of Memory: Holocaust Memorials in History,* "Every memory inevitably depends both on distance and forgetting, the very things that undermine its stability and reliability."[7] To forget part of the past leaves one more open to other aspects of history. National communities, like individuals, are constantly reshaping both past and present. The alchemy between the two depends on the needs of the moment. Jews, like survivors of the Nanking Massacre, have found that their connection to trauma is not always welcome in the public mind. Israel— like China—became more open to narratives of victimization only when it no longer needed heroes larger than life.

At first Jews, too, turned away from the "black milk" of history in favor of narratives more congenial to the tasks of state building. In 1942, six years before official Israeli independence, one can already detect great ambivalence about historical memory among Jews who settled the Land. A short story by Haim Hazaz, "The Sermon," captures this inclination toward amnesia quite effectively. It is the tale of a kibbutznik named Yudka—an everyman kind of Jew. A hard-working socialist whose virtues would be readily recognizable by the architects of peasant revolution in Yenan, Yudka asks to meet with the central committee to talk about a matter that weighs heavily on his heart. A man of few words, not unlike China's guerrilla warriors, Comrade Yudka ends up delivering a prophetic indictment of Jewish history:

> Oppression, defamation, persecution, martyrdom. And again oppression, defamation, persecution and martyrdom. And again and again and again, without end . . . that's what's in it and nothing more! . . . It bores you to death, it's just plain dull. . . . Jewish history is dull, uninteresting. It has no glory of action, no heroes and conquerors, no rulers and masters of their own fate, just a collection of wounded, hunted, groaning and wailing wretches always begging for mercy. . . . I would simply forbid teaching our children Jewish history.[8]

This rejection of historical consciousness is rooted in an aversion to suffering. Yudka, an Eastern European Jew, knows only too well the facts of oppression and martyrdom that he wants to withhold from Israel's new generation. Having heard too much groaning, he wants to fill their ears with more inspiring sounds. Such sounds were not forthcoming from Auschwitz—nor from the Nanking Massacre. So the dilemma for comrades who wanted less "boring" tales deepened after the war.

In Israel the discomfort with unheroic "wretches" grew more manifest after 1948. With the end of the Holocaust and the establishment of the new state, the country became filled with survivors who carried with them terrible memories of having begged for mercy to no avail. The new homeland, caught in a series of wars, had no use for such memories. It needed the bodies of survivors to fight Arab armies bent upon destroying the new Jewish state. It had little empathy for their pain-riddled souls. As a result, many Holocaust survivors changed their names with more Hebraicized sounds. With new names, it was easier to leave the past behind. Yet it kept coming up. In 1953, the Knesset established the official Yad Vashem Memorial Authority, which was to generate and monitor Israel's narratives of the Holocaust. Under the mandate of this institution, Israel also began commemorating the official *Yom Hashoah*—or Holocaust Day, as it is known in English. This occasion, however, was consciously linked to the heroism of the fighters of the Warsaw Ghetto—rather than to the millions of Jews exterminated in the death camps. Yael S. Feldman, an Israeli literary scholar, recalls this selective remembering as follows: "For us, *Yom hashoah vehagvurah* [Day of Holocaust and Heroism] was not "Martyrs' Day," as my current Israeli calendar translates it, but rather a celebration of resistance and national pride, a prolegomenon to the Israeli Day of Independence."[9]

What changed between the 1950s and the 1980s? Certainly more than the accumulation of historical evidence. The main breach in the official narratives of heroic resistance came with the Eichman trial of 1963. Fifteen years after the founding of the state, survivors began to tell their own story in public. Nothing that they said was new but their tales suddenly fell on more receptive ears. The decade and a half of distance from the trauma seemed to have lessened the burden of guilt and shame. Suddenly there was room in public rhetoric for some interest in the "groaning of wretchedness." More historical details now made an impact upon the distaste for old-world Jews who supposedly went into the crematoria "like sheep to slaughter." In the 1970s, especially after the Yom Kippur War of 1973, Israeli historical narratives became increasingly complex as public criticism about state policy became more widespread. The fervent need for the sort of larger-than-life heroes that had animated Yudka in "The Sermon" (and also in the Six-Day War of 1967) lessened, and there emerged a more pervasive interest in and sympathy for victims—be they Jews or Palestinians. Israeli historical consciousness was no longer so defensive—identifying all complex narratives of suffering with the mentality of *Galut* (exile) Jews. Stories heard and gathered abroad began to have moral weight at home.[10]

This process of circling back to memories of victimization is not unlike that of the memorialization of the Nanking Massacre. Immediately after 1949 China, too, was consumed with the challenge of state building. With the outbreak of the Korean War, the need for grandiose narratives of heroic fighters grew even more intense. Stories and films like *Songhua Jiang Shang* (On the Sungari River) began to popularize images of ordinary Chinese villagers successfully repelling well-armed Japanese troops. Fighters with homemade weapons were a more useful "memory" than was the slaughter of Nanking's helpless civilians and the repeated raping of naked women. If the Rabe diaries and John Magee's film lay dormant in private archives it was not simply because family members had not publicized their importance. There was no receptivity (yet) for their images of a China all too prone to Japanese aggression. The ordinary citizens who had been left behind in the city as well as the terrified soldiers who tore off their uniforms to get into the foreigners' Safety Zone were like blank spaces on a screen crowded by vivid images of heroic resistance. For a while it seemed as if China "forgot" the events of 1937–1938—and not only because of Japanese suppression of historical facts.

To understand this turn away from what Yudka termed the "groan of wretches," it is useful to look at artistic representations of historical events and figures. On the Israeli side, there is the towering statue of Mordechai Anielewicz, the fallen leader of the Warsaw Ghetto Uprising that occupies the central public space in Kibbutz Yad Mordechai. This kibbutz was named after the fallen hero and takes its inspiration from the larger-than-life image of a strong man who faces his enemies with a fierce look and a homemade bomb in one fist.[11] On the Chinese side, an equally heroic message soars out of Chen Yifei's 1972 canvas "Eulogy of the Yellow River." Produced in the decade of the Cultural Revolution, this painting continues the official remembrance promoted by the Communist Party in the 1950s: One lone peasant-soldier stands on a high cliff while cranes fly by him with no power to disturb his serene, fighting gaze. The man and his huge bayonet are one.[12]

In a world in which single heroes overcame irresistible forces there is little room for the depiction of "wretches." Like Israel, China had to experience an interruption of state-sponsored narratives before turning more sympathetically to the victims of the Nanking Massacre. The death of Mao Tse-tung in 1976, and the decade of doubt that followed, nurtured the literature of the "wounded" as well as a more complex appreciation of history. Single-minded focus on the evils of "imperialism" began to wane, along with faith in Maoism. An outpouring of details about the horrors of the Cultural Revolution followed. If people could imagine themselves as victims of the Red Terror (a more convenient alternative than recalling one's own participation in the brutal events of 1966–1976), then the specter of helpless Chinese in the past became conceivable as well. By the late 1970s the need for larger-than-life heroes had diminished considerably. Chen Yifei's 1979 painting "Thinking About History from My Space" shows the shift of mood quite dramatically. This canvas is even larger than the 1972 one of the lone soldier. It too has a central figure—but this time it is the image of an intellectual. We see him mostly from the back. His white shirt sleeves are rolled up—to show us he is hard at work, having left the ease of the empty armchair that occupies the front right. Historical contemplation is painful labor and the canvas does not shy away from brutality. In fact its most striking images are a man being led off in chains by Japanese soldiers and a bare-breasted young woman being led away from what we can only imagine as rape and humiliation.[13]

Side views and tangential details mark this painting in the same way as they do the new historiography after the death of Mao. Instead of single, frontally idealized heroes, we are drawn closer to the subject of helpless victims. In the late 1980s, almost a decade after Chen Yifei's "Thinking About History from My Space," the Association for Asian Studies launched a new research project "to commemorate the Chinese Holocaust." Michael Lestz, one of the early participants in the discussions of the "Chinese Holocaust," wrote about the striking amnesia that seemed to have colored Chinese reactions to the Nanking Massacre in earlier decades. Commenting about Chinese reticence in comparison to Jewish memorializations of the Holocaust and Japanese commemorations of Hiroshima and Nagasaki, Lestz wrote:

> It is almost as though Chinese memories of the war have been rocketed into a barely accessible psychic outer space where they occasionally can be referred to, generally in a highly polemical or emotionally exaggerated way, but usually ignored. China's collective war memories are a bit like a photo album: stored away in the attic, when pictures happened to be looked at they evoke pain and rage and tears but they are rarely taken out and examined that [sic] over time these reactions become irrelevant or stereotyped emotional frisson.[14]

These remarks, written less than three months before the Tiananmen Square massacre of 1989, contain a warning about overidentifying the Nanking events as the "Chinese Holocaust." After the bloody events of June 4, interest in the "family album" grew more intense. Far from being consigned to the "attic" of historical consciousness, the Nanking Massacre moved into the foreground, especially after the Chinese government found it to be a useful tool for "patriotic education."[15] Whereas, before the Tiananmen events, Chinese historian Wu Tianwei could ask (rather open-endedly), *"Zhongguo de huojie?"*[16] ("Is there a Chinese holocaust?") after 1989 film director Wu Ziniu consciously styled himself as "China's Stephen Spielberg" and publicized his new work—*Rape of Nanking*—in a manner clearly reminiscent of American Holocaust education programs: "Not long ago, officials would have denied Wu permission to make this film, never mind screening. . . . They prohibited public debates about the massacre and forbade survivors to seek compensation. Perhaps because now they felt the need to bolster their credentials as nationalistic Chinese, China's leaders gave the film the go-ahead."[17]

Interest in the album in the attic keeps growing each year, both in China and abroad. New leaves are being added to the album: Reverend John Magee's film (rediscovered at the Yale Divinity School) and diplomat George Rosen's report to Hitler, as well as John Rabe's diaries, now augment our images of the carnage in Nanking. Iris Chang makes a direct analogy between these documents and the movie *Schindler's List:* Here we have another German businessman who protected helpless victims. Rabe was the leader of the local Nazi Party and Safety Zone chairman in Nanking. This double role provides some creative tension in the process of historical memorialization. Chang's book details the echoes between the predicament of Japanese soldiers in search of food, and the destitute Chinese in need of protection as well as Rabe's own hunger in Berlin during the early years after Germany's defeat. When the Nazi businessman confronts Japanese looters on the streets of Nanking, he had learned that their supply column did not arrive and they could not count on the column for any nourishment.[18] In 1948, when Rabe himself was suffering from malnutrition and unemployment (because of his Nazi Party membership), the mayor of Nanking brought the funds collected in China to Switzerland to buy "milk powder, sausages tea, coffee, beef, butter and jam"[19] for the former rescuer in Berlin. This cycle of need and compassion, however, cannot be conveyed in all its complexity once the public memorialization process gains momentum. The moving of Rabe's tombstone from Berlin to the Memorial Hall for the Victims of the Massacre in Nanking in April 1987 cemented a simply heroic version of the Nazi "Buddha."

For those who seek a more nuanced view of the past, museums provide little space for augmented critical reflection. The search for history's true face is further impeded by the fact that the Japanese government is still suppressing the facts about the Nanking Massacre. Researchers such as those who travel to Princeton, New Jersey, from Japan are making an impact on policy and textbooks, and are slowly opening up this painful chapter of Japanese history. The collaboration of the U.S. government after the war in protecting war criminals is also being discussed, along with the fallacy of the postwar Guomindang policy of *yide baoyuan* (repay cruelty with virtue). In light of these developments, it is too simplistic to blame the Japanese, the Americans, or the Nationalists for the longstanding "silence" about the Nanking Massacre. If we are to understand China's own aversion to a victim-laden image of history, we must look beyond the politics of commemoration. We must begin to excavate the lower regions of cultural ambivalence about suffering. In this endeavor, Jewish comparisons may be useful as well.

Jewish tradition, on one hand, places great value on historical memory. The current slogan "Never again" is rooted in a religious commitment that goes back to the Passover ritual that commemorates Jews' exodus from Egypt. Each year Jews are called upon to recall their redemption from slavery as if it were a personal experience. The Passover *Hagaddah* (a story that Jews retell each spring) insists on this immediate identification with the past. At the same time, there are Jewish prophets like Isaiah who speak about forgetting as a blessing from God precisely because it helps one get over the pain and rancor of history.[20] Similarly, in Chinese tradition there is a tension between the Confucian commitment to historical memory and the Daoist concern with troublesome emotions aroused by painful remembrance. For those who would inscribe the Nanking Massacre in the consciousness of the Chinese people (and of the world) there is no better place to start than the Analects' own tribute to recollection that is found in Book II, Chapter 11. Here, the Master is quoted as saying: "*Wengu er zhixin, ke yi wei shi ye*" (One who remembers history [literally, warms up the embers of the past] can be truly considered a teacher.)

To blow new life into the ashes of the past is a difficult task shared by Chinese and Jews alike. In the wake of historical trauma, it is not surprising that both cultures turned away from suffocating images. Daoists in China understood and warned about the dangers of historical memory as early as the Han dynasty: "*Qing you yi sheng, bu yi ze wu qing*" (Feelings rise out of memory; if there is no memory, feelings dissolve as well). This passage from the *Jin Shu* is still relevant today.[21] It is a reminder that the sense-defying brutality of the Holocaust as well as of the Nanking Massacre is inherently disturbing. It was an obsession with distressing memories that led the German-Jewish poet Paul Celan to write about the "black milk" of historical consciousness. This is what we must turn to now in order to explore the similarities *and* the differences between the Jewish and the Chinese "holocausts."

A Tale of Two Holocausts

To call the Nanking Massacre and the Japanese occupation of China a "holocaust" is to assume that the Jewish Holocaust is a knowable, translatable quantity. This assumption also suggests that Germany remembers, whereas Japan does not; that Jews commemorate with the world's approval, whereas Chinese are still making their way to public acknowledgment of a wounded history. To stretch the reason-defying annihilation of European Jews to the Asian continent sets up a terribly dangerous competition for numbers and scars:

> In terms of measure and cruelty of the genocide, its duration and large numbers of people killed, says a professor of history of Southern Illinois University, "Neither Hiroshima nor Jewish Holocaust can rival the Nanking Massacre." The international community estimated that more than 300,000 Chinese were killed and 20,000 women raped [*sic*] within six weeks of continuous Massacre.[22]

What is gained by such comparisons? Or rather, what is being asked for through this insistence that Chinese suffering rivaled and surpassed that of the Jews and the Japanese? Surely the attention and sympathy of the world is part of what is demanded here—but also the reassurance that quantifiable trauma is reasonable (that is to say, understandable by a professor of history). What is being masked in this competition for numbers is the dread that suffering of this magnitude will not fit into existing categories of historical understanding; that it will expose our certainties about the European Holocaust—and the Chinese one as well. Such doubts may cast one into a desolate darkness between collective amnesia and personal grief.

When Paul Celan wrote about "black milk" he was pointing to this shadowy realm. He knew, already in 1944–1945, that his contemporaries disbelieved the survivors' reports. Celan also understood that the linguistic and conceptual universe of postwar Europe could not accommodate the truths he had seen. He persisted in writing elusive, dark poems because he could not stop remembering and because he was infuriated by the German public's repeated efforts to read his work as metaphorical. When "Deathsfuge" appeared in Germany, one reviewer praised it for "its removal of everything concrete" (hounds? iron rods? graves in the air?) and "its absorbing rhythms, romanticizing metaphor, lyrical alchemy."[23] The will to blindly misread history never ceased to amaze— and to wound—the German-Jewish poet. It is this conscious misperception of "iron rods" and "graves in the air" that must also concern those of us who seek to understand China's "holocaust."

At the end of our panel presentation for the Princeton Conference, the audience was asked to submit questions in writing. A flood of notes came toward the podium. One addressed in blue ink to me captured this concern with metaphorizing the Nanking Massacre. At the top of a white sheet, there was a box marked "Important Question!!!!!!!!!" Below, in neat handwriting I read:

> It's easier to write a poem from one of those whose anger and pain were somehow soothed by sincere apologies and redress money. Whereas there is no luxury of playing with words but swallowing tears for those who suffered in the Rape of Nanking.

> Dr. Schwarcz, can you comment on that?

I took the microphone with trepidation. I did not know the person who dared to unveil this grief in words. I understood the practical implications in the demand for reparation payments and a formal gesture of regret by the Japanese government. Nonetheless, the statement revealed something more. I chose to speak about that: "Why keep on swallowing tears?" I asked. Jews like Paul Celan who wrote bitter poems did not do so because Germans gave them money or psychological permission to speak. Rather, they wrested the right to memory from their own wounded hearts through a huge effort. They had not been "playing with words." In fact, Celan's language eventually became a knife turned against his own identity and he ended up committing suicide, as did so many other publicly prominent survivors of the Holocaust (for instance, the Italian chemist-writer Primo Levi and his bunkmate from Auschwitz, the Belgian philosopher Jean Amery).

Jewish testimonies after the war were not "soothed" by anything: not by reparations and not even by the sympathy of other Jews. Too often survivors spoke about their dark secrets into the ears of an unhearing, unforgiving world. We are now more aware of the importance of their recollections because we no longer need heroic images. This is what I emphasized in my answer to the "important question" at the Princeton Conference: that Chinese intellectuals of the older generation must also stop swallowing their tears and start speaking more often and in more detail to the younger generation. Only by delving into the crevices of helplessness and dread will they be able to pass on the true gift of historical consciousness.

The world needs to grapple with more than the question of how many were killed or raped in Nanking in 1937–1938. It is time, sixty years after the event, to explore the strategies used to evade, allegorize, and romanticize genocide. Because of time limitations, I pointed out only one: the notion that Japan's apology for the Massacre would somehow set it to rest. Can one government's words (and perhaps reparation payments) patch up the gaping wounds in the past of another nation? This possibility lies at the core of the German word—and policy—of *wiedergutmachung*. Literally, this term means "to make good again"— as if the money that the German government pays survivors of the Holocaust could repair the severed lives torn apart in the death camps.

What words—or money—could ever bring back the miscarried child from the womb of Li Xiuying, the survivor who has already testified in Tokyo courts? I am not saying that Li and thousands of other Chinese do not deserve reparations and should not make every effort to compile legal cases against the Japanese government. I know from my own parents' experiences how difficult (and important) it is to partake of the *wiedergutmachung* process: Often you cannot remember what really happened until you try to quantify and verify it for a foreign government. At the same time, wounds within cannot be somatized by doctors hired to estimate the culpability of a regime far removed from the events that still haunt you. To fight for reparations is to persuade ourselves that the past can indeed be made whole again. But it cannot. This is one of the lessons of the Jewish *Shoah*. Public words and government funds cannot heal the wounds of memory.

The other warning concerns the overuse of images of cruelty. In the fight against amnesia it is tempting to parade newly discovered photographs of cruelty inflicted by the Japanese upon helpless Chinese men and women in Nanking. In the Jewish context, this is exactly what the Israeli government is doing each time it insists on taking visiting foreign dignitaries to Yad Vashem. It has become a fixed ritual: If you want to understand and befriend us, you must first come and look at these photographs on the hill outside Jerusalem. Here you will shed some well-publicized tears; here you will lay a wreath of flowers on one of the stones bearing the names of various death camps. Then, and only then, can we proceed to business. Snippets of horrifying history thus become an appetizer for the meal of friendly diplomacy to follow.

Some Israelis who witness this ritual are revolted by its implications. One of my friends, the curator of a private archaeological museum in the old city of Jerusalem, put it this way: "Why do they keep on dragging these foreign men to gape at our naked women? Did you ever notice how they always stop in front of that enlargement of the four women about to be shot into the mass grave at Babi Yar? Their breasts point to the camera, their hands seek to cover their pubic hair, the children, naked too, hang on for dear life. All this right at eye level! I hate to see the visitor's eyes on these women. They were killed once. Was that not enough? Does the degradation have to go on, and on? And what do we get by being seen as forever naked? Forever frightened? Forever on the verge of being shot dead?"

My friend's reaction to the Yad Vashem ritual is not unique. Nor is it simply a contemporary echo of Yudka's indictment of the lachrymose version of Jewish history. It is very much a post-Auschwitz critique of the political and erotic manipulation of genocidal images. Naked women are also becoming the main currency in commemorations of the Nanking Massacre. The most famous one seems to be the one that is reprinted as the largest image on the front cover of *Nanjing datusha tuzhen*.[24] It is the photograph on the bottom right. The eye follows the thread of smaller images of beatings, decapitations, and dead bodies until it comes to a Chinese woman with her pants lowered, genitals exposed while a seemingly proud Japanese soldier kneels alongside her. The pain and shame on the woman's face are blurred by the poor quality of the black and white. But the central expanse of white flesh is very clear. Is this what we want the world to see? Know? Think about? Is this why so many histories of the Japanese occupation of China condense the events of 1932–1938 into the ever-tantalizing phrase "Rape of Nanking"? Is rape the only metaphor for massive pain?

In turning away from such prurient language and images, we may find it useful to think about the prolonged Jewish struggle to create a narrative of the Holocaust. Paul Celan was not alone in his quest to find words for what could never be truly expressed. Every writer who has circled the *Shoah* has come up against the limits of representation. The French survivor Pierre Vidal-Naquet described this predicament when he wrote: "I was convinced that . . . everything should necessarily go through discourse . . . but beyond this, or before this, there was something irreducible which, for better or worse, I would still call reality?"[25] Reality in this case is not something assumed but a vague entity to be sought after. As with the careful reconstruction of the facts of the Nanking Massacre, so too, the Jewish Holocaust has to be continuously excavated out of public rhetoric. Numbers, however, do not necessarily strengthen reality. Photographs of naked woman, however gripping, do not necessarily deepen understanding of pain. Often, small (very small) details arrest and alert us to what really happened back then.

Let me give you one example used to great effect by Saul Friedlander in his introduction to *Probing the Limits of Representation.* It concerns Lithuania—where in 1942 one Nazi troop, Einsatzkommando Number 3, under the command of SS Colonel Karl Jaeger, executed 137,000 Jews, among whom there were 55,000 women and 34,000 children. As Friedlander puts it, "This is the apocalyptic background"[26]—a snippet of a huge canvas that can only shock but not really move us. Instead, he focuses our attention on a single page of the "Kovno Ghetto Diary," dated January 14, 1942: "An order to bring all dogs and cats to the small synagogue on Veliuonos Street, where they were shot." A footnote adds: "The bodies of cats and dogs remained in the synagogue on Veliuonos Street for several months; the Jews were forbidden to remove them.[27] To redirect our attention from 137,000 massacred Jews to the stinking corpses of cats and dogs is a masterful rhetorical feat. We are thereby invited—and enabled—to get closer to the heart of the inferno. The idea of 55,000 women and 34,000 children numbs us into helpless wonder. But the fact that Nazis could be so cruel as to prevent Jews from claiming the remains of their pets from a ravaged house of worship can provoke outrage. From outrage may grow the seeds of new understanding.

How to Translate "Knowing" into "Telling"

The task of trimming facts according to the needs of narrative design is familiar to all historians. This task acquires moral urgency when the subjects happens to be the *Shoah* or the Nanking Massacre. Given the oversaturated space of public discourse, numbers and photographs are of limited use. This was the reason, for example, that the filmmaker Claude Lanzmann refused to use documentary footage in his epic *Shoah*. Coming after the wildly successful public television series *Holocaust*, Lanzmann's film sought to overcome the commodification of Auschwitz. Therefore he simply lets survivors speak. Nothing more than their words, the close-ups of their faces, and a few long shots of the landscape of the death camps as it lies covered by grass today.

Grassy fields are more than metaphors for our inevitable distance from the events of the *Shoah*. They represent the cultural phenomena of social amnesia that surrounds survivors of the Holocaust. Those who speak out in various forms of testimony know the ultimate power of grassy fields. Yet they hope to set up a stony path with their words. The Yale University Fortunoff Video Archive, for example, provides a useful model for this kind of guardianship of survivor memories. To be sure, there are many other, more lavish projects under way at the Washington Holocaust Museum and through funds currently provided by Stephen Spielberg. Yet the chief virtue of the Yale Archive is its unadorned commitment to recording simply the words of those who have been "there." Geoffrey Hartman, cofounder of the archive, has summarized its mission as follows: "Oral history does not try to turn the survivor into a historian . . . but to value him as a human witness to a dehumanizing situation. We cannot allow only images made by the perpetrators to inhabit our memory."[28]

The Nanking Massacre is not yet as well documented through oral history materials as the Jewish Holocaust. The search for images other than those provided by the perpetrators is well on the way. The Magee film and the Rabe diaries are an important beginning. The photographic history of Japanese carnage published by James Yin and Shi Young also moves the documentary process along. Here we have not only the familiar images of naked women and decapitated men, but also the faces and voices of individual survivors. The gaunt cheeks and drawn mouth of Xu Ziqian, for example, confirms the simple tale in the passage that follows:

> In the winter of 1937 my family moved to Yihe Road in the International Safety Zone . . . we bumped into Japanese soldiers. A soldier picked up my grandfather's hat with his bayonet and threw it away. Then he stabbed Grandfather's chest with the bayonet. Putting his hands over the wound, Grandfather tried to stop the blood which stained his clothes. I helped Grandfather struggle back to the Safety Zone. He died a few days later.[29]

An aged man's recollections of what he witnessed as a young boy cuts through many layers of generalization about Japanese brutality and Chinese pain. The hat that was pierced before the body speaks volumes about wanton cruelty. Keeping our gaze on such small details helps us understand the larger picture. But we need more voices, more detailed recollections before we can truly grasp—and appreciate—the distinction between historian and survivor. The first will always be committed to adding up the total picture, to providing explanations. The latter will invariably complicate and untangle the artful designs of the first.

This tension between the "knowing" of the historian and that of those returning from the death camps is also the subject of several essays by Dr. Dori Laub, also a founder of the Yale Video Archive. A psychiatrist and a survivor, Laub is especially well suited to reflect on the problems of narrative. Trauma, in his view, is defined by its assault upon the conventional structures of knowing. The more extreme the anguish, the fewer the resources for translating it into conveyable discourse. Yet the effort to push against this barrier is compelling for the survivor and his audience alike:

> Knowing is dependent on language—not only our knowing the Holocaust through hearing the survivor's language, but the ability of the survivor to grasp and recall his experiences through formulating it. Because of the radical break between the Holocaust and what culture is, the survivor often cannot find categories of thought or words for his experiences. . . . He cannot make sense of it; he cannot know it. Indeed, he may not even be able to remember it, except for haunting, fragmented visual precepts. That he cannot integrate effectively into his personality.[30]

Assembling such fragments is the joint task of the doctor and of the historian. Neither is served well if he or she imagines the gap between experience and language to be less than vast. Those of us who are "witnesses-through-the imagination"[31] have to acknowledge our indebtedness to the absent language of the dead and the halting cadence of survivors.

Reassembling the Nanking Massacre, in this context, is a difficult and delicate operation. The needs of public commemoration are amply evident. Clear images of atrocity are demanded to educate subsequent generations about the dangers of war. The "lessons" of the Nanking Massacre, like those of the Holocaust, may yet be inscribed in stone—as in the case of the Simon Wiesenthal Museum of Tolerance in Los Angeles. The English name of this site promises explicit understanding through an instructive narrative. In Hebrew, however, the museum's name is Beit Hashoah, which suggests something else: an awkward home for a story of ravage that can never be fully told, for which there are no reparations and which is far from certain to nurture humanistic values like "tolerance."

Commemorating the Nanking Massacre presents similar dilemmas. Which story to tell: The one needed (and generated) by China's currently nationalistic government? The one pieced together from fragments of evidence gathered in a climate of reflection abroad? Looking at Jewish memorializations of the Holocaust with such questions in mind should, I hope, complicate the picture. As in the Chen Yifei canvas "Thinking About History from My Space," we are accosted first by images of disturbing helplessness—so different from the myths of heroic resistance generated in the early stages of state building both in Israel and on the Chinese mainland. How long do we allow ourselves to dwell on dark shadows from the past? In the painting, a young man who has left his armchair seems to have endless time for the contemplation of disturbing narratives. We may feel more pressured to stand back from the bewildering collage.

Nonetheless, it may be useful to remember the "black milk" of Paul Celan. To know history in the ways that Celan and Dori Laub know it is to come face to face with something harsher than a nursing mother who provides nourishing "lessons." This kind of historical consciousness is, first and foremost, disturbing. It disrupts tales of heroism and resistance. Its only virtue, if it may be called that, is to keep us from ever assuming that we can return to normalcy—to the world as it was before the Holocaust, before Nanking. In the words of Geoffrey Hartman, "Before Auschwitz we were children in our imagination of evil; after Auschwitz, we are no longer children."[32]

Reparations, actual or metaphorical, do not restore our innocence. Japan may end up, like Germany, paying money to the victims; but that does not make *wiedergutmachung* a moral reality. No funds, apologies, or words repair the breach between past and present. The lost lives, like that of Xu Ziang's grandfather, are gone, along with the pierced hat. The loss endures. This impossibility of "making good again" lies at the heart of the poetry of Dan Pagis, who, like Paul Celan, was born in Bukovina. Pagis chose to write in Hebrew, the language of the new state of Israel. This tongue, like the new nation, demands optimism and didactic messages. Despite such pressures, Dan Pagis wrote in modern Hebrew about broken survivors who shared a dream of normalcy. His poem "Draft of a Reparations Agreement" (below) gives voice to this futile wish. It shows the absurdity of trying to turn the clock back to a pre-Auschwitz world. It is this sense of painful irony that we, too, must nurture as we contemplate the passage of the Nanking Massacre from history into memory.

> All right, gentlemen who cry blue murder as always,
> nagging miracle makers,
> quiet!
> Everything will be returned to its place,
> paragraph after paragraph.
> The scream back into the throat.
> The gold teeth back to the gums.
> The terror.
> The smoke back to the chimneys and further on and inside
> back to the hollow of bones,
>> and already you will be covered with skin and sinews and
>> you will love,
> look, you will have your lives back,
> sit in the living room, read the evening paper.
> Here you are. Nothing is too late.
> As to the yellow star:
> it will be torn from your chest
> immediately
> and will emigrate
> to the sky.[33]

Nothing is too late? Pagis seems to assert as fact what all survivors know to be a question: "The smoke back to the chimneys"? "The scream back into the throat"? "The hat back on grandfather's head"? Such odd questions are memory's troubling bequest to subsequent generations. To some, this may seem a paltry or even a dangerous gift. Yet it is the only "light" that Jewish remembrance can cast on the gaping wound that is the Nanking Massacre even today.

Notes

1. Paul Celan, *Selected Poems*, transl. Michael Hamburger (New York: Persea Books, 1972).

2. Historical consciousness is a willful connectedness to one's cultural inheritance. We are all born into our own temporal frameworks, bounded by family and
society. This initial objective fact needs to be appropriated in a subjective fashion as
each individual reaches his or her maturity. Initially, one may be tempted to emphasize personal definitions of cultural identity only—for example, "I am a scientist" or
"I am an artist." Later comes the more complex wrestling with the fact that I am also
"Chinese," "Jewish," or "Black." These larger contexts can often be burdensome,
especially if they are framed by experiences of terrible victimization such as the
Holocaust, apartheid, or the Nanking Massacre. Young people in the early stages of
self-definition may wish to avoid the history of utter helplessness and shame that
often marked relatives who went through such trauma. When, finally, one lays claim
to one's lineage in such pain-ridden cultures, it is with a particularly complex sense
of historical consciousness. This is the "black milk" that Celan wrote about in his
poem "Deathsfuge." The knowledge that one must come to terms with terrible grief
leaves its mark not only on immediate survivors but also on generations that come
later. Those of us born after the actual events that constitute the trauma of the Holocaust and of the Nanking Massacre have to redefine the meaning of "history" and of
"consciousness" to accommodate the nightmares that are our collective inheritance.

3. See the chapter called "May Fourth as Allegory" in Vera Schwarcz, *The
Chinese Enlightenment: Intellectuals and the Legacy of the May Fourth Movement
of 1919* (Berkeley: University of California Press, 1986), pp. 240–282.

4. Elie Wiesel, *Discours d'Oslo* (Nobel Prize acceptance speech) (Paris: Genre
Humain, 1991).

5. Iris Chang, *The Rape of Nanking: The Forgotten Holocaust of World War II*
(New York: Basic Books, 1997).

6. For a fuller discussion of the role of overseas intellectuals in commemora-
tions of the Tiananmen Massacre of 1989, see Vera Schwarcz, "No Solace from
Lethe," in *The Living Tree: The Changing Meaning of Being Chinese Today*, ed. Tu
Wei-ming (Stanford, CA: Stanford University Press, 1994), pp. 64–87.

7. Andreas Huyssen, "Monument and Memory in a Postmodern Age," in *The
Art of Memory: Holocaust Memorials*, ed. James Young (Munich: Prestel-Verlag,
1994), p. 9.

8. Haim Hazaz, "The Sermon," in *Modern Hebrew Literature*, ed. Robert Alter
(New York: Behrman House, 1975), pp. 274–275.

9. Yael S. Feldman, "Whose Story Is It, Anyway? Ideology and Psychology in
the Representation of the Shoah in Israeli Literature," in *Probing the Limits of Representation*, ed. Saul Friedlander (Cambridge, MA: Harvard University Press, 1992),
p. 223.

10. I am indebted to two Israeli colleagues and friends—Professor Richard Cohen
and Sidhra Ezrahi (both of Hebrew University) for their help in finding sources and
identifying themes in Israeli narratives of the Shoah.

11. Saul Friedlander, "Memory of the Shoah in Israel: Symbols, Rituals and Ideological Polarization," in *The Art of Memory*, ed. Young, p. 149.

12. *The Homecoming of Chen Yifei: Retrospective Exhibition* (Hong Kong: Press-
room Printer and Design, 1997), p. 37.

13. Ibid., p. 39.

14. Michael Leszt, "War and Memory: The Chinese Holocaust," paper delivered
at the Association for Asian Studies Convention, Washington, DC, March 18, 1989,

p. 3. For a fuller version of this argument, see Michael Leszt, "Lishi de mingji" (History's inscriptions), *Jiuzhou* (Chinese culture quarterly) vol. 1, no. 4 (Summer 1987), pp. 97–106.

15. Ian Johnson, "Breaking the Silence: Beijing Permits Screening of Nanjing Massacre Film," *Far Eastern Economic Review* (August 24, 1995), p. 40.

16. Wu Tianwei, "Zhongguo de huojie?" (Is there a Chinese holocaust?) *Jiuzhou*, vol. 1, no. 4, pp. 107–110.

17. Johnson, "Breaking the Silence."

18. Chang, *Rape of Nanking*, p. 115.

19. Ibid., p. 193.

20. Benjamin Blech, *The Secret of Hebrew Words* (Northvale, NJ: Jason Aronson, 1991), p. 187.

21. I am indebted to Professor Yu Ying-shi of Princeton University for drawing my attention to this Han dynasty source about memory and for conversations that inspired and sustained my work on a comparative study of the Chinese and Jewish commitment to historical memory. See Vera Schwarcz, *Bridge Across Broken Time: Chinese and Jewish Cultural Memory* (New Haven, CT: Yale University, 1998).

22. "The Other Holocaust: Nanjing Massacre," http://www.smn.cojp/gallery/nanjing/. This essay had the added posting "15,028 readers have visited NJ Massacre page since September 20, 1996" (as of August 26, 1997).

23. John Felstiner, *Paul Celan: Poet, Survivor, Jew* (New Haven, CT: Yale University Press, 1995), p. 71.

24. Zhongguo Dananguan, *Nanjing datusha tuzhen* (Pictorial documentary of the Nanjing Massacre) (Changchun: Jilin Remin Chubanshe, 1995).

25. Friedlander, "Introduction," *Probing the Limits of Representation*, p. 20.

26. Ibid.

27. Ibid., p. 21.

28. Judith Miller, *One, by One, by One: Facing the Holocaust* (New York: Simon and Schuster, 1990), p. 269.

29. James Yin and Shi Young, *The Rape of Nanking: An Undeniable History in Photographs* (Chicago: Innovative Publishing Group, 1996) p. 167.

30. Dori Laub, "Knowing and Not Knowing the Holocaust: Prologue," *Psychoanalytic Inquiry*, vol. 5, no. 5 (1995), p. 3.

31. Ibid., p. 6.

32. Geoffrey Hartman, "The Book of Destruction," in *Probing the Limits of Representation*, ed. Friedlander, p. 333.

33. Dan Pagis, "Draft of a Reparations Agreement," in *Points of Departure*, transl. Stephen Mitchell (Philadelphia: Jewish Historical Society, 1981), p. 27.

10

The Tokyo War Crimes Trial, War Responsibility, and Postwar Responsibility

Onuma Yasuaki

When we step back from the Nanking Massacre itself and observe the larger environment of the postwar era, it becomes clear that much of the debate is related to the Japanese people's response to their ignominious defeat, including the judgments of the Tokyo War Crimes Trial. Although it was easy for the Allied powers to view Japan as the defeated nation and themselves as the victors, it has not been nearly so easy for the Japanese to understand this "victors' mentality," to say nothing of the considerable complications involved in accepting their responsibility for the war. How much blame should fall to the emperor? How much to high military and governmental officials? Or even to some civilian workers? Should any blame fall to the common people themselves? How much responsibility does each of these parties bear? How much should each pay, both emotionally and in restitution?

Onuma Yasuaki examines these difficult questions and peels through layer after layer of complication, thus providing an invaluable perspective into postwar sensibilities in Japanese society, and into the Japanese people's struggle with the past. —Eds.

Introduction

Conceptualizing the War Experience

No other event in Japanese history left as deep a mark on the Japanese people as the so-called Greater East Asian War, for never before had a total war engulfed the entire people, subsuming almost every aspect of their lives over four long years. Yet, little has been achieved by transforming this awareness of the profundity of the war experience to the

205

Japanese people as a whole. Experiences remain mere experiences, and thoughts and ideas always circulate as abstract thoughts unrelated to experience.[1] The Tokyo War Crimes Trial and the issue of Japanese war responsibility might have been able to offer one important clue in establishing meaningful thoughts and ideas based on experience.

The Japanese people fought the Greater East Asian War in China and Southeast Asia with their entire might. After the war, when it became apparent that this was an unforgivable war of aggression, the Japanese people as a whole by necessity had the task of questioning and clarifying the meaning of each person's involvement in the war. What in the world had the Japanese people done wrong such that a war that they had participated in and believed in as a holy war had turned out to be a war of aggression? What was their own responsibility for their participation? What was the meaning of the death of 3 million compatriots?

It is well known that the Tokyo War Crimes Trial was a "judgment" by the Allied powers and not by the Japanese people themselves. However, the Tokyo Trial presented a unique opportunity to publicly pass judgment on all aspects of the "Fifteen-Year War," with evidence that was hard to deny. Even if the Japanese people did not themselves stage this trial, we should at least discuss and seek to understand their view of this judgment. Moreover, we should also question the meaning of the people's lack of action. Why did they not even try to create for themselves a public stage on which they could pass judgment on the war, but instead remain only *bystanders* at war crimes trials administered by the Allied powers?

The Insufficiency of the "War Responsibility Debate"

It is true that these problems have already been touched upon in works dealing with the issue of war responsibility.[2] However, these works have not occupied a central place in the discourse on war responsibility. What is more, it is clear to everyone today that the theories and discussions on the responsibility of the war failed, as a postwar philosophy, to provide a framework for and give direction to the Japanese people in the postwar period. "Although 'freedom of speech' has been loudly asserted, it has not borne much fruit,"[3] These lamenting words by Kasuya Kazuki contain a fundamental criticism of postwar thought in general, including that on the war responsibility debate.

Japan was supposedly reborn by defeat. To put it simply, during the postwar era we abandoned the policy of "rich country, strong army" [fukoku kyohei] which had been followed since the Meiji period, and has since traveled only the path of "rich country." However, despite a difference between these two paths, the Japanese people's disposition has not so fundamentally changed. Just as the old Japan already carried the germ of catastrophe when it became a military power "ranking among the Great Powers," does it not already carry a new germ of catastrophe now that Japan has become an economic power "ranking among the developed countries in the world"?

In the same way as the Japanese people once allowed the militarists to run the nation's affairs exclusively, they now allow those in charge of the economy to do the same. By letting this happen, have the intellectuals, who ought to be responsible for an appropriate understanding of the world, not once again demonstrated that they are ineffective in their discourse? In a sense, the intellectuals have continuously criticized the postwar Japanese system. But doesn't their criticism lack effectiveness? Was there not a fundamental lack of perspectives at the outset of the postwar era which was supposed to be the beginning of total self-criticism? Recognizing this deficiency, isn't it important now to inquire into the Japanese people's behaviorial pattern which has remained unchanged throughout the prewar and postwar eras? Shouldn't we change these characteristic features or search for a way to control them?[4]

Kasuya Kazuki's "lack [of] effectiveness" of the "intellectuals" is no doubt valid in the debate on war responsibility. What does this lack consist of? In the following I will seek to answer the question by clarifying how the Tokyo War Crimes Trial was perceived in Japanese society, as well as the subsequent debate on war responsibility. In addition to exploring already familiar issues, I seek to shed light on some points that remain untouched.

1. The Tokyo War Crimes Trial—Its Historical Significance

I have already written about the Tokyo War Crimes Trial and its meaning in history.[5] The following points should be stressed, however.

The Tokyo War Crimes Trial was a trial in which the Allied powers as the victors of World War II judged and punished a part of the defeated Japanese political and military leadership allegedly under international law within the framework of the American occupation in the name of civilization. In more concrete terms, this means the following:

First, the Tokyo Trial was "victors' justice" in that the victorious nations unilaterally passed judgment on the defeated nation. This in itself is contrary to the notion of a fair trial. Justice should be exercised by an independent third party. Moreover, those who judged in the Tokyo Trial could be accused of the same kind of faults upon which they passed judgment. This is apparent in three aspects of the trial: (a) the aspect of the modern history of colonization, that is, the acquisition of and rule over worldwide colonies by the European powers; (b) Allied wartime operations, namely the strategic bombing of a number of cities and the dropping of atomic bombs over Hiroshima and Nagasaki by the United States, as well as a number of violations of international law by the Soviet Union; and (c), postwar military activities such as the U.S. involvement in the Vietnam War; the Soviet Union's invasion of Hungary, Czechoslovakia, Afghanistan, and so on; and other interventions by the former Allied powers in various countries. Of course, these aspects of the trial do not weigh as heavily as the wars Japan had waged from 1931 to 1945, and the Japanese war cannot be justified on this basis. Nonetheless, they raise serious doubts about the judges who claimed to act on the moral basis that "aggression should be punished," which was so highly advertised as the ideology of the trial, because they themselves disregarded this imperative.

Second, the Tokyo trial was in actuality part of the U.S. Occupation policy. The Trial was thus heavily influenced by U.S. policy considerations. Concrete evidence for this includes the lack of an indictment of the emperor and the selection of defendants predominantly on grounds of their involvement in the "attack on Pearl Harbor."

Third, the Tokyo Trial was carried out under the name of civilization. In the imperialistic era of the nineteenth and twentieth centuries, European nations colonized various regions of the world by claiming that their own culture was universal civilization and regarding other cultures as "barbarian" or "uncivilized." Civilizing the "barbarians" then became their "sacred mission." The Tokyo Trial followed this ideology.[6] Yet the Tokyo Trial also showed undeniably that the schema "civilization versus barbarism" had a certain basis in that it shed light on the barbarous acts of the Japanese military, for example, the Rape of Nanking.

Fourth, as part of the "outlawry of war" in the twentieth century, embodied in the League of Nations Covenant of 1919, the Kellogg-Briand Pact of 1928, the United Nations Charter of 1945, and Article 9 of the

Japanese constitution, the Tokyo Trial implemented the notion of the illegality of war in the form of imposing criminal responsibility on the state leadership. Heretofore, the notion of the leadership's responsibility had not been recognized in international law; instead, the entire people had been made liable in the form of the state's responsibility for reparations payments. Compared with the former law, which virtually exempted the leadership from responsibility, the Tokyo Trial thus did have positive significance.[7] On the other hand, the judgment and severe punishment of a part of the old political and military leadership was ill conceived, for the trial failed to prosecute people in leading positions in economic, cultural, and other areas, and never questioned the participation of the common people in the war.

Finally, the Tokyo Trial was a way of judging Japan's Fifteen-Year War by way of a judicial trial. Because the defendants were people in high positions who had used the entire state mechanism, and because the investigations covered the entire war from the late 1920s to 1945, a strict implementation of the Anglo-American legal principle of evidence was almost impossible. Still, since the Allied powers had decided that there was to be a judicial trial, they had to present evidence that could be admitted in accordance with the law. As a result, the exposure of what had actually happened during the war was more massive and overwhelming an experience for the Japanese people than any before or since. Herein lies perhaps the greatest significance of the Tokyo Trial for contemporary history.[8]

2. Reactions to the Tokyo War Crimes Trial (Part One: The Bystanders' Passive Endorsement)

Neither Wholehearted Acceptance Nor Wholehearted Rejection

How did the Japanese people perceive the Tokyo Trial? At one extreme there was an almost total rejection of any positive meaning of the Tokyo Trial, on the grounds that it was seriously flawed. One prominent argument in this camp was that the Greater East Asian War was justified as an act of self-defense or liberation of Asia. This view has been advocated by some leading scholars since the trial.[9] Yet such reasoning could not attract the sympathy of the general Japanese populace.

Many arguments have spoken against such a position. First, the actual facts revealed by the Tokyo Trial could not possibly be denied, be they the conspiracy of the Kanto Army in the "Manchurian Incident" or the atrocious actions of the Japanese Army in various regions of China and Southeast Asia. Second, the wholehearted rejection of the Tokyo Trial tended to buttress political restorationism and disturbed the future-oriented psychology of postwar Japanese, who were primarily concerned with economic development. Last, there was hardly any support among the Japanese people for the defendants. For a great number of people the war had meant hell on the battlefield; loss of family members; fear of air raids; hunger; and, finally, defeat. Thus it was a matter of course in most people's eyes that Tojo and the other leaders, who had failed to spare the people such a dreadful experience, should be punished. Although many Japanese held some doubt of the judgment as well as the verdict, they regarded it as acceptable that the former leaders were put on trial.

If the total rejection of the Tokyo Trial failed to capture the people's hearts, neither did arguments of wholehearted affirmation win general support. In 1947, just at the time of the Trial, Yokota Kisaburo published his book *Senso hanzairon* (On war crimes). At the time Yokota was the leading professor of international law at Tokyo Imperial University. Thereafter he became a member of the International Law Commission of the United Nations and then chief justice of the Supreme Court in Japan, among other posts. As such he was the leading scholar in the field of international law in Japan. Yet, his defense of the Trial, which was basically in line with the majority opinion in the judgment, received little support despite his great influence in scholarly circles. Still more, his view left almost no trace among the general populace.

The Images of Evil Tojo and the Common People's Exemption from Responsibility

In contrast, Maruyama Masao, in his essay "Gunkoku shihaisha no seishin keitai" (Psychological patterns of Japan's militarist leaders) (1949), echoed the Japanese people's generally approving disposition toward the Tokyo Trial. In using the record of the examination of defendants such as Tojo, Shimada, and Togo as his material, Maruyama composed an impressive picture of "the system of irresponsibility," and an attitude of "hiding behind the formal public authority" on the part of the old leadership with the emperor at the top. Comparing the Tokyo Trial with the

Nuremburg Trial, he characterized the answers of Goering, a defendant at the latter trial, as "explicitly nihilistic and self-consciously defying the European traditional mind," while depicting the defendants at the Tokyo Trial as "slippery as eels, vague as mist." He sought to demonstrate the dwarfishness of Japanese fascism in this way. Maruyama's work was not a defense of the Tokyo Trial itself. Rather, his contribution is significant in that it offered a theoretical framework—although a very Westcentric one in its basic tenets—to analyze these facts.

The Tokyo Trial was carried out in an atmosphere that completely rejected the Japanism of the wartime years in favor of the wholehearted acceptance of Westcentric modernism, captured in the one word "democracy." Moreover, this atmosphere has dominated postwar Japan for a long time until today. Thus the prewar and wartime Japanism, which was nothing but an inferiority complex vis-à-vis Western civilization turned inside out, was characterized as totally wrong. In such an atmosphere, Japan's old leaders, whom Maruyama described in contrast with Germany's leaders as taking refuge under the invisible mantle of public authority, were despised as merely bad dwarfs, not even great evil figures.[10] Despite Maruyama's explanation that in his view "it is not a question of individual corruption . . . but the characteristics of the decadence of the 'system,'" it was difficult to avoid the impression that the dwarfishness he described was actually a characteristic of each individual defendant.[11]

On one hand, this image of the old leadership corresponded exactly to the ordinary people's perception of the Tokyo Trial. As I stated earlier, for the Japanese people the war was a terrible experience. With the terror of the deteriorating war situation, Tojo had already become the object of secret resentment. However, it was defeat that made the Japanese people really feel like victims of the war. The great majority of the Japanese people were now convinced that the old leadership bore the responsibility for this dreadful situation.[12] Thus they undoubtedly approved of the Tokyo Trial based on such psychology.

On the other hand, Tojo had already been frowned at for prying into the people's trash cans during the war and, when he failed to commit suicide after the war, everyone was even more appalled. The portrayal of the defendants as coarse villains at the Tokyo Trial had the reverberating result that the common people thought themselves exempted from responsibility for having participated in the war. The Tokyo Trial passed judgment by categorically divorcing the old leadership clique from the rest of the Japanese people. It helped to portray the leaders as jingoistic militarists and punished them for the crime of waging aggressive wars. The general populace, neither judged nor punished, watched the Tokyo Trial merely as bystanders who had nothing to do with the responsibility for the war.

3. Reactions to the Tokyo War Crimes Trial (Part Two: Cynicism Toward the Hypocrisy of the Allied Powers)

Distrust of the Trial as "Victors' Justice"

The Japanese people's response to the Tokyo Trial is best characterized as passive approval, centering on their affirmation of the old leadership's judgment and punishment. Yet there lurked a feeling among many people that may be called silent distrust of the Trial. This distrust is inseparable from the problematic flaws in the Tokyo Trial; above all it is related to the fact that the Trial was victors' justice. Doubts existed from the very beginning of the Trial, and with the subsequent developments in international politics it became ingrained as deep distrust of the former Allied powers as judges.

As to the issue of the guilt of colonial rule by the former Allied powers, there was not much awareness of the fact because Japanese people themselves did not feel guilty about their own history as a colonial power. In contrast, almost everybody in Japan knew that the United States dropped atomic bombs over Hiroshima and Nagasaki. Many were also aware of the fact that the Soviet Union attacked Japan at the very last phase of the war in violation of the neutrality treaty between the two countries. This perception of the treaty violation by the Soviet Union contributed to suspicion about the Tokyo Trial, which included a Soviet judge, mainly among anticommunists.

However, it was above all the postwar military actions of the former Allied powers that fed the sense that those who had judged Japan exhibited their own share of faulty behavior. The Soviet Union mercilessly invaded Hungary and Afghanistan and engaged in large-scale human rights violations domestically. The United States fought the infamous Vietnam War and constantly dispatched troops into various Central and South American countries. England and France sent troops to the Suez Canal. All these facts planted among the majority of the Japanese people a sense of distrust of the fundamental principles of the Tokyo Trial, in which the Allies as "peace-loving countries," acting in the name of civilization, passed judgment on the Japanese militarists for their aggressive war. "Despite all their noble words, aren't they doing the same thing that we were doing back then? After all, might makes right, doesn't it?" This distrust became deeply rooted in people's minds as a sense of betrayal, all the more so because the ideology of the Tokyo Trial as "trial by civilization" had been so attractive.

The Disposition Toward Hirota Koki

How deeply this distrust is rooted in Japanese society was revealed by the popular reaction to the novel and TV drama *Rakujitsu moyu* (The Setting Sun Glows), whose leading character was Hirota Koki, the only civil servant sentenced to capital punishment by the Tokyo Tribunal. It was also revealed by the popular reaction to the film *Tokyo saiban* (The Tokyo War Crime Trial), which was first shown in 1983 and invoked a great controversy. *Rakujitsu moyu* portrayed Hirota as a tragic figure who resisted the arbitrariness of the military but in the end could not stop the war and then received the death penalty. He won the sympathy of a wide range of readers and viewers. Against this background the film *Tokyo saiban* depicted the faults of both sides, namely Japan's Greater Asian War and the United States' atomic bombing of Hiroshima and Nagasaki. The viewers gave the latter much greater weight than the former. Moreover, the reaction of the Japanese public to the visit of Dr. B.V.A. Röling in 1983, who was the only former Tokyo Trial judge still alive at that time, is telling in that it focused solely on the inappropriateness of Hirota's death sentence.[13]

This reaction is symbolic of the complex feelings on the war and war guilt in Japanese society. In the devastating situation after defeat, many Japanese felt bitterness against the leaders of the old system who had "trapped" them, and approved of their punishment in the Tokyo Trial on this basis alone. At the same time they continued to have their criticism of the hypocrisy of the former Allied powers on other grounds. This Janus-faced attitude among the people singled out Hirota's death sentence as the symbol for the problematic features of the Tokyo Trial.

Many Japanese today on one hand still maintain an inferiority complex vis-à-vis Western nations, symbolized by their slogan "Datsua myuo" (Parting from Asia and joining Europe). On the other hand, they gradually developed a superiority complex—the reversal of the former—

because Japan has become an economic superpower. At the same time as they downplay their own involvement in the Greater East Asian War, they are tempted to advertise their distrust of the Tokyo Trial and use it as a lever to reject the fact that the Fifteen-Year War was a war of aggression.

The Responsibility of Postwar Thought

People involved in the creation of postwar thoughts and ideas bear half the responsibility for this situation. The Japanese government, the leaders of the Liberal-Democratic Party (LDP), the financial world and the bureaucracy have not participated in such an exchange of thoughts and ideas. Instead they have concentrated their entire energies on economic prosperity. Conversely, many intellectuals who were the producers of thoughts and ideas in their writings and theories were scholars and literati who resisted the LDP power structure for a long time. However, they failed to face the Tokyo War Crimes Trial.

It is true that some were dissatisfied with the fact that the Tokyo Trial was "victors' justice" and pointed that out. However, the overwhelming majority of intellectuals dared not take a critical position that in the Tokyo Trial the victors judged the Japanese military leadership for having started a war of aggression. Behind this passive endorsement of the Trial was a fear that a full investigation of the "victors' justice" aspect of the Tokyo Trial would diminish the positive value of the Tokyo Trial and might contribute to justifying the old leadership of prewar and wartime Japan.

This was nothing but a politicized attitude which ignored critical important aspects of reality. It was similar to the argument by the "progressive" and "liberal" intellectuals that uncovering the strong pressure of the Occupation forces on the promulgation of the new constitution was undesirable because it would jeopardize the legitimacy of the new constitution. These intellectuals also turned a blind eye to Japan's economic prosperity and social stability under the postwar conservative leadership but only criticized negative aspects of postwar Japan. They further kept silent on suppression in the socialist countries such as the U.S.S.R. and China. Such a chain of thought had a counterproductive effect and resulted in the exact opposite of what these people had intended. This is all too apparent in almost the entire scope of the issue, not only the Tokyo War Crimes Trial. The Japanese people did not appreciate this type of shallow politicism; the people were far more critical than the "conveyers of thought" who concerned themselves with such self-serving arguments.

Hence the majority of Japanese approved the punishment of the leadership from the standpoint of disengaged bystanders, thereby sidetracking the problem of their own participation while maintaining their cynicism against "the judges' soiled hands."[14] In the following sections I will seek to clarify the thoughts and emotions of the postwar Japanese people by analyzing the debates on war responsibility.

4. The Debate About War Responsibility

The Old Leadership's Evasion of Moral Responsibility

The debate about war responsibility in postwar Japan was first conducted during the period immediately after defeat, between 1945 and 1947. This debate had the following characteristics. First, the debate was conducted in the situation where people whose responsibility for the war was relatively great either remained completely silent or evaded their own responsibility. The most prominent of these people was, of course, the emperor. But apart from him, most of those in the old military leadership, the political leadership, the high bureaucracy, and the financial world took this evasive attitude.

There were exceptions, of course. Some people tried to stand up to their responsibility by making public statements to that effect or even committing suicide; but what these people held themselves responsible for was that they had led Japan to defeat, not that they had started and carried out an unjust war. They also placed responsibility on the emperor, not on the people who suffered unbearable misery as a result of their misleading the nation. Nor did this mean responsibility to the foreign victims of the war, namely the more than 10 million people killed by the Japanese Army in China and in Southeast Asia.

The manner in which those who bore relatively heavy responsibility approached this issue was typically demonstrated by the Higashikuni cabinet's appeal, *ichioku sozange* (one hundred million repenting together). While silence does not necessary mean a denial of responsibility, this strategy of the evasion of responsibility is much worse. It is true that the whole nation must take responsibility for having cooperated in the war. Even those who opposed the war must take responsibility because they failed to stop the aggression that resulted in the death of more than 10 million people in innocent nations. The appeal for collective repenting, however, obscures the important differences in degree between those who bear the most and those who bear the least responsibility. It also absolves the responsibility of the leaders toward the Japanese people, who lost 3 million countrymen and had to endure such misery and pain as a result of the critical failures of the wartime leaders. Morever, "one hundred million taking responsibility" in reality comes down to nobody being responsible. Thus the Higashikuni cabinet's *ichioku sozange* argument in effect absolved the responsibility of the entire wartime leadership, many of whom revived their political careers after the war. It demonstrated precisely the moral decay of those in power. The *senso sekininron* (idea on war responsibility) of those in power, especially the cabinet's call for repentance, was not only unconvincing in everyone's eyes, it was downright scandalous.

The Problem with Party-Political Debates About War Responsibility

The first discourse about war responsibility during the period immediately after the end of the war developed against this background, where people with relatively less responsibility vehemently accused those bearing heavier responsibility. The accusers belonged to the political left, centered on the Communist Party. Given the fact that they had been subject to the most violent oppression before and during the war, their accusations were understandable. They had legitimate grounds for accusing those in the establishment. Nonetheless, their approach to war responsibility proved to be highly problematic. It had been looked down upon with distrust from the outset and later met with severe criticism. The intertwinement of the war responsibility issue with party politics rendered inquiries into other responsibility morally doubtful and ultimately failed to convince the ordinary people.

The involvement of political parties in this issue was problematic in two ways. First, those politically oriented accusers ignored the past behavior of their colleagues and allies. Second, they argued that past mistakes had to be compensated for by present actions and that these actions must be political ones for the benefit of the people. This logic of having to compensate for one's war cooperation by working for the benefit of the people after the war was not that of the Communist Party alone. Nor was it necessarily wrong. Since past actions could not be undone, one's responsibility for prewar and wartime mistakes could be fulfilled only through postwar conduct. This leaves open the question of what type of postwar activity is an appropriate way of taking responsibility.

With the benefit of hindsight—and it is not only a privilege but a duty to learn from the past when judging it from our present-day perspective—it is apparent that the notion of taking responsibility through "working for the people," which was equated with the establishment of a government by the Communist Party or the political left, was mistaken. However, this mistake may have been excusable at a time when socialism, communism, and Marxism-Leninism still had meaning as creative symbols for a better future, and their negative aspects were not yet known. The problematic feature of the factionalism was that the Communist Party strategy of dealing with war responsibility by way of accusations refused to take into consideration the wartime behavior of its supporters and regarded them as innocent during the war period, although some of them cooperated with the war.

If individuals recognize their own cooperation before and during the war as an unredeemable matter, and on this basis decide to work "for the people" as a way of making up for it, then others will continue to have respect for these individuals, even if these others differ in their opinions of the individuals' postwar activities. Inquiries into other people's war responsibility will then retain a moral basis. However, when this premise is lost, there will only be attacks and counterattacks among political opponents. This will result in the loss of trust by the people in the accusations by the leftists of those responsible for the war. This is a major reason why the Communist Party–centered war responsibility debate in the immediate postwar period could not prevail.

Thoughts of the Saint, Thoughts of the Common Person

During the period immediately after the end of the war, a few voices did carry important and lasting messages. One of them was the attempt to accuse themselves for their own cooperation with the war, although their cooperation was much less than that of others. They criticized themselves, saying that their noncooperation had merely been a matter of accident. They argued that they had to take responsibility for having allowed themselves to be so easily deceived as to lose their critical sense.[15]

Perhaps this was an ineffective undertaking, because it could not directly influence politics. Nonetheless, it may eventually make a real impact in one way or another. Sometimes an idea that initially seems to have almost no actual relevance may seep deeply into people's hearts and ultimately acquire an important role in shaping reality. In that sense, the undertaking described above may touch later generations and gain relevance through its gradual influence. Even if it does not have such an actual relevance, this self-reflection threw some light into the gloomy picture of the debate on war responsibility, either that of accusations warped by party politics or that of the government's intellectually and morally desolate *ichioku sozange*.

However we admire this intellectual project and respect it, it still cannot be our own. Such a lofty undertaking can only be done by the saint, not by an ordinary person. Does this mean that there is no hope for the common people? Not necessarily.

We can find another type of war responsibility debate that merits attention. It is the attempt by people who actively participated in the war effort to confront their mistakes in a self-critical manner by offering their own experiences as lessons for the future. Okuma Nobuyuki's work had such an agenda. Okuma criticized himself severely after the war for his participation in the Greater East Asian War as a member of the *genron hokokukai* (Patriotic Literati Committee) and, based on his war experience, tried to work out a principle of disobedience to the state and loyalty to humanity.

As I have laid out in detail elsewhere,[16] Okuma could not establish this principle as a coherent theory. He considered the "nation" and "home" as a person's more realistic basic community than "humanity." Okuma strongly advocated building a theory on the experience of war; but in reality he also depended on a transcendental approach to the war experience such as his own "recollections" of Tolstoyan pacifism, which he had believed in when he had been young. The theory of disobedience to the state was thus introduced by him in the form of absolute pacifism, which was dissociated from the experience of the war.[17] His appeal to absolute pacifism was thus not based on his *experience* during the war period. Consequently, he himself could not rely on the abstract form of absolute pacifism, and he later had to seek more concrete bases to ground his theory of disobedience to the state. He thus ended in relying on the "family" and the "nation" in the ethnic sense as such bases. In this way, Okuma could not establish a coherent theory of disobedience to the state.

Nonetheless, I consider Okuma's attempt to theorize war responsibility extremely valuable. Cooperation in the war effort was rather natural for ordinary Japanese people. Later, when it occurred to them that this had been a mistake, the question of what to do in order to compensate for this mistake became of utmost importance for the war responsibility debate. Okuma's capability as an intellectual and an artist was no doubt far beyond that of the ordinary people's; but Okuma was a common person in that he was inclined to make mistakes and he actually committed errors. Okuma's intellectual project of admitting his own mistakes and seeking to derive from this a principle to avoid repeating these mistakes is highly suggestive. It is important for the great majority of us, precisely because he was not a person of particularly high ethics but an ordinary person like us.

The Second Phase of the Debate on War Responsibility

The second phase in the discourse on war responsibility, centering around 1956, arose out of an almost desperate bitterness toward the apparent failure of the immediate postwar discussions of this issue, which had taken the form of accusations on the part of the left. This second debate developed as a critique of the wartime and postwar activities not only of those accused of war responsibility, but also of those who had participated in the earlier debate.[18]

Yoshimoto Takaaki, who along with others raised this issue, drew on Okamoto Jun's words, "Only historical story-mongers say that the masses overwhelmingly supported the military and their supportive members in the Diet. While the masses pretended to agree with the wartime leaders, they in fact turned away from them." Yoshimoto regarded this as a typically empty ideology of "today's vulgar communism." He characterized such an attitude as a major reason for the defeat of the postwar democratic revolution. He said, "The problem is clear. Now that the postwar democratic revolution in Japan has finally failed, the vanguard communists try to distract attention from their own postwar responsibility."[19]

Yoshimoto advanced two points as indispensable prerequisites for dealing with the problem of war responsibility, first, "to recognize that the failure of Japanese wartime poetry and literature lay in the interconnection of vices in literary style and the deficiency of the Japanese social structure," and second, "to come to terms with the wartime experience as one's own problem and its transformation into practice (in a literary sense, but it can also mean social practice) during the ten years since the end of the war; in short, one's attitude towards postwar responsibility."[20] Takei Teruo held the same view as Yoshimoto. Takei found Kiyooka Takuyuki's confessions of his war experience "truthful," but he wondered why Kiyooka never talked about how his postwar views were formed by his wartime experience, and how he dealt with the postwar reality during the ten years since the end of the war. [21]

Yoshimoto and Takei added depth to the war responsibility debate of the immediate postwar period. They left no doubt that war responsibility was *not* an issue of *ex post facto* evaluations of past actions, that is, of confessing and apologizing for a past that could no longer be retrieved. Rather, the past had to be rendered significant within the practical reality of the present day, and that could not be done simply through party political activities. This argument naturally aroused a strong reaction in the literary community, but did not end there. Some participants in this debate pointed out that it was wrong to limit the discussion to the intellectuals' war responsibility. They raised questions concerning the various subjects of responsibility, including the responsibility of the emperor and of the Communist Party.

Compared to the first phase of the war responsibility debate, the second phase offered richer perspectives and reflections on humanity. Important works during the second period included Honda Shugo's rebuttal of Yoshimoto and Takei in "Senso sekinin no mondai" (The question of war responsibility), in which he warned of "the arrogance of asking perfection in mortals"; Sada Ineko's "Jibun ni tsuite" (About myself), in which she voiced her feelings of responsibility towards the war dead in terms of her own war cooperation, but wondered whether the living were qualified to criticize her own responsibility; Fukuda Tsuneari's essays "Senso sekinin to iu koto" (On so-called war responsibility) and "Jiko hihan to iu koto" (On so-called self-criticism), which criticized the "righteous theories" of pursuing war responsibility; Tsurumi Shunsuke's "Chishikijin no senso sekinin" (The war responsibility of intellectuals)[22]; and Maruyama Masao's "Shiso no kotoba" (The language of ideas), in which he made a case for the responsibility of the emperor and the Communist Party for the political consequences of the war.

5. The Failure to Acknowledge Responsibility Toward Foreign Peoples in the Debate on War Responsibility

"Peace Settlements" and War Responsibility

The second phase in the discourse on war responsibility around 1956 both widened and deepened the immediate postwar debate. Yet many of the problems that had plagued the earlier discussions remained unchanged. First, those who focused on the subject of war responsibility were concerned with the leaders in the nation, whether they were the emperor, the military, the literati and intellectuals, or the vanguard Communist Party. They were not concerned with the ordinary people, who did not have a voice of their own. Second—and the first problem basically originates from this second one—they were not aware of the fact that who was most responsible *in Japan* was not a crucial problem for the foreign peoples who had suffered the immense human and material casualties that Japan had inflicted on them. Those who were involved in the war responsibility debate had almost no sense of the reality that Japanese people as a whole had invaded Asian territory, that Japanese soldiers had killed millions of Asians.

This subject was, of course, not altogether ignored, but it never became common knowledge in Japan. The debaters did not consciously abstract the issue of responsibility toward foreign peoples; rather, the narrow-minded, inward-directed perspective, focusing on nothing but their home country, made it difficult for them to be aware of the very existence of the problem. This narrow perspective was not at all limited to the war responsibility debate. It merely exposed to broad daylight the general characteristic tendency of Japanese society to ignore Asians as non-Westerners. Herein lies the most serious problem of contemporary Japanese society: lack of sensitivity toward the hearts and minds of non-Westerners.

An example of this lack of sensitivity was revealed in the issue of peace settlement with the countries with whom Japan had been at war. One would naturally expect the discussions on the peace treaties with these countries to include some assessment of Japan's aggressive war, its recognition of Korea's independence, its surrender of former colonies, and the payment of reparations to the Allied powers. In fact, the earlier drafts of the peace treaty made by the U.S. government had tended to be critical of Japan's responsibility for its aggressive war. The fact that it was replaced by a "more generous" peace treaty by no means indicates that the former Allied powers denied Japan's responsibility for the war. Rather, they, especially the United States, sidetracked the issue of war responsibility in order to win Japan as a member of the anticommunist bloc. This matter was decided purely from considerations of international politics.[23] Moreover, by giving preference to this decision, the United States took the wind out of the sails of various Asian countries, such as China and the Philippines, which demanded that Japan's war responsibility be pursued.

Moreover, Japan itself neglected to think about the problem of its own war responsibility at the time of the San Francisco Peace Treaty. Japan avoided this discussion by taking advantage of the fact that the problem of its war responsibility was not provided in the treaty. This was not even a conscious avoidance. Although the Peace Treaty was the settlement between Japan and the nations with which the Japanese people had fought, the Japanese were not aware of the very problem itself. What actually was questioned and discussed in earnest were the rights and wrongs of the Japan-U.S. Security Treaty. It is true that this issue was of great importance because it would affect the fundamental position of Japan in international society for some time thereafter. Yet, the very fact that there was almost no mention of the war which had ended only six years earlier reveals the Japanese people's fundamental lack of sensitivity toward the huge number of Asian victims. This attitude stood in vivid contrast to the attitude of the various Asian countries who observed Japan closely with memories of the past that were painfully alive.

"Reparations" and War Responsibility

The same kind of problem arose in another conspicuous way at the time of reconciliation with Southeast Asian countries who did not participate in the San Francisco Peace Treaty, such as Malaysia, Singapore, and Indonesia.[24] This was the issue of reparations and compensations to these nations.

The situation here was different from that of China, on which Japan had inflicted the greatest damage during the war, but which had also influenced Japan culturally throughout history and thus enjoyed Japan's interest and respect. In the debate about the peace treaty, there was an awareness of the lack of Japanese responsibility taking toward the Chinese people because mainland China was not invited to the Peace Conference and did not sign the San Francisco Peace Treaty. With respect to Southeast Asia such an awareness had no chance to develop, because Japan was trapped in the image of these nations as "uncivilized and backward." In particular, the issue of reparations was regarded as a purely economic one, as if it had nothing to do with the war. It was viewed as economic aid "granted" to the "backward" Southeast Asian countries by a "developed" Japan. The nation that had inflicted great damage fighting an unjust war of aggression thus transformed the meaning of reparations from money and services offered as compensation to a notion of assisting the "underdeveloped people" of Southeast Asian to develop under its guidance. This image, generally held by contemporary Japanese, was basically not different from the idea of the Greater East Asian Co-prosperity Sphere held by Japan during the war period.

Furthermore, the reparations payments became the spur for the recovery and growth of Japanese postwar capitalism, because they were all paid in Japanese services and products. They not only served the purpose of stimulating production by securing markets for such mainstay products as automobiles and electrical appliances, which could not yet compete with other developed countries, but also guaranteed markets for domestic surplus products like porcelain and rayon. In this way, the goods and services provided as reparations opened markets in the region, and thus became the priming water for guaranteeing Japanese enterprises a secure share in exports to Southeast Asia.[25] Thus the payment of reparations, which was meant to be one way of taking responsibility for the "Greater East Asian War," has resulted in Japan's overwhelming economic control of Southeast Asia today.

"Japan-Korea Normalization" and the Memory of Colonial Rule

The conclusion of the Japan-Korea Normalization Treaty of 1965 shows the same characteristics as we have observed in the San Francisco Peace Treaty and the reparation agreements with the Southeast Asian countries. When the normalization treaty was concluded, a violent opposition movement led by students erupted in Korea. At the root of this movement lay resentment of Japan's thirty-six-year-colonial rule over Korea. In Japan, Foreign Minister Shiina Etssaburo said, "If one regards Japan's project to protect Asia from the powerful Western imperialism, maintain Japan's independence . . . and annex Korea . . . as Japanese imperialism, then I would say that it is a glorious imperialism."[26] How little Japan reflected on its colonial rule is symbolized by the words of Shiina, who said that apologizing for Japan's colonial rule of Korea "sounds too humiliating."[27]

As suggested by these words, there was hardly any sense among the Japanese people that Japan, which had once been a colonial power, should have been blamed for its colonial rule over Korea and Taiwan. Koreans and Taiwanese had been rounded up as imperial subjects during the war and some of them had even been punished as war criminals after the end of the war. Nevertheless, these Koreans and Taiwanese were not treated as Japanese after the war as far as pensions and compensations were concerned. This double standard was not questioned during the early years of the postwar period.

6. The Notion of Responsibility Toward Asia: Recognizing Japan's Invasion of China

"Asia as a Method"

There are several reasons for the Japanese lack of a sense of responsibility toward other Asian nations and the lack of sensitivity to them that can be observed in the debate about war responsibility, the San Francisco Peace Treaty, the reparation treaties with the Southeast Asian countries, and the normalization with South Korea: (1) the Japanese people's sense of victimization, which originated in total defeat, impoverishment and exhaustion; (2) the feeling among the common people of having nothing to do with the responsibility of the war, generated by the sense that those responsible had been punished by the Tokyo War Crimes Trial and the minor war crimes trials; (3) the consolidation of this sense of victimization in the peace movement originating from the experience of Hiroshima and Nagasaki (reminders that Japan was the first and only nation to suffer a nuclear bomb attack); (4) the intellectuals' ambiguous feelings of guilt toward the masses as seen in the war responsibility debate; (5) the lack of a comprehensive approach to the basis, degree, and manner of war responsibility; (6) the disengagement of the problem of war responsibility from other issues, such as economic questions, due to an overly moralistic and individualistic understanding of war responsibility; (7) the lack of a concrete and accurate analysis of the "viciousness" of the Greater East Asian War, because this "viciousness" was regarded as self-evident; and, most important, (8) the fundamental lack of interest in the Asian peoples as victims of Japanese aggression, which originated in the common idea of "parting from Asia and entering Europe," which is deeply rooted in Japanese society.

It was Takeuchi Yoshimi who pointed out the lack of analysis of the viciousness of the Greater East Asian War and the lack of concern for Asia, thereby calling into question the Japanese people's sense of victimization and their lack of the sense of responsibility. In "Kindai no chokoku" (Overcoming modernity),[28] he distinguished between two aspects of the war, namely the war between Japan and Western imperialist powers such as the United States and Great Britain, and the war in which Japan invaded Asian countries. In his opinion, Japan was to bear responsibility only for the latter.

I do not necessarily agree with him. It is true that an international "peace" that reflected the power structure of the advanced imperialist countries was at best a negative peace. The "peace" was certainly another type of status quo based on the Westcentric colonial system. Still, this does not legitimize Japan's resorting to force against imperialistic powers. However, one cannot deny that the war did have these two aspects. The importance of Takeuchi's argument for understanding the question of war responsibility in its relationship to other nations lies precisely in his identifying these two kinds of responsibility.

The "Fifteen-Year War" View of History

Since Takeuchi's critique, the recognition of Japan as perpetrator of the war in Asia has gradually widened and deepened through efforts of fact finding, and through a shift in the intellectual framework. The former is represented by the attempt at the time of the normalization of Sino-Japanese relations in 1972 to bring to light the atrocities of the Japanese Army in China.[29] The latter is represented by Tsurumi Shunsuke's claim for viewing the war historically as the Fifteen-Year War.

According to Tsurumi, "it would be impossible to understand the structure of the war if one understands it as the 'Manchurian Incident,' the 'Sino Incident,' and the 'Greater East Asian War' separately."[30] Rather, the ordinary people living in those days felt that the war continued, with intermissions from time to time. This view is close to Takeuchi's unique view of "Asia as a Method."

With regard to the issue of how to name and characterize a series of wars Japan fought from the 1930s to 1945, "Greater East Asian War" was the term that caught the feelings and experiences of the widest range of people. However, after this term was prohibited by the Occupation forces, the term "Pacific War," which was prevalent in the United States, was substituted and continued to be in use even after the Occupation ended. Yet the very term "Pacific War" strongly implied Japanese-American enmity and referred to nothing but the war between Japan and the

United States. Such a view only strengthened the Japanese tendency to ignore its aggression in Asia. This tendency is further strengthened by the fundamental desire in Japanese society to "part from Asia and join Europe" (*Datsua nyuo*).

Regarding the war as the Fifteen-Year War placed emphasis on the continuity between the "Manchurian Incident" and the Greater East Asian War, and made clear that the Greater East Asian War was an almost inevitable result of Japan's military interventions in China. Further, the focus on the war against China shed light on its aggressive nature. The historical view of the Fifteen-Year War gradually became common knowledge in the latter half of the 1960s and in the 1970s. It bears important meaning for the question of war responsibility because it helped correct the lack of consciousness of Asia in Japanese society.

The Restoration of Sino-Japanese Relations and the Common People's War Responsibility

The consciousness of the Japanese as perpetrators against the Chinese was greatly enhanced by a second wave of research that unearthed much of the Japanese Army's activities in China. Honda Katsuichi's works *Chugoku no tabi* (A journey to China) and *Chugoko no Nihongun* (The Japanese Army in China) played a central role in this enhancement of the Japanese consciousness. Neither of the two books was theoretical, but rather both presented facts with a clear sense of the problem at stake. Still, they laid the essential foundation for the development of a sound theory about Japanese aggression in China through their selection of the subject matter and through their fact finding, and as such they were of great significance.

As I stated earlier, the problem of responsibility for Japan's aggression in Asia touched very few people at the time of the San Francisco Peace Treaty. This did not change with subsequent treaties with Southeast Asian nations and the "normalization" of Korean-Japanese relations, but with the restoration of Sino-Japanese relations and Honda's work, the problem of war responsibility toward China became an issue on many different levels. While the Southeast Asian countries and Korea could be silenced with the candy of economic aid, the Japanese government had to respond concretely to this issue because it was impossible to ignore China as a "great power." On the part of the ordinary Japanese people, human and material damages that Japan inflicted upon China were horrendous, and the Japanese people continued to feel, deep down, "the pain of Japanese aggression against China" (Takeuchi's words). According to Takeuchi, it meant "a natural feeling of responsibility in the people's emotions,"[31] although it did not usually come to surface.

Some journals at that time put together a series about Sino-Japanese relations during the Fifteen-Year War, and showed the activities of the Japanese Army in China based on the voices of various ranks of the military personnel present at the time, from the commander down to soldiers.[32] Of course, there was an element of sensationalism involved in this project, especially for popular magazines, and there were problems with regard to strict evidence of the historical facts. However, the voices this project brought out were of a wide and varied kind rather than purely intellectual, which showed that the discourse had come a long way since the earlier ones on war responsibility.

7. War Responsibility Toward Asia

The Concept of National Responsibility

Honda's work (mentioned in Section 6) and the reconstruction of the people's war experience at the time of the normalization of Sino-Japanese relations put on the agenda the facts about the Japanese presence on the Chinese mainland and hence the responsibility for Japanese activities there. As I mentioned earlier, this problemization of the Japanese responsibility was made possible because of (1) the importance of China in Japanese history; (2) the sheer enormity of the human and material damage inflicted on China by the Japanese Army during the war; and (3) the feeling of atonement toward China among some people that has existed from early on, albeit without ever becoming an explicit trait in postwar society.

This, however, was true only with respect to China. No such popular awareness has had an opportunity to develop with regard to other Asian nations. Yet, starting in the second half of the 1960s, the problem of responsibility toward Asian nations other than China gradually became an issue. It started with the theory that an accomplice can be defined as a perpetrator by omission. This was a central part in the criticism of the "normalization" of Japan-Korea relations in 1965, the anti–Vietnam War movement beginning in the second half of the 1960s, and the Japanese student revolt in the late 1960s and early 1970s.

This theory questioned not only past behavior but also the meaning and actual consequences of everyday forbearance in the present. It asked every Japanese whether he or she was a perpetrator, since adherence to the status quo included one's own failure to act against the status quo. It asked every Japanese whether he or she committed a sin of acquiescing in the Vietnam War and the suppression by many Asian nations in the 1960s and 1970s. This view criticizing the sin of omission did not directly address the problem of responsibility for the Greater East Asian War. However, I believe that this notion can and should be applied to the issue of war responsibility.

The Psychology that Sustained the "Fifteen-Year War"

In the Greater East Asian War, Japan challenged the Western powers and was forced to surrender by the military strength of the United States. At the same time, the aspect of international power politics was apparent in this war. These are certainly important aspects of war that should be kept in mind.

However, as the Fifteen-Year War view of history made clear, Japan used continuous military force against China, albeit with some intermissions, and maintained a great number of troops there. The Greater East Asian War became almost inevitable because of the firm determination of the Japanese military and government not to withdraw troops from China under any circumstances and at any cost. This policy was supported by the anti-Chinese sentiment in Japanese society, which sanctioned stationing a huge amount of troops in the northeast of China, claiming a part of China as the Japanese "lifeline," regarding the resisting Chinese as "bandits," and not questioning the legitimacy of using military force against them as "punishment."

Kamei Katsuichiro once criticized the view that laid the blame for the Fifteen-Year War solely on the ruling class, pointing to "the contemptuous attitude towards Orientals which had been deeply rooted among the Japanese population since the Sino-Japanese war." He argued that "had there not been an ingrained ignorance of and disinterest in China, the invasion of China would probably not have taken place so easily and in such a conspiratory manner."[33] Of course, this factor alone could not have prompted the invasion of China. It might be difficult to assert that the invasion of China inevitably led to the Greater East Asian War. However, the significance of Kamei's words becomes clear when one recognizes that these words were prompted by the true self-examination of a man who once glorified the Greater East Asian War.

This contempt was directed not only toward the Chinese. We have only to retrace how Korea was subjugated under Japan's "sphere of influence," how after its annexation the Japanese entirely ignored Korea's highly developed culture and imposed cruel rule on it, and how the anti-Korean sentiment in Japanese society manifested itself in the massacre of Koreans after the Kanto earthquake in 1923. Furthermore, the Japanese have regarded Southeast Asia as culturally undeveloped and nothing but a supply area of oil and raw materials. Seen from this perspective, the Greater East Asian War was the culminating point of modern Japan as a belated imperial power. Japan had followed a straight line toward the goal of an unlimited rise to power in order to "part from Asia and enter Europe," and stand on an equal footing with the Western powers as the leading power in Asia. In this sense, the underdeveloped peoples of Asia existed merely as a means for Japan to elevate its status in the international hierarchy of nations.

It is true that characterizing the Greater East Asian War as merely a result of Japan's goal to rise to power is too simplistic. However, one cannot deny that this aspect of Japan's modern development has been neglected for too long. Thus the historical view of the Fifteen-Year War and the notion of Japan's national responsibility toward Asia compensated for the one-sidedness of the earlier views of the war that were shared by many people discussing the issue of the Greater East Asian War. The two concepts should provide the basic framework for correcting this distortion.

Common Characteristic Features Underlying the Prewar, Wartime, and Postwar Periods

It is important to keep in mind that this contemptuous view of Asia in Japanese society has not fundamentally changed in the postwar era. I have discussed the one-sidedness of the Japanese people's reaction to the Tokyo War Crimes Trial, the lack of recognition of responsibility toward foreign nations in the first and second phases of the discourse on war responsibility, and the lack of the notion of war responsibility at the time of the San Francisco Peace Treaty and other treaties providing for reparations to Southeast Asian countries. All these basically originated in the lack of sensitivity to the concerns of other Asian nations. In this way, the basic state of mind in Japanese society that underlay the Greater East Asian War has not fundamentally changed in the postwar era. Even with the replacement of the militarists by economists, postwar Japan has repeated its unlimited striving to power based on the belief of "parting from Asia and entering Europe." Inasmuch as the economic version of the Greater East Asian Co-Prosperity Sphere is almost a reality today, the problem of war responsibility for the Greater East Asian War certainly has contemporary relevance.

Neither an "apology" for an unretrievable past nor a monetary substitute in the form of reparations payments can be Japan's true form of taking war responsibility. War responsibility can be taken only when the Japanese can dissolve the basic structure that caused the war. If this basic structure of thoughts and ideas still remains today, then it is the responsibility of the entire Japanese people during the postwar period that makes such a persistence of the structure possible.

Almost forty years after the war, the generation that was directly involved in the Fifteen-Year War as adults has become the minority in Japanese society. The postwar generations now make up the majority of Japanese society. This means that most Japanese today have nothing to do with the Fifteen-Year War as a person and accordingly do not bear any responsibility. However, to the extent that the basic attitude that underlay the cause of the Fifteen-Year War persists in contemporary society, the Japanese people share the experience of the war on a daily basis.

This is not merely an abstract argument. As I mentioned earlier, although postwar Japan ceased to be a colonial power with the end of the war, there has been no awareness of this critical fact. The failure to recognize this fact has been a major cause for a variety of problems in postwar relations with former colonies. Thus the Fifteen-Year War has remained an acute contemporary problem for many Japanese today, in several respects, including the restoration of diplomatic relations with the Democratic People's Republic of Korea, the discrimination against some 700,000 Koreans in Japan, the failure to pay reparations to the Koreans and Taiwanese who served as soldiers in wartime Japan, and Koreans who were sent to Sakhalin by the Japanese government and yet abandoned after defeat and have been unable to repatriate to their own homeland. Many of these problems tie into Japan's responsibility for its colonial rule, and in the sense of our discussion above, they are part of the issue of postwar responsibility toward Asian peoples.

The Contemporary Relevance of the Concept of Postwar Responsibility

No exhaustive discussion of these various issues can be rendered here, but I want to note at least the following fact. When Japan recognized the independence of Korea according to the San Francisco Peace Treaty, the Japanese government did not grant the Koreans who were at that time living in Japan the right to opt for citizenship, although that was the generally accepted rule when former colonies gained their independence. The rationale underlying this denial was, in line with the San Francisco Peace Treaty, to repudiate Japanese aggression and return to the *status quo ante* Japan's invasion. Thus, the Japanese government withdrew from the ethnic Koreans as a whole their Japanese citizenship regardless of their residence.

In fact, the actual reason for this measure by the Japanese government was as follows. If the Koreans in Japan had been allowed to opt for Japanese citizenship as a right, it would have been impossible for the Japanese government to exclude "undesirable" Koreans from becoming Japanese citizens. Conversely, once they were deprived of Japanese citizenship, the Koreans would have to apply for naturalization to obtain Japanese citizenship. In this case the state would have a wide discretion to grant naturalization and could weed out undesirable Koreans. That was the government's true intention.[34]

Does this idea not resemble the anti-Oriental notions before the war, as Kamei expressed them in his words of self-reflection? Further, in accordance with these measures, Koreans and Taiwanese who performed "public services" as soldiers for imperial Japan or civilians under military employ were excluded from wartime compensation. Koreans who died in the atomic bombing of Hiroshima were not included among the "people who suffered an A-bomb attack," and Koreans who were left in Sakhalin during the war were denied the right to return to their homeland, but grew old and died without being reunited with their families.[35]

Postwar responsibility toward Asia is not merely an abstract speculation. It is the cumulative result of each person's failure to act in postwar Japanese society. Such inaction was perhaps unavoidable immediately after the war, when the great majority of Japanese had neither food nor places to live. Even though people do not live on bread alone, they must have bread first to survive. Nevertheless, the problem is that even today, after forty years, when bread is abundant, we still refuse to do what is necessary. It is easy to criticize the policies of the postwar Japanese government on the issues discussed here, but these policies do not exist separately from the general perceptions in Japanese society. It follows, then, that if postwar thought is to be sufficiently effective, we need to try to turn around the conceptual trends in our society that brought about such apathy.

This is not an attempt to create a high and idealized meaning for the Japanese word *shiso* (thought). Rather, I think it is a more fundamental theoretical project in the sense of filtering out what controls our every-day activities.

* * *

This chapter is an abbreviated English translation of the article "Tokyo saiban, senso sekinin, sengo sekinin" (The Tokyo Trial, war responsibility and postwar responsibility), which first appeared in *Shiso,* no. 719 (May 1984), and was reprinted in Onuma Yasuaki, *Tokyo saiban kara sengo sekinin no shiso e* (From the Tokyo war crimes trial to the philosophy of postwar responsibility) 4th ed., Toshinado: 1997.

This English translation is based on the translation by Ms. Franziska Seraphin. The author is grateful to her for her time-consuming work. All names of Japanese, including that of the author, follow the proper order of the Japanese name, surname preceding given name.

Notes

1. I do not mean to say that there has been no awareness of this profundity. The postwar peace movement and the thoughts behind it were expressions of such awareness. Moreover, postwar Japan's efforts to become a pacifist-oriented economic power can be characterized as an expression based on the negative appraisal of the war. The issue I want to raise here is that the response to the war took its form only in such a manner and not in a way that the idea of war responsibility, let alone the problem of responsibility for the foreign peoples who were victims of aggression, was to be shared by the Japanese people as a whole.

2. Kinoshita Junji is one of those exceptional writers who have continued to address these questions. See, for example, his "Kami to hito to no aida" (Between God and man), *Gunzo* (December 1970); his *Bokyaku ni tsuite* (On oblivion) (Heibonsha 1974); and his report at the International Symposium on the Tokyo War Crimes Trial, in Hoshoya Chihiro, Ando Nisuke, Onuma Yasuaki, eds., *The Tokyo War Crimes Trial: An International Symposium* (Kodansha International, 1984).

3. Kasuya Kazuki, "Sengoshi no soten ni tsuite" (Points of controversy in postwar history), *Shokun!* (October 1978), p. 103.

4. Ibid.

5. Onuma Yasuaki, " 'Bunmei no sabaki' 'Shosha no sabaki' wo koete" (Beyond "trial by civilization" versus "victors' justice") *Chuo Koron* (August 1983); reprinted in *Tokyo saiban kara sengo sekinin no shiso e* (Yushindo, 1987; 4th ed., Toshindo, 1997), pp. 15–66. A summary translation is published in *Japan Echo*, vol. 11, special issue.

6. Nagao Ryuichi demonstrated and criticized this point in his essay "Bunmei wa sabaita no ka sabakareta no ka" (Did civilization judge or was it judged?), *Chuo Koron* (August 1975).

7. See Onuma Yasuaki, *Senso sekininron josetsu* (An introduction to the theory of war responsibility) (Tokyo University Press, 1975).

8. From the perspective of *today's* standard of historical studies it is easy to criticize the documentary value of the Tokyo War Crimes Trial. However, the historical value of the documents is still undeniable.

9. Representative for this argument is Kiyose Ichiro, *Hiroku Tokyo saiban* (Secret memoirs of the Tokyo Trial) (Yomiuri shinbun sha, 1968).

10. As a researcher who has read the records of both the Tokyo Trial and the Nuremberg Trial, I have serious doubts about Miruyama's contrasting of Nazi leaders and Japanese militarists. One can certainly see among Japanese militarists an attitude characterized as "hiding behind the public authority." This point is well taken; but in many ways the same can be observed in the Nazi leadership. It was not the Japanese leadership alone who hid behind public authority.

On the other hand, Goering, as Maruyama sketches him, gives a "great" impression in his consistent "evilness." It is difficult to deny the impression from him that "even though both are evil, Europeans are superior!" However, Goering not only sought to hide behind authority in his trial; he also sought to shift his responsibility over to Hitler. In contrast, Tojo's attempt to stop responsibility in his own person in order to avoid the pursuit of responsibility toward the emperor may be characterized as more courageous and impressive!

11. A student wrote in an essay on the movie *Tokyo saiban* (Tokyo war crimes trial) by the director Kobayashi Masaki: "I used to have the impression from Maruyama's 'Psychological Patterns of Japan's Militarist Leaders' that all defendants were timid and mean because of their own dwarfishness and irresponsibility. But this was not the case. Starting with Tojo Hideki, all defendants had a commanding presence. They were a little self-righteous, but they did make their points."

12. With regard to the Japanese people's hatred of Tojo after the defeat, Hosaka Masayasu described an episode in which a radio actor who had played the role of Tojo on a radio program received a number of intimidating letters. Hosaka wrote, "Suppose Tojo had not been in prison but in his own house, he would probably have been killed." *Tojo Hideki to tenno no jidai* (The era of Tojo Hideki and the emperor) vol. 2 (Dento to gendai sha, 1970), pp. 169–170.

13. News reports of Dr. Röling's arrival in Japan, as well as interviews and the questions from the general audience at the international symposium on the Tokyo War Crimes Trial, amply demonstrate this tendency. Dr. Röling died on March 16, 1985, after this manuscript had already been completed. (See also Onuma, *Tokyo saiban kara sengo sekinin no shiso e*, pp. 79–84.)

14. There are a few exceptional works dealing with the Tokyo War Crimes Trial. See, for example, Isoda Koichi, " 'Tokyo saiban' ron" (On the Tokyo Trial), *Bungakkai*

(August 1975), later reprinted in *Showa e no chinkon* (Yomiuri shinbun sha), 1976; Asada Mitsuteru, "Nihon gendaishi ni okeru senso sekinin no mondai" (The question of war responsibility in Japanese contemporary history), *Shizuoka daigaku bunri gakubu kenkyu hokoku*, no. 6 (1957). I am indebted to these works, which have inspired much of my thinking.

15. See Itami Mansaku's article, "Senso sekinin no mondai" (The problem of war responsibility), *Eiga shunju* (August 1946), which he wrote shortly before his death. Iwasaki Akira, who was imprisoned during the war as a pacifist, also devoted himself to dealing with war responsibility. He rigorously faced his own responsibility, calling himself "a potential war criminal."

16. Onuma Yasuaki, "Kokka, senso, soshite ningen" (The state, the war, and the human being), *Kokkaron kenkyu*, no. 15, 1978; reprinted in Onuma, *Tokyo saiban kara sengo sekinin no shiso e.*

17. Okuma did not necessarily treat the issue from the viewpoint of responsibility toward foreign peoples either. This is a problem common to the whole war responsibility debate and will be discussed later.

18. Yoshimoto Takaaki's essay "Takamura Kotaro noto" (An essay on Takamura Kotaro) was published in *Gendai shi* (July 1955).

19. Yoshimoto Takaaki and Takei Teruo, *Bungaku no senso sekinin* (War responsibility of the literati) (Awamiji shobo, 1956), p. 13.

20. Ibid., pp. 16–17. For Yoshimoto, the critical issue was not whether the poet in question wrote a war poem or not. Rather, the problem was "how one has come to think about one's own war experience during the ten years since the war."

21. Ibid., p. 242.

22. Tsurumi Shunsuke established four categories to explicate the meaning of the methods of dealing with war responsibility: (1) the "method of the detective" informing on those in power; (2) the "I-novel method"—writing about and criticizing one's own war cooperation as an example of how this could happen; (3) the "method of problem-solving"—explaining how one came to cooperate in the war and how one can prevent such a mistake; and (4) the "historical method"—measuring the actions of war cooperators against the development of world history. Yet more important than his categories of dealing with war responsibility was that Tusurumi set forth various ways of assuming responsibility with regard to four personality types, namely (1) capable people without integrity, (2) upright people without capability, (3) people who have both integrity and capability, and (4) those who because of their lack of integrity could not maintain their capability. According to Tsurumi, capability and reasonableness go hand in hand under stable social conditions, but in a situation of social chaos, capability is often contrary to reasonableness. Under such circumstances, integrity, considered of no practical use and unreasonable, supports reasonableness. The intellectuals who remained reasonable during the Fifteen-Year War were such people. Under the stable conditions of the postwar period, when capability once again became the highest value for intellectuals, "it is doubtful whether capable intellectuals can improve reasonableness through a mutual bond of capability."

23. Onuma Yasuaki, "Zainichi Chosenjin no hoteki chii ni kan suru ikkosatsu," Part 4 (A study of the legal status of Koreans in Japan), *Hogaku kyokai zasshi*, vol. 97, no. 2 (1980), pp. 104–107.

24. Although Indonesia signed the San Francisco Peace Treaty, it did not ratify it.

25. Yano Toru wrote, in *"Nanshin" no keifu* (Geneology of the "southward advance") (*Chuo Koron sha*, 1975), "There is something curious about postwar Japan's advance into Southeast Asia. It is a miracle that Japan, who fought and was defeated in the Pacific War, should after the war have had the 'freedom of action' to march back into Southeast Asia" (p. 178). He mentioned this only in passing, but the connotation of his words is important.

26. Shiina Etsusaburo, *Dowa to seiji* (Fairy tales and politics) (Toyo seiji keizai kenkyujo, 1963), pp. 57–59.

27. Nakamura Takahide et al. *Gendaishi o tsukuru hitobito* (People who have made contemporary history), vol. 4 (Mainichi shinbun sha, 1972), p. 308.

28. Takeuchi Yoshimi, "Kindai no chokoku," *Kindai nihon shisoshi koza*, vol. 7 (Chikuma shobo, 1959).

29.The facts about the Japanese Army's massacres, arson, and violence in China were brought to daylight in *Sanko* (Three lights) (Kobunsha, 1957). *Akuma no hoshoku* (Pleasing the devil) (Kobunsha, 1981) disclosed the existence of Unit 731. Important for their continuous influence in Japanese society were Gomikawa Shunpei's works, *Ningen no joken* (On human conditions) (San-ichi shobo, 1954–1957), *Senso to ningen* (The war and human beings) (San-ichi shobo, 1965–1982), and *Kyokugen jokyo ni okeru ningen* (Human beings in extreme situations) (San-ichi shobo, 1973), as well as the activities of people who had been interned as war criminals in China and then returned home. Gomikawa's works raised the question of the "inner war criminal," directed at the reader, and are important intellectually also in that respect.

30. Tsurumi Shunsuke, *Senjiki Nihon no seishinshi* (Spiritual history of Japan during the war period) (Iwanami shoten, 1982), pp. 241–242.

31. Takeuchi Yoshimi, "Senso sekinin ni tsuite" (On war responsibility), in *Gendai no hakken* (Discoveries of the contemporary), vol. 3 (Shunjusha, 1960), p. 14.

32. The journal *Ushio* was particularly enthusiastic about this project.

33. Kamei Katsuichiro, *Gendaishi no kadai* (Agenda for contemporary history) (Chuo koron sha, 1957), p. 23.

34. See Onuma, *"Zaincichi Chosenjin no hoteki chii ni kan suru ikkosatsu* (A study of the legal status of Koreans in Japan), pp. 109–110, 122 (note 157).

35. See Utsumi Aiko, *Chosenjin BC kyu senpan no kiroku* (Records of Korean war criminals) (Keiso shobo, 1982); Tanaka Hiroshi, "Ajia ni tai suru sengo sekinin" (Postwar responsibility toward Asian people), in *Kikan sanzenri* (1983); *Sengo sekinin* (Postwar responsibility), first issue (Ajia ni tai suru sengo sekinin wo kangaeru kai, 1983); Onuma Yasuaki, *Tan'itsu minzoku shakai no shinwa wo koete* (Beyond the myth of a monoethnic society) (Toshindo, 1986), to name but a few.

11

Toward a Common Historical Understanding: The Nanking Massacre as a Challenge of Transnational History[1]

Daqing Yang

It is no accident that we end this book with Daqing Yang's essay, "Toward a Common Historical Understanding." The title itself reflects our hopes and the challenges we envision. While considerable disagreement has been presented in the foregoing essays, both directly and indirectly, in a larger sense a healing process continues to work. Yet, as Yang reminds us, it is naive to hope for a simple, fixed view of history. It would be too pessimistic as well to accept the current disparities and, because of them, to give up the effort for a higher historical understanding.

Daqing Yang, who is a graduate of Nanjing University, strives for this kind of "common historical understanding" and presents some theoretical approaches to the problem of achieving it. —Eds.

Introduction

Whither a Common Historical Understanding?

The debate over the Nanking Massacre raises an important question for historians as well as for the general public: Is a common historical understanding (or, in Japanese: *kyōtsu no rekishi ninshiki*; in Chinese: *dui lishi de gongshi*) that transcends national boundaries still possible? Needless to say, national boundaries are not the only fault lines to be crossed in the field of historical understanding. Historians within the same nation-state can be equally divided on issues related to the nation-state's wartime history, as in the case of Japan today. However, it is perhaps in the context of international politics that the need for common historical understanding is more acutely felt than ever before.

An increasing number of politicians in the region are calling for such a historical understanding in recent years. A few examples from around the fiftieth anniversary of the end of the Asia-Pacific War will suffice. Japan's Socialist Party declared in July 1995 that "an Asian common historical understanding" regarding the war was one of its policy objectives during the upcoming Diet elections. In the Peace Proclamation issued on the anniversary of the dropping of the atomic bomb, Mayor Hiraoka of Hiroshima stated that "it is necessary to face the war from the sides of both perpetrators and victims, in order to achieve a common historical understanding." A few days later, in an interview with Japan's leading liberal newspaper, *Asahi Shimbun*, President Jiang Zeming of China emphasized that "a common historical understanding is needed" to overcome the historical problems between China and Japan.[2]

There are good reasons for this phenomenon. Economic and technological forces are bringing societies closer together, for better or for worse. If in the past we could afford to ignore what people in a neighboring country thought about the history of bilateral relations, that is no longer the case. Frequently, the difference of views is heightened in this day and age of transnational media and cross-cultural communication; even history (in the broad sense) produced primarily for a national audience (such as history textbooks) or for a local audience often has international repercussions. When the Japanese press revealed in 1982 that the Ministry of Education had ordered revisions in high school history textbooks to minimize aggression (the revisions had been made earlier), it ignited waves of protests from neighboring Asian countries and the resulting controversy escalated into a diplomatic crisis for Japan. When the city of Nanking opened Nanjing datusha yunan tongbao jinian guan (Memorial in commemoration of the victims of the Nanjing Massacre) in 1985, Tanaka Masaaki, a leading voice in denying the Massacre ever took place, immediately published an extended objection in a Japanese monthly magazine.[3] More recently, in March 1996, when the city of Nagasaki succumbed to the demands of conservative and right-wing groups and replaced photographs of the Nanking Massacre in the city's new Atomic Bombing Museum, the Chinese press fired another round of criticism.[4] Indeed, through translations, journal articles, and newspaper editorials, both Chinese and Japanese pronouncements on the Nanking Massacre have profoundly affected the other country's discourse on the event. Even publications by Tanaka had been translated into Chinese in order to, as pointed out in the lengthy introduction by a Chinese writer, "provide a negative example" for Chinese readers.[5]

With additional statements by a few Japanese politicians denying the Massacre and claiming it is a Chinese fabrication, it is not surprising that an event like the Nanking Massacre is casting a long shadow over relations between China and Japan. According to a 1997 poll in China, the Nanking Massacre tops the list of things or events the Chinese associate with Japan.[6] Given such a glaring "gap" in historical understanding between Japan and its Asian neighbors, as one American current affairs analyst has pointed out, any new confidence-building initiative in the region will be predicated on addressing issues from the past.[7] A common historical understanding is seen by many in this region as an ultimate solution.

To be sure, not everyone is convinced that such a common understanding of history is desirable. Some are opposed to the idea because a transnational historical understanding would undermine a nation-centered narrative, thus injurious to national pride and damaging to national identity. In the People's Republic of China (PRC), although the idea of universality based on historical materialism still has some popularity among historians, the government is also placing renewed emphasis on using historical education to strengthen patriotic feelings among its citizens. The Memorial of Victims of the Nanjing Massacre has been designated as one of the numerous Aiguozhuyi jiaoyujidi (Sites of patriotic education) in China. Two lessons to be learned from the Nanking Massacre, we are told, are "Backwardness leads to humiliation" and "If the country is not strong, its people suffer." The national orientation is quite clear.

In Japan, once considered by many to be a model of postindustrial society, an increasingly vocal segment of the population is arguing that historical education should serve to instill pride in Japan among the country's young generation. Professor Fujioka Nobukatsu and his supporters in the Atarashii Kyōkasho o Tsukuru-kai (Society for Writing New History Textbooks), for example, see little good in sharing a view of Japanese history with other countries. In fact, he is calling for a Japan-centered perspective in historical education to replace what he terms "historical views of Japan based on the interests of foreign countries" (or former enemy countries).[8] Consequently, any Japanese who strive to reveal Japan's war crimes in Asia or the darker side of its past are branded "masochistic," while non-Japanese who do so are branded "anti-Japanese." Such tendencies toward self-centered national histories are still going strong in certain quarters in both China and Japan.

In a sense, such tendencies cannot be separated from efforts elsewhere in the world to wrestle with the difficult questions concerning history, memory, and identity. If history and collective memory are essential to the formation and maintenance of national identity, some would argue, then they become properties impossible for two different nations to share. Moreover, the end of the Cold War has brought with it the decline of old ideological battlefronts that have dominated much of the postwar international political landscape, but it has also created new lines of allegiance in its place. Intensifying ethnic conflict as well as a heightened sense of ethnic identity may further erode universalistic views of the history of human interaction. However, the intensification of ethnic conflicts since the end of the Cold War also serves as a timely reminder that a common historical understanding that transcends national boundaries is all the more important, as we enter the new millennium.

A Framework for Common Historical Understanding

Even if we can agree that a common historical understanding may be desirable, many would find it a noble ideal that is impossible in practice. The new emphasis on different historical experience or even cultural background, as well as the highly questionable existence of a single "historical truth," all make a common historical understanding across national borders a daunting task. The recent and not entirely successful efforts by some Japanese and Korean scholars to narrow the gap between their history textbooks seem to have largely proved this point.[9] While reiterating the need for better mutual understanding between Japan and China, Hirayama Ikuo, a well-known Japanese painter and the current president of Nitchū yūkō kyōkai (Japan-China friendship association), also noted that cultural differences influence how the Chinese and the Japanese view the past.[10] In fact, many of the skeptics are non other than academic historians. The Enlightenment idea of universal truth based on rational discourse has lost much of its potency with the declining popularity of positivism in Western historiography. Just as objectivity in historical writing is now regarded as a mere "noble dream,"[11] a "single truth" that is acceptable to all regardless of their experience may be nothing more than pure fantasy. As extreme relativism would have it, everyone is entitled to his or her own truth.[12]

Historians, especially those working in the field of international history, need not despair, however. A common historical understanding may indeed be a fantasy if our goal is to reduce the event in the past to a body of "facts" beyond any contention, or to impose a singular version of history across nations. Inevitably, different people with different values, experience, and viewpoints at different times, looking at the same phenomenon, draw different conclusions from even the same body of evidence. In this sense, some differences in understanding and assessing the Nanking Massacre are not going to disappear entirely, nor do they need to.

Some of the differences can be narrowed to pave the way toward an understanding of the past that transcends national boundaries. However, what is needed is an interpretive framework for understanding a shared past, even if it was experienced in drastically different ways (in the extreme sense, perpetrator vs. victim).[13] Such an interpretative framework would have to consist of at least three dimensions: historical, political, and humanistic. Whereas the historical dimension is concerned primarily with the historicity of the event itself, the political and humanistic dimensions deal with its moral-ethical implications, in both particularistic and universal manifestations respectively. The relationship among them may be loosely visualized as three concentric circles: whereas we cannot speak of historical understanding without its historicity as its core, both particular and universalistic perspectives are required to achieve a full understanding of this center.

The Nanking Massacre, a highly controversial subject that belongs to the annals of *both* modern Chinese and Japanese history, is a most appropriate example to investigate how such an interpretative framework may help contribute to a common historical understanding. It is important to note that these three dimensions are closely interconnected, and none of these dimensions can stand alone. The unresolved polarization of the current debate, I would argue, is in part due to the fact that most existing interpretations of the Nanking Massacre have often failed to incorporate all three dimensions. I would like to discuss why each of these dimensions is indispensable in this context, and in the meantime offer some suggestions for a transnational dialogue.

1. Historical Inquiry

In its historical dimension, the Nanking Massacre was above all an event at a particular time in the past, made up of a particular set of historical circumstances. Unlike a fictional event, it was both real and definite. This may sound obvious, but its implication for practice is nevertheless crucial. We can only know the past through reconstruction based on existent historical evidence. Therefore, if we care to know what happened in history and ground our subsequent discussion on such a knowledge, we need to be critical-minded and be willing to overcome preconceived assumptions in conducting historical inquiries.

We need to remember that historical inquiry is never an unproblematic process of uncovering the facts. Not all historical events have left records, especially of the written kind. Sometimes no evidence remains, either because of the passage of time or through deliberate destruction. Furthermore, there may be considerable dispute over what constitutes reliable evidence, since, to a certain degree, all historical documents were human creations. Therefore, historical evidence can be as illuminating as it can be limiting.[14] However, this condition should not lead to the abandonment of the empirical approach to historical inquiry. On the contrary, it highlights the importance of historical methodology and calls for the sharpening of the historian's own craft. In this sense, historical inquiry should be the combined study of what happened and how it is passed down to us.[15]

To understand what actually happened and how it happened over sixty years ago in Nanking, there is no substitute for meticulous historical research, although it need not be limited to professional historians. Faithfully accounting for every bit of historical particularities is no easy task, but failure to do so has grave implications. It is not uncommon for an exhibitor to feel perfectly justified in using a photograph of a Japanese atrocity in another part of China for an exhibit on the Nanking Massacre, since the message about the brutality of Japanese aggression seems to be the same. However, such a practice brings in the danger of disregarding actual historical evidence and can only provide detractors with easy targets and undermine the effectiveness of a moral cause, however justified it may be.[16]

Holocaust deniers have long deployed the argument of extrapolation. By highlighting certain testimonies at the Nuremberg Trial, such as mass electrocution or soap making from human fat, which has since been discredited, the Holocaust deniers seek to challenge the entire credibility of all evidence presented at the Trial and the verdict of the Trial itself.[17] By discrediting isolated piecemeal evidence, the nationalistic historians in Japan also hope to erode the entire evidential basis of the

Nanking Massacre and ultimately to remove what they consider to be a dishonoring stain from modern Japanese history. It has become a preoccupation of some to expose the technical discrepancies in existing accounts of the Japanese atrocities in Nanking, however minor they may be, and to immediately claim, explicitly or implicitly, that the whole incident was "made up." The recent backlash against inclusion of records of Japanese aggression and atrocities in many war museums in Japan largely deployed similar tactics. Inaccurate photographs or video clips showing Japanese atrocities became an excuse to remove entire sections.[18] The argument of extrapolation works best with the uninitiated, which partly explains their success in Japan among many young people on issues like the Nanking Massacre. Such a condition suggests that historians simply must sharpen their craft and be empirical-minded to meet the strictest criteria possible.

Given the circumstances of the atrocity in Nanking, inevitably most of the evidence collected in China after the war, as well as some collected in Japan, consisted of reminiscences. The Japanese public was confronted with Chinese survivors' accounts for the first time in 1971 when Honda Katsuichi published his interviews in Japan. At the same time, a few Japanese soldiers have also come forward to bear witness or to tell their own participation. One such Japanese was Azuma Shirō, a former Japanese solider who confessed to various atrocities in his memoir and in many public speeches. His book, *Our Nanjing Platoon*, based on his wartime journal, made reference to fellow Japanese soldiers killing innocent Chinese by putting them into a mail bag and setting it on fire with hand grenades and gasoline. As a result, Azuma was sued by other soldiers in his platoon, who denied the incident and claimed to be emotionally distressed over Azuma's allegations. In April 1996, the Tokyo District Court found his description "without objective evidence" and ordered Azuma and his publishers to each pay 500,000 yen to the plaintiff.[19]

Here we need to raise the issue of how to evaluate memory as credible historical evidence. In the absence of written or other forms of evidence, reminiscences are in some cases the only way to know what has happened.[20] Although still without a consensus on this subject, scholars have found memory to be often quite resilient after years of repression. At the same time, they also point out that memory is subject to distortion, both willful and unconscious.[21] Azuma lost his case, but not necessarily because he fabricated the episode; memory may have failed him on that particular detail many decades ago. Therefore, while we should make use of postwar testimonies in reconstructing events like the Nanking Massacre, we cannot afford to make use of them uncritically.

Finally, reconstructing historical events is not the same as simply adding up all available evidence. Nor is historical understanding static. A historian should possess an open mind and be prepared to revise earlier assumptions and hypotheses in the face of new, credible evidence. Moreover, if we include interpretation as a part of the historical inquiry, the meanings of past events are even less constant. In the public media, however, the term "revisionism" is usually associated only with those who seek to deny or minimize Japanese atrocities in Nanking and aggression in general. Such use may be convenient considering the self-proclaimed missions of these writers, but it is nonetheless misleading, since critical and scrupulous revision is the lifeblood of historical reflection and inquiry. Needless to say, it is perhaps easier to revise the history of seventeenth-century weather patterns than that of a major atrocity, but even with the Holocaust, as one leading American historian has noted, "After fifty years the question is no longer whether or not to reappraise and historicize . . . , but rather how to do so responsibly."[22]

There has been a tendency among some Chinese writers to equate previous conclusions (or verdicts) on the Nanking Massacre with "historical facts," off limits to reinterpretations. This is often a reaction to attempts—both real and perceived—to "whitewash" Japan's war crimes in history. From a purely historiographical point of view, however, the Nanking Massacre as well as the postwar Tokyo War Crimes Trials verdicts need to be reexamined in light of new evidence just as any other event in history. Only by reconstructing past events on the basis of solid evidence can one best guard the truths in history from their real assailants.

The Nanking Massacre cannot be reduced to a body of incontrovertible facts, unless we are referring to such examples as "Nanking was the capital of China in 1937." Such "facts" on their own quite simply would allow no interpretation, thus no meaning of the event at all. Moreover, contrary to the conventional wisdom, historical facts cannot speak for themselves; historians do. As Benedetto Croce used to say, events in the past become historically known when they "vibrate in the historian's mind." Ultimately, then, there are no distinct and separate categories of veritable facts on the one hand and pure interpretation on the other. Evidence and interpretation exist in a continuum.

In the meantime, even if there is value-free science, there is no such thing as value free history. Writing a history of atrocities has moral and ethical implications. In fact, as Hayden White has argued, historical narrativity always involves moralization, since what he calls historical emplotments (the way a historian arranges narrative into a "plot") invariably embody ethical judgments.[23] A good historian should be fair and strive to be objective but cannot be completely impartial on issues like war atrocities. As one British historian put it, if historians shun all the moral aspects and write "objective" or nonmoral history, "the best intention of historians may result in what they would not desire; namely, a slide from a non-moral attitude in historians to attitudes in their readers that are, first, amoral, and then, perhaps, immoral."[24]

In his book on the "historians' debate" in former West Germany, historian Charles Maier has reminded us that "[historical] interpretations must simultaneously be political interpretations in that they support some beliefs about how power works and dismiss others. But they need not be politicized interpretations; they need not be weapons forged for a current ideological contest."[25] This is an important insight. To arrive at a full understanding of the Nanking Massacre requires us to go beyond simply the empirical dimension to explore the moral-ethical aspects of the event. To do this right, I emphasize that we should approach the subject from both particularistic and universalistic levels.

2. Perpetrators and Victims

At the particularistic level, the moral dimension calls for a distinction between the victim and the perpetrator. Such distinctions are not just moral but also political, because they refer to a specific power configuration—the context of political institutions and nation-states—in which perpetrators overpowered victims. In studying the Nanking Massacre, they are not only still necessary, but indeed indispensable to our understanding of the event itself as well as its postwar repercussions. Imperfect as these designations may be due to our own political limitations, failure to make such a distinction amounts to a grave injustice to the victims. While it would be naive to ignore political interference, it would be equally wrong to believe that remembrance of the Nanking Massacre can be divorced entirely from politics (as opposed to politicization or use by political authorities). After all, there is always going to be a political aspect to the continuing discourse on the Nanking Massacre as long as the term "aggression" remains a relevant concept in international affairs.

This immediately begs the question of whether the perpetrators and victims could be extended to national levels, and whether they are represented by present-day Japan and China. This is a complicated issue. To the extent that the atrocities in Nanking took place during the military conflict between the two countries and reflected characteristics of that international conflict, the national perspective is necessary. Moreover, since neither of these nation-states has withered away after the war, it is unrealistic to ignore the national framework completely in discussing the lingering repercussions of the Nanking Massacre today. As I will argue later, however, it would also be wrong to consider perpetrators and victims as fixed designations or solely at the national level.

It is worth remembering that the event known as the Nanking Massacre took place in the context of Japan's military invasion of China. That kind of brutality—wanton killing, raping, and looting—could not be separated from the war of aggression Japan was waging against its Asian neighbors. In particular, the institutionalization of terror against surrendered soldiers in the Japanese military and contempt for other Asians that had permeated the prewar Japanese society contributed decisively to the Japanese atrocities in Nanking.[26] Here is how the unequal power relationships made the difference. In his provoking analysis of the wartime Japanese mentality in relation to the Nanking Massacre, Japanese author Tsuda Michio cites the following example: During the war in south China, a Japanese sergeant who had raped and killed numerous Chinese women became "impotent" as soon as he found out to his shock that one of his rape victims was actually a Japanese woman who had married a Chinese and emigrated to China.[27] Apparently, the national difference mattered! In short, taken out of the context of Japan's aggression, the Nanking Massacre would become a mere accident, as claimed by many apologists in Japan. It is also in this sense that the Nanking Massacre is rightfully considered a symbol of Japanese brutalities during the entire war.

Perhaps more importantly, the perpetrator-victim distinction has implications for the evidence upon which historians reconstruct history. It would be naive to believe that the field of historical evidence is ever a neutral playground. In the case of war and atrocities, the nature of written evidence tends to privilege the powerful and disfavor the vanquished. That perpetrators tend to conceal incriminating evidence is hardly a novel idea. This is true of the Nazi perpetrators of the Holocaust, as it is true of Japanese perpetrators of the various atrocities in Nanking. There were good reasons for the wartime Japanese authorities to exercise strict censorship control over both foreign correspondents and their own writers at home. *Manchester Guardian* correspondent Harold Timperley was prevented by Japanese censors in Shanghai from sending out reports about Japanese atrocities in Nanking. Japan's prize-winning writer Ishikawa Tatsuzō was given a four-month sentence for writing a work of fiction with references to brutal killings by the Japanese soldiers in the Nanking area. The April 1938 issue of the monthly journal *Chūō Kōron*, which contained a sanitized version of his novel, was immediately withdrawn.[28] Incriminating evidence at the scene of the atrocities was either destroyed or suppressed. Bodies of killed Chinese POWs had to be burned or thrown into the river, so that there could be no traces of the massacre. At the lowest level, it was common for Japanese soldiers to kill their rape victims so that they could not live to bear witness.

Morality continues to influence how evidence is produced, or if it is produced at all, even after the war. As Japanese historian Hata Ikuhiko pointed out in his well-researched book on the Nanking Massacre, those who believed they were guilty tended to keep quiet while those who believed in their innocence spoke out. Even those who admitted guilt would talk about killing POWs or looting, but hardly anyone admitted to raping and killing rape victims.[29] Another writer working on the subject told of a Japanese captain who recorded the details of critical events in Nanking in his diary, but insisted that his dairy be buried with him.[30] Even the indefatigable Ono Kenji was not able to recover all the former soldiers' wartime diaries, since not a few of them refused to cooperate. At the same time, the few Japanese soldiers who have come forward to tell their stories of the event were derogatorily dubbed *zange-ya* (professional confessors), or even threatened with personal harm. When former Japanese soldier Sone Kazuo stepped forward in the mid-1980s and published three books on the Nanking Massacre and other Japanese atrocities, all based on his own experience, he was labeled a "professional confessor" and a liar, since there were some discrepancies in his books.[31]

The victim-perpetrator dichotomy continues to affect their posttraumatic experiences, which is becoming a subject of study in its own right. "The obligations of memory thus remain asymmetrical," as Charles Maier put it succinctly in discussing the Jewish-German relations, "The appropriateness of each position depends on who utters it."[32] According to two scholars involved in a Jewish-German Seminar at Yad Vashem— the Heroes and Martyrs Memorial Authorities in Israel—the Israelis and the Germans approach the issue of Holocaust rather differently. The former tend to seek response from Germans on a political level, "responses deriving from elements of deep soul-searching and the resolve to take a moral stand, such as combating contemporary anti-Semitism or increasing sensitivity to Jewish forms of memory."[33] The parallel to Chinese views on Nanking is striking in that most Chinese accounts of the Nanking Massacre have ended on a political note: The revival of militarism in Japan must be stopped and the Japanese government must atone for the country's past aggression against China.

It is usually those on the side of the perpetrators who either deny or downplay such a political distinction. One manifestation in Japan is the obsession with historical particularities such as death figures with hardly any attention to the greater political and moral implications of the event as a whole. When asked by an American historian why it is *so* difficult for the Japanese to accept the Nanking Incident and to admit the shameful behavior in Nanking, a prominent Japanese historian replied, "For me, to apologize for things that can't be ascertained as *facts* is very difficult. To apologize for something that can't be ascertained like Japan killed 300,000 or 400,000 people, what does it become?" He may be right as far as the "facts" are concerned, but as the American historian then pointed out, the question was not obtaining the exact figure but admitting that what happened in Nanking was tragic and shameful. As another American historian added, the solution for Japan is not whether the figure claimed by the victims or their government is appropriate, but to admit the shameful behavior in the past did happen.[34] Historians who place excessive attention to facticity become incapable of seeing its moral implications. Some would go even further, as in the case of Fujioka, who has argued that if historian Hata's estimate of 40,000 Chinese "unlawfully" killed was true, then the 300,000 figure claimed by the Chinese amounts to a grave injustice to the Japanese people, just as if someone who might have killed only 1 person was accused of killing 100.[35]

While some in Japan have sought to evade this political-ethical aspect altogether, many do consider the moral implications of an atrocity like the Nanking Massacre, but only in a universalistic way to the extent perpetrators and victims became indistinguishable. Many Japanese ex-soldiers who testified to the atrocity in Nanking put the blame on the war. As former Sergeant Ide Junji, who recalled brutal killings in Nanking by the Japanese troops, put it, "Human beings are capable of being god and demon. It is war that induces human beings to become demons."[36] There is certainly truth in such a statement. Moreover, sentiments like this, I believe, are genuine and have contributed to the strong pacifism in postwar Japan. Not surprisingly, seen from the Jewish-German relationship, pacifism is also the code of contemporary behavior many Germans deduce from their understanding of the past.[37] As an ideal type of historical approach, however, this is close to what Charles Maier calls Bitburg History, named after President Reagan's visit to the German Military Cemetery at Bitburg. Such an approach "unites oppressors and victims . . . in a common dialectic," and makes it difficult to pin down any notion of collective responsibility.[38] Blaming everything on the war is at best inadequate and at worst an escape from accepting responsibility since war does not of itself kill or rape, but humans do. Acknowledgment of the dehumanizing impact of war cannot replace the analysis of the responsibilities of individuals as well as the institutions they have created.

In an effort to clear the name of General Matsui Iwane, Tanaka Masaaki made much of the fact that after his return to Japan, Matsui built a Buddhist altar near his home, which he dedicated to the fallen soldiers in Nanking, both Chinese and Japanese. Tanaka thus argues that Matsui was a peace-loving humanist, equally concerned with the loss of Japanese and Chinese lives in the war.[39] The same Matsui, however, refused to take any personal responsibility for the Nanking Massacre, although his feverish push to take Nanking and his failure to control his subordinates were its important causes.[40] Without first acknowledging the human agency for atrocities, however, the claim to universal mercy rings hollow and the implied apology insincere to the victims.

Finally, the political dimension is also relevant to analysis of the politicization of historiography of the Nanking Massacre in Japan and China. Arif Dirlik, a historian of modern China, noted that the two kinds of rewriting of history—in People's Republic of China and in Japan, respectively—were not identical in their political implications.[41] He was probably right, although from a strictly historical or empirical point of view any deviation from "facts" amounts to tampering with history. While it would be naive to ignore political manipulation and mistaken to justify any distortion on political grounds, we need to keep in mind that politicization of the Nanking Massacre historiography in China resulted partly as a response to the perceived political agenda of some Japanese deniers. To victims, denial of the crime—assault on memories—by perpetrators amounts to a new assault. As German journalist Ralph Giordano put it, if war of aggression and oppression of other peoples in the past can be regarded as the "first guilt," denial of such transgression after the war constitutes "the second guilt."[42]

3. A Human Catastrophe?

Necessary as they may be, politically determined ethical yardsticks are not the final criteria for judging events such as the Nanking Massacre in human history. In fact, neither the history of the West, with its mixed record of enlightenment and colonial exploitation, nor the history of China, with its own share of imperial expansions as well as barbarity, can serve as a final point of reference to condemn Japanese aggression and atrocity in World War II. Such a final judgment must be anchored on a common ideal of humanity.

A "humanistic" history seeks to deepen understanding of human behavior through investigation of specific events, including war atrocities. In this endeavor, the particularistic—in this case, national—designations are less important than the kinds of universal patterns. It reminds us that, ultimately, the Nanking Massacre is not simply an atrocity by the Japanese against the Chinese, but a human catastrophe, for it took place in a brutal war (though an undeclared one), fanned by racial hatred and contempt, sanctioned by male domination over women, among other things. Unfortunately, from these undesirable traits no single nation-state can claim total immunity in the past. In other words, the Nanking Massacre or other war crimes in the Asia-Pacific War, however hideous, were by no means uniquely Japanese. As John Dower has reminded us in his well-documented study of the Pacific War, the Allies had their share of racism and atrocities that had to be accounted for.[43]

In particular, a humanistic approach to history requires penetrating the world of perpetrators to understand their behavior and calls for the rejection of their demonization. Scholars of the Holocaust, such as Robert Jay Lifton and Christopher Browning, have made a special point of trying to understand the Nazi doctors and executioners in human terms. To Lifton, Browning, and others, demonizing the perpetrator is a dead end, since it "cuts us off from a deeper, more complete understanding of human behavior, of our capacity for evil, and, therefore, of our ability to guard against future atrocities."[44] Making carefully constructed comparisons or even seeking to understand the perpetrator does not necessarily excuse the perpetrator of a particular crime in the past. As German philosopher Karl Jaspers warned immediately after the war, there can be no collective guilt of a people or a group within a group—except for political liability. To pronounce a group criminally, morally or metaphysically guilty is an error akin to the laziness and arrogance of average, uncritical thinking.[45] What must be done instead is to condemn the kind of behavior and prevent it from recurring, not the least in our own actions.

Comparison is usually the historical method used to achieve such goals, but not all comparison can bring us closer to a humanity-oriented historical understanding. In an article published in 1985, intellectual historian Matsumoto Ken'ichi made poignant references to what he called two earlier "Nanking Massacres." The first one took place during the Taiping takeover of the city in 1853, in which over 30,000 were allegedly killed. The second was the massacre of 1,000 students by warlord Zhang Xun in September 1913.[46] Professor Hata Ikuhito also referred to these earlier "Nanking incidents" in his 1986 book bearing the same title, adding another one that took place during the Northern Expedition in March 1927, when the Kuomintang troops attacked foreign legations, including the Japanese embassy.[47] So far, so good. The Chinese indeed have a lot of accounting to do themselves, especially with regard to what one American scholar has called "China's bloody century."[48] While such a juxtaposition of the Japanese atrocities in Nanking with earlier killings at the hands of the Chinese can demonstrate that what happened in 1937 was not a *uniquely* Japanese behavior, it also opens the possibility for apologists. In fact, this is exactly what Tanaka Masaaki has argued in his book: namely, that mass killing has been commonplace throughout Chinese history, but has never been a Japanese characteristic, and thus the 1937 massacre was a Chinese fabrication.[49] Comparison of this sort contributes little to advancing our understanding of human wrongs under various circumstances, and in less controlled hands can only serve to relativize one's own wrongs and to avoid taking responsibility.

On the other hand, there is also a tendency for victims to emphasize their own suffering as greater than that of others. This may be understandable, for each experience is unique. However, if "comparative criminology" can be misleading, we also need to guard against what might be called "comparative victimology." Some writers, in an effort to bring attention to an atrocity that has been relatively underacknowledged in the West, make the argument that the Nanking Massacre was a bigger calamity than Hiroshima and Nagasaki or other atrocities in history, because of the death toll and the manner in which the victims perished.[50] Such an approach is misguided, in that it treats unfairly the suffering of other peoples and thus prevents the genuine understanding of what war does to individuals. Moreover, by according death figures such a centrality in the discourse on the Nanking Massacre, this approach also precludes healthy historical revision and, in fact, falls perilously close to the logic of deniers that if the exact number cannot be substantiated, the massacre must not have taken place.

In the meantime, while each victim's experience may be unique, being a victim should not prevent one from going beyond the particularistic perspective to reach out for more universal meaning of their suffering. This is a difficult, but necessary first step toward reconciliation. The painting career of the Marukis in Japan offers an encouraging example illustrating the path from seeing oneself as simply a victim toward a more universal understanding. For many years after World War II, Maruki Iri and Toshi painted the sufferings caused by the atomic bombing in Hiroshima and Nagasaki. In fact, their names became associated with their famous "Hiroshima Murals," which were shown around Japan and even in the United States. During their American tour in the early 1970s, they were confronted with questions about the Nanking Massacre. This was around the time when the debate in Japan had just begun. After much soul-searching, the Marukis decided to create another mural of human suffering depicting Japanese as brutal killers, entitled "The Nanking Massacre." The painting was based on extensive research into the subject, and Mrs. Maruki made a special point of painting Chinese rape victims herself. The painting had a powerful impact on Japanese viewers, including many schoolchildren. From there, the Marukis went on to paint the Nazi Holocaust at Auschwitz, and the battle of Okinawa, where local civilians either perished under American shelling or were killed or ordered to commit suicide by the Japanese troops.[51] Since then, the Marukis have lent their support to efforts to redress Japan's wartime wrongs, and have exhibited works on the Nanking Massacre in Japan, along with a Chinese painter.[52]

Although one may raise a possible objection that placing different atrocities in the same gallery runs the risk of leveling them, we cannot overlook the important message they convey: It is possible to overcome a narrow victim consciousness by becoming a true humanist who faces up to the dark episodes in one's own national history. In doing so, the Marukis help bring down the barrier of national history without completely ignoring the issue of identity and subjectivity of being Japanese. As philosophy scholar Takahashi Tetsuya would argue, for a Japanese to take responsibility for Japan's past crimes need not lead to a total submission to nationalism or nation-state. This is because the individual "self" is a multilayered, multidimensional entity that can identify with a nation-state but also with a locality as well as with "world citizenship."[53] In this sense, the possibilities for transnational history are best found at nonnational levels.

Conclusions and Recommendations

What I have sought to do in this chapter is to transcend a singular, fixed and "flattening" view of history, which is both futile and counterproductive. I have tried to visualize a multifaceted framework consisting of several indispensable aspects—historical, political, and humanistic dimensions. The event known as the Nanking Massacre needs to be viewed from all three perspectives. Together these perspectives promise to offer a more nuanced perspective and enable a truly reflective and critical attitude toward past events.

Such a framework itself is by no means static. It is a continuing process and changes as our society evolves and as each generation examines the past through new lenses. Moreover, healthy differences and divergent approaches to remembrance are needed, since ultimately everyone is his or her own historian. Otherwise, memory would be the purview of the state and the search for facts and explanations would remain subject to political objectives and regimes.[54]

This framework is not static also because the three dimensions are addressing the past, the present, and the future aspect of the event. The historical dimension calls for the respect for its historicity and application of a critical awareness in our reconstruction and understanding of an event in the past, while the political dimension addresses the issue of historical justice in the present world still consisting largely of the same nation-states. The humanistic dimension of the Nanking Massacre suggests that to prevent future reoccurrence of such crimes requires not only reconciliation but also guarding against evils that are universal.

In this sense, such a framework is not meant for a purely academic exercise, but intended to bring about constructive dialogue. What is most important now is the first step, which involves commitment from all parties to open dialogue based on critical scholarship, explicit Japanese acknowledgment of the Japanese responsibility for the atrocities against Chinese people in Nanking, and recognition by all of the universal lessons of atrocities in Nanking.

The last point is particularly relevant to the postwar generation that, though removed from World War II atrocities such as the Nanking Massacre, has witnessed the continuing destruction of human lives and violation of human dignity, be it Rwanda or former Yugoslavia. A deeper understanding of the Nanking Massacre that took place over sixty years ago will not be complete, in my view, if we simply condemn it as a product of Japanese militarism and refuse to draw any wider implications that are universal.[55] It is incumbent upon us to realize that one of the ultimate goals of studying the Nanking Massacre today is to learn the proverbial lessons of the past so as to prevent such violence from happening again, anywhere in this world. In his Japanese Web page on the Nanking Massacre, a Chinese student at the University of Tokyo describes the Massacre, the dropping of atomic bombs, and other causes of wartime sufferings as "human tragedies" that brought shame not only upon the aggressors but upon all humankind. People all over the world must strive, he wrote, to prevent such tragedies from recurring.[56] To succeed in this endeavor first requires that we reject the demonization of the other, as well as applying the humanistic moral standard to everyone, ourselves included.

At the present, however, the greatest obstacle to a common historical understanding is at the second level, namely, the political resistance in Japan to fully coming to terms with its wartime past.[57] This effect has become obvious in dialogues between Chinese and Japanese scholars. It is not that such exchanges of views are not frequent; there have been many. Participation by those Japanese historians who confront the dark pages of their national history help break down national barriers. There are structural problems, however. Some Japanese scholars have noted that there is not yet the "psychological basis" among the Chinese for acceptance of new interpretations related to the Sino-Japanese War based on academic research.[58] Although there are many factors behind this phenomenon, the continued denial of past aggressions in Asia by a vocal segment of Japanese society is a leading cause. In other words, the

Chinese would be more likely to consider these new conclusions were it not for virulent denials in Japan. As Japanese scholar Yoshida Yutaka pointed out, the nationalistic rhetoric of some scholars and politicians in Japan is doing more damage by inviting anti-Japanese nationalism from Asian countries, and thus stimulating nationalism among the Japanese, creating a vicious cycle. To break this cycle, he argued, the foremost task is for Japan to "settle the past" in an unmistakable way at the political level. That such "settlement" is not sufficiently achieved is the greatest obstacle to free discussion transcending national boundaries.[59]

Although some may fear that admitting Japan's war crimes such as the Nanking Massacre amounts to making history a "political toy," this need not be the case. Such recognition is likely to bring the Chinese and the Japanese researchers closer to genuine and meaningful collaboration on such an intrinsically divisive subject. Such collaboration is more likely to create the kind of "psychological basis" needed for new findings and interpretations. In fact, this is borne out by an emerging agreement among some historians in both China and Japan. As Sun Zhaiwei, a leading Chinese historian on the Nanking Massacre, pointed out in a recent book, even the sensitive subject of the death tolls in Nanking is open to discussion as long as "one respects and recognizes the historical fact that the invading Japanese troops wantonly slaughtered the Chinese people on a large scale."[60] On the other hand, a popular history writer in Japan, who is not known for radicalism, also acknowledged that while the often-proposed joint Chinese-Japanese investigation of the Nanking Incident would be useful, the Japanese should first of all admit that "the Nanking Massacre did happen."[61] Pragmatic statements like these from both countries offer hope that it is indeed possible to work toward a common historical understanding, even about such an emotionally charged subject as the Nanking Massacre. Indeed, when Kasahara Tokushi, a Japanese historian who has painstakingly documented Japanese atrocities and offered in-depth explanations, reported to a recent symposium in Nanking that his best estimate so far is that between 100,000 and 200,000 Chinese died in Nanking, he did not encounter the same objections that have characterized other occasions when lower figures were raised by the Japanese.[62]

Only by taking this first step and continuing such a process of dialogue can we expect to approach, reach, and eventually secure a real common ground of historical understanding. In this sense, the Nanking Massacre should serve as a useful, if sobering, lesson about our shared humanity.

Notes

1. This chapter draws heavily from my other current work on the Nanking Massacre, in particular my essay "The Challenges of the Nanjing Massacre." I would like to thank Joshua Fogel and Okiyoshi Takeda for their helpful comments on an earlier version of this chapter.

2. *Asahi Shimbun* July 5, 1995, July 28, 1995 (Osaka, evening), August 7, 1995, August 13, 1995. For examples of use by private citizens, see June 4, 1990, September 8, 1994, March 3, 1995, July 31, 1995, October 18, 1996 (Kanagawa), September 30, 1997 (Hiroshima), December 25, 1997 (Hiroshima). Unless indicated otherwise, these are national morning editions.

3. Tanaka Masaaki, "Nankin daigyaku kinenkan' ni monomosu," *Seiron* (December 1985), p. 160.

4. "Nagasaki Genbaku Shiryōkan no kagai tenji mondai," *Kikan Sensō Sekinin Kenkyū* 14 (Winter 1996), pp. 22–31.

5. For example, Honda Katsuichi, *Chugoku no tabi* (Tokyo: Asahi Shinbunsha, 1972); Hora Tomio, *Nankin daigyakusatsu no shōmei* (Tokyo: Asahi Shinbunsha, 1986); Tanaka Masaaki, *"Nankin daigyakusatsu" no kyoko* (Tokyo: Nihon kyōbunsha, 1984); and Hata Ikuhiko, *Nankin jiken: Gyakusatsu no kōzō* (Tokyo: Chūō shinsho, 1986) have been translated into Chinese. In addition to Nankin-shi Bunshishiryō kenkyūkai comp. *Shōgen: Nankin daigyakusatsu* (Tokyo: Aoki shoten, 1984), which is translated from the Chinese by Kakami Mitsuyuki and Himeta Mitsuyoshi, Gao Xinzu, *Nanjing datusha* (Shanghai: Shanghai remin chubansha, 1987) as well as many Chinese-language sources have been translated into Japanese.

6. Nearly 84 percent cited the Nanjing Massacre when asked "What is associated with Japan?" This percentage is higher than "Japanese aggressors and the War of Resistance" (81.3 percent), "Cherry blossoms," "*bushidō*," and "Mount Fuji" (all around 50 percent). *Asahi Shimbun* (February 17, 1997) (evening).

7. William Lee Howell, "The Inheritance of War: Japan's Domestic Politics and International Ambitions," in *Remembering and Forgetting: The Legacy of War and Peace in East Asia*, ed. Gerritt W. Gong (Washington: Center for Strategic and International Studies, 1996), p. 97.

8. See Fujioka Nobukatsu's speech at a recent symposium on the writing of new history textbooks. "Atarashii rekishizō o motome," *Seiron* (August 1997), p. 78. Professor Sakamoto Takao of Gakushuin University, another core member of the society and a speaker at the same symposium, emphasized the formation of national consciousness and the state in Japan as a foremost theme in modern history education. Curiously (or perhaps revealingly), a major publication by the self-proclaimed "liberal" organization rendered its own title in English as "Japanese Institute for Orthodox Education." See Atarashii Kyōkasho o Tsukuru-kai comp, *Atarashii Nihon no rekishi ga hajimaru* (Tokyo: Gentosha, 1997), copyright page.

9. Some Korean participants, such as Seoul National University Professor Yi Wonsun, opposed the idea of a common history textbook on the ground that (history) education is tied to the subjectivity of a nation. See *Kyōkasho o Nik-Kan kyōryoku de kangaeru* (Tokyo: Ōtsuki shoten, 1993), p. 143; also Kimijima Kazuhiko, *Kyōkasho no shisō: Nihon to Kangoku no kingendai shi* (Tokyo: Suzusawa shoten, 1996).

10. According to Hirayama Ikuo, whereas the Chinese are practical and rational

in seeing and speaking about the truth, the Japanese are unique in being able to understand (each other) even without saying everything. "Yūki o motte rekishi to mukiaou," *Ronza* 31 (November 1997), p. 196.

11. See Peter Novick, *That Noble Dream: The Objectivity Question in American History* (New York: Cambridge University Press, 1988). As the postmodernists like to remind us, the language itself imposes a limit on the representation of a traumatic experience, just as the debate on the Holocaust has raised the issue of representation and historical evidence on numerous occasions.

12. Indeed, the standard line deployed by those defending the neo-Nazi revisionists is that all history is mere opinion, and there is no such thing as even a bare minimum of incontrovertible historical facts. This is pointed out in Christopher R. Browning, "German Memory, Judicial Interrogation, History Reconstruction: Writing Perpetrator History from Postwar Testimony," in *Probing the Limits of Representation: Nazism and the "Final Solution,"* ed. Saul Friedlander, (Cambridge: Harvard University Press, 1992), p. 31.

13. As Norma Field stated recently, history (of atrocities) belongs neither to perpetrators nor victims solely. "Kyōiku genba de no sensō: Higai to kagai no kioku tsunagaru mono," *Sekai* (October 1997), p. 269.

14. For a brief but useful "text critique" regarding sources on the Nanking Massacre, see Hata Ikuhiko, *Nankin jiken*, pp. 108–111. For a more detailed discussion with a different perspective, see "Nankin gyakusatsu jiken," in Kasahara Tokushi et al., *Rekishi no jijitsu o dō ninteishi do oshieru ka* (Tokyo: Kyōiku shiryō shuppankai, 1997), pp. 64–147.

15. James E. Young, "Toward a Received History of the Holocaust," *History and Theory* 36.4 (December 1997), p. 41.

16. Tanaka Masaaki devotes a chapter to "fake photographs on the Nanjing Massacre" in his *Nankin jiken no sōkatsu* (Tokyo: Kenkōsha, 1987), pp. 323–338. The book had been through six printings by 1994.

17. For a careful analysis of extrapolation by Holocaust deniers, see Carlos C. Huerta and Dafna Shiffman-Huerta, "Holocaust Denial Literature: Its Place in Teaching the Holocaust," *New Perspectives on the Holocaust*, ed. Rochelle L. Millen (New York: New York University Press, 1996), especially pp. 189–190.

18. "Nagasaki Genbaku Shiryōkan no kagai tenji mondai," pp. 22–31.

19. Azuma Shirō, *Waga Nankin puraton* (Tokyo: Aoki shoten, 1987); for extensive coverage on the suit, see *Sankei Shimbun* (November 22, 1995), (March 22, 1996) (evening), (April 26, 1996) (evening).

20. Carlo Ginzburg, "Just One Witness," in *Probing the Limits*, pp. 82–96.

21. See, for example, Michael Schudson, "Dynamics of Distortion in Collective Memory," in *Memory Distortion: How Minds, Brains, and Societies Reconstruct the Past*, ed. Daniel L. Schacter (Cambridge, MA: Harvard University Press, 1995). Historian Michael Kammen notes that not all distortions are cynical in nature and further emphasizes that distortion or even manipulation does not always, or inevitably, occur for cynical or hypocritical reasons

22. Arno J. Mayer, *Why Did the Heavens Not Darken: The "Final Solution" in History* (New York: Pantheon Books, 1988), p. xiii. I quote from him with the full awareness that his revisionist conclusions were not accepted by many historians and might be misused by others.

23. Hayden White, *Content of the Form: Narrative Discourse and Historical*

Representation (Baltimore, MD: The Johns Hopkins University, 1987), pp. 21–25. As White argues, " 'Pure' interpretation, the disinterested inquiry into anything what-soever, is unthinkable as an ideal without the presupposition of the kind of activity that politics represents. The purity of any interpretation can be measure only by the extent to which it succeeds in repressing any impulse to appeal to political authority in the course of earning its understanding or explanation of its object of interest" (p. 59).

24. Michael Stanford, *The Nature of Historical Knowledge* (Oxford: Basil Blackwell, 1986), p. 178.

25. Charles S. Maier, *The Unmasterable Past: History, Holocaust, and German National Identity* (Cambridge, MA: Harvard University Press, 1988), p. 32.

26. Hata Ikuhiko, interview in *Sankei Shimbun* (January 14, 1994). For more critical views, see Yoshida Yutaka, *Tennō no guntai to Nankin jiken* (Tokyo: Aoki shoten, 1987).

27. Tsuda Michio, *Nankin daigyakusatsu to Nihonjin no seishin kōzō* (Tokyo: Shakai Hyōronsha, 1995), pp. 161–162.

28. For a complete version with deleted passages restored, see Ishikawa Tatsuzō, "Ikiteiru heitai," in *Zōkan: Chūō Kōron—Shōwa-ki no bungaku* (1997), pp. 274–350.

29. Hata Ikuhiko, *Nankin jiken*, pp. 108–109.

30. "'Nankin daigyakusatsu' no kakushin," *Shokun!* 17:4 (April 1985), p. 76.

31. For example, see Itakura Yoshiaki, "'Nankin gyakusatsu' no zangeya 'Sone Kazuo' no shōtai," *Shokun!* 20:12 (December 1988), pp. 126–146; Ara Ken'ichi, "Nankin jiken 'jūgun nikki' no maboroshi," *Shokun!* 28:7 (July 1996), pp. 136–144.

32. Maier, *Unmasterable Past*, p. 166.

33. See Yaacov Lozowick and Rochelle L. Millen, "Pitfalls of Memory: Israeli-German Dialogues on the Shoah," in Millen, ed., *New Perspectives on the Holocaust*, p. 267.

34. Kojima Noboru et al., *Jinrui wa sensō o fusegeru ka* (Tokyo: Bungei shunjusha, 1996), pp. 293–295.

35. Fujioka Nobukatsu, "'Tokyo saiban shikan" (2): Meiji no henkaku e kyōkan no ketsujō," in his *Kingendaishi kyoiku no kaikaku* (Tokyo: Meiji Tosho, 1996), pp. 35–36.

36. Ide Junji, "Watashi ga mokugekishita Nankin no sangeki," *Rekishi to Jinbutsu* (Zōkan) (1984), p. 276.

37. Lozowick and Millen, "Pitfalls of Memory," p. 270.

38. Maier, *Unmasterable Past*, p. 14.

39. Tanaka Masaaki, *Nanjing datusha de xugou* (Beijing: Shijie zhishi chubanshe, 1985), pp. 51–54. This is the Chinese translation of his *"Nankin gyakusatsu" no kyokō*.

40. For a thorough analysis of Matsui's role in the battle of Nanking, see Kasahara Tokushi, *Nankin jiken* (Tokyo: Iwanami shinsho, 1997), pp. 45–72.

41. Arif Dirlik, "'Past Experience, If Not Forgotten, Is a Guide to the Future'; or What Is in a Text? The Politics of History in Chinese-Japanese Relations," in *Japan in the World*, eds. Masao Miyoshi and H.D. Harootunian (Durham: Duke University Press, 1993), p. 72.

42. Ralph Giordano, *Daini no tsumi*, transl. Nagai Kiyohiko et al. (Tokyo: Hakusuisha, 1990). The book was originally published as Ralph Giordano, *Die zweite Schuld oder Von Last Deutscher zu sein* (Hamburg: Rasch und Rohring Verlag, 1987).

43. John Dower, *War Without Mercy: Race and Power in the Pacific War* (New York: Pantheon, 1986).

44. See Donald G. Schilling, "The Dead End of Demonizing: Dealing with the Perpetrators in Teaching the Holocaust," in Miller, ed., *New Perspectives on the Holocaust*, pp. 196–211.

45. Karl Jaspers, *The Question of German Guilt*, transl. by E.B. Ashton (New York: Dial Press, 1947), p. 42.

46. Matsumoto Ken'ichi, "Shinwa toshite no Nankin daigyakusatsu," *Seiron* (March 1985), pp. 110–122.

47. Hata, *Nankin jiken*, p. 242, and "A Numerical Study of the Nanjing Incident," paper presented at the Nanking 1937 conference, Princeton University, Princeton, NJ, November 22, 1997. Noting that the Japanese should be ashamed of the atrocities in Nanking, Hata nevertheless suggested recently placing the Nanking Massacre on the scale of world history by quoting a Russian broadcast that stated that the numbers killed by Nazi Germany and Japan (12 million and 6 million respectively) pale in comparison with the victims of communist countries (62 million in the Soviet Union, 35 million in China, and 2 million in Cambodia under Pol Pot). "Nankin daigyakusatsu 'Rabe kyoka' o sokutei suru," *Shokun!* (February 1998), pp. 88–89.

48. R.J. Rummel, *China's Bloody Century: Genocide and Mass Murder since 1900* (New Brunswick, NJ: Transaction Publishers, 1991). Based on mostly secondary sources in English, Rummel's study concludes that the majority of the Chinese victims died at the hand of their own governments.

49. See Tanaka Masaaki, *Nankin daigyakusatsu no kyokō*, and *Nankin jiken no sōkatsu*, pp. 12–15, 240–255.

50. For instance, Chang notes that the Japanese "outdid the Romans of Carthage [*only* 150,000 died in that slaughter; emphasis added], the Christian armies during the Spanish Inquisition, and even some of the monstrosities of Timur Lenk." Iris Chang, *The Rape of Nanking: The Forgotten Holocaust of World War* II (New York: Basic Books, 1997), pp. 5–6.

51. John Dower and John Junkerman, *The Hiroshima Murals* (New York: Kodansha, 1985). Also based on author's visit to the Maruki Gallery, located in rural Saitama, in 1992. Recently, Maruki Iri and Toshi have been accused of using a photograph of Chinese executions as the basis for drawing Japanese soldiers in Nanking. *Sankei Shimbun* (June 17, 1995).

52. *Asahi Shimbun* (April 25, 1996) (Hyōgo). Maruki Iri passed away in 1995.

53. Takahashi Tetsuya, "Tasha no sensō kioku o mazukara no kakushinbu ni kizamu," *Ronza* 32 (December 1997), pp. 188–191.

54. Judith Miller, *One, By One, By One: Facing the Holocaust* (New York: Touchstone/Simon Schuster, 1990), pp. 286–287. On the need to move away from nation-centered narratives in history-writing, see Prasenjit Duara, *Rescuing History from the Nation* (Chicago: University of Chicago Press, 1995).

55. Lisa Yoneyama recently has also emphasized both particular (Japan) and universal (cross-space) aspects regarding memories of the Asia-Pacific War. See "'Hikokumin' no kioku to kioku no hi-kokuminka," *Sekai* (October 1997), p. 269.

56. Jiang Dali, Preface to Web page "Nankin daigyakusatsu" (September 1996).

57. As Ian Buruma has noted, the "Nanjing revisionists" were not confined to an extremist fringe, but have a large audience and are supported by powerful right-

wing or conservative politicians. Ian Buruma, *Wages of Guilt* (New York: Meridian, 1994), p. 122.

58. Cited in Hata Ikuhiko, "Seiji no omocha ni sareru rekishi ninshiki," *Shokun!* (September 1997), p. 39. When reappraisal is done responsibly, however, such conclusions are not rejected by the Chinese. Hata's own 1986 book, in which he carefully analyzed the Nanking Massacre and offered an apology to the Chinese people, was translated and published in Hong Kong with due respect, despite its much lower estimate of the total number of Chinese victims. See Introduction to Hata Ikuhiko, *Nanjing shijian* (Hong Kong: Commerial Press, 1995).

59. Yoshida Yutaka, "Heisai suru nashonarizumu," *Sekai* (April 1997), p. 82.

60. Sun Zhaiwei, *Nanjing datusha*, pp. 9–10.

61. Hosaka Masayasu, "Chū-Kan no 'tai-Nichi hihan' ga okiru toki," in *Bokyaku sareta shiten* (Tokyo: Chūō Kōronsha, 1996), p. 107.

62. *Asahi Shimbun* (September 7, 1997).

Contributors and Advisers

Ian Buruma has been a research fellow in Japanese cinema at Nihon University College of Arts, Tokyo; cultural editor of the *Far Eastern Economic Review*; foreign editor of the *Spectator*, and a fellow at Wissenschaftskolleg, Berlin, and the Woodrow Wilson Center, Washington, D.C. His books include *God's Dust: A Modern Asian Journey* (1989); *Playing the Game*, a novel (1991); *The Wages of Guilt* (1994); *The Missionary and the Libertine* (2000); and *Anglomania* (2000). He is also a contributor to the *New York Review of Books*, the *New York Times*, the *New Yorker*, the *New Republic*, and *Newsweek*.

Haruko Taya Cook teaches Japanese history, and war and society at Marymount College in Tarrytown, New York. She is the author of *Japan at War: An Oral History* (1992). Her present project is a book provisionally titled *Japanese Women in the "Greater East Asian War": A Social and Cultural History*.

Richard Falk is the Albert G. Milbank Professor of International Law and Practice at Princeton University, Princeton, New Jersey, where he has been a member of the faculty since 1961. He is a coeditor of *Crimes of War* (1971) and the author of *On Humane Governance: Toward a New Global Politics* (1995), *Law in an Emerging Global Village* (1998); *Predatory Globalization: A Critique* (1999); and *Human Rights Horizons: The Pursuit of Justice in a Globalizing World* (2000). He is also a member of the editorial boards of a number of magazines, including the *Nation* and the *Progressive*.

Sheldon Marc Garon is currently professor of history at Princeton University, Princeton, New Jersey. His numerous awards include the John K. Fairbank Prize (American Historical Association) in East Asian History (1988), for his book *The State and Labor in Modern Japan*; a

National Endowment for the Humanities Fellowship for University Teachers; and a Japan Foundation Professional Fellowship. His most recent publications include *Molding Japanese Minds: The State in Everyday Life* (1997).

Higashinakano Shudo is professor of intellectual history at Asia University, Tokyo. He has been visiting scholar at the University of Hamburg in Germany and visiting professor of Japanese intellectual history at Western Washington University. His publications include *The Overview of the Entire "Nanking Massacre"* (1999), *The Thorough Examinations of "Nanking Massacre"* (1998), *A Study on the Socialistic System in East Germany* (1996), and *18 Lectures on* the *History of Social Thought* (1989).

Kasahara Tokushi is professor of modern history of China and East Asia at Tsuru Bunka University in Thuru, Japan. He has extensively researched the Nanking Massacre since the early 1980s and has visited Nanking three times (in 1984, 1987, 1997) as a member of the Study Group for the Nanking Massacre. He published *One Hundred Days in the Nanking Safety Zone* (1995), in which he portrayed Nanking during the event based on oral history documents of Japanese perpetrators, Chinese civilians who experienced atrocities, and bystanders such as American missionaries. His most recent book is *Nanking Massacre Incident* (1997).

Lee En-Han is a research fellow at the Institute of Modern History, Academia Sinica, Taipei, and adjunct professor at the School of Diplomacy of the Chengchi University, Taipei. His publications include seven books in Chinese; one book in English, *China's Quest for Railway Autonomy* (1977); and more than eighty scholarly articles in such publications as the *Journal of Asian Studies* (U.S.), the *Journal of Oriental Studies* (Hong Kong University), and the *Bulletin of IMH, Academia Sinica*.

Perry Link has taught Chinese language and literature at Princeton University, Princeton, New Jersey, and at the University of California–Los Angeles. He has coauthored two Chinese-language textbooks and is the author of *Mandarin Ducks and Butterflies: Popular Fiction in Early Twentieth Century Chinese Cities* (1981); *Evening Chats in Beijing:*

China's Predicament (1992); and *The Uses of Literature* (2000). He is on the boards of several human rights groups. He contributes essays on Chinese culture, society, and politics to the *Times Literary Supplement*, the *New York Review of Books*, and a number of Chinese-language magazines in Hong Kong and the United States.

Onuma Yasuaki is professor of international law at the University of Tokyo and has been a visiting scholar at such institutions as Harvard Law School, Cambridge, Massachusetts; Princeton University, Princeton, New Jersey, Yale Law School, New Haven, Connecticut; and the Max Planck Institute, Heidelberg, Germany. He is a coeditor of *The Tokyo War Crimes Trial: An International Symposium* (1986), and the author of *International Law: The United Nations and Japan* (1987); *Koreans Left in Sakhalin* (1992); and *Human Rights, States, and Civilizations* (1998). His article "Towards an Intercivilizational Approach to Human Rights" appeared in *The East Asian Challenge for Human Rights* (1999).

Vera Schwarcz is the Mansfield Freeman Professor of East Asian Studies at Wesleyan University, Middletown, Connecticut, and she received a 1989–1990 Guggenheim Fellowship. Her numerous books include *Long Road Home: A China Journal* (1984); *The Chinese Enlightenment: The Legacy of the May Fourth Movement in Modern China* (1986); *Time for Telling Truth Is Running Out: Conversations with Zhang Shenfu* (1992); *Bridge Across Broken Time: Chinese and Jewish Cultural Memory* (1998); and *Scoop of Light* (2000). Her article "A Brimming Darkness: The Voice of Memory/The Silence of Pain in China After the Cultural Revolution" appeared in the *Bulletin of Concerned Asian Scholars* (1998).

Sun Zhaiwei is researcher and vice-director at the Institute of History at the Jiangsu Academy of Social Sciences, Nanking, China. He is also vice-chairman of the Jiangsu Provincial Association of Chinese Modern History and vice-chairman of the Research Association of the History of Japanese Aggressor Troops' Massacre in Nanking.

Daqing Yang is assistant professor of history and international affairs at the George Washington University, Washington, D.C., and has been a visiting scholar at Keio University, Japan. His specialty is modern Japanese history, especially its external relations. He is currently writing a book on telecommunications in the Japanese empire.

Takashi Yoshida is a visiting lecturer at Yale University, where he teaches modern Japanese history. He received his Ph.D. in history from Columbia University in 2001. His recent publications include "A Battle Over History: The Nanjing Massacre in Japan," in *The Nanjing Massacre in History and Historiography* (2000). He is currently completing a book on the history and memory of the Nanjing Massacre in Japan, China and the United States from 1937 to the present.

Editors

Fei Fei Li grew up in Chengdu, Sichuan, China, and is a 1999 graduate of Princeton University with a degree in physics and certificate programs in applied and computational mathematics and in engineering physics. She was cochair of the Princeton University Nanking 1937 Conference in 1997. She recently spent a year as a Martin Dale Fellow doing research on traditional Tibetan medicine in Lhasa, Tibet. She is currently pursuing graduate studies at California Institute of Technology, Pasadena, California, supported by a National Science Foundation fellowship and a Paul and Daisy Soros Fellowship for New Americans.

Robert Sabella, a graduate of Seton Hall University, South Orange, New Jersey, is currently teaching secondary school mathematics. He was secretary of the Princeton University Nanking 1937 Conference and chaired a spinoff conference in Parsippany, New Jersey. He was formerly a member of the editorial board of the *New Jersey Mathematics Teacher* and is currently editor of the literary journal *Visions of Paradise*. He has published an analysis of twentieth-century speculative fiction, *Who Shaped Science Fiction?* (2000).

David T. Liu graduated in 1999 from Princeton University, Princeton, New Jersey, with a degree in electrical engineering and certificate programs in engineering biology and East Asian studies. He was a member of the steering committee of the Princeton University Nanking 1937 Conference. A native of Taiwan, he is currently working as an analyst at Goldman, Sachs & Co. in New York City.

Index

866-540-4968